DEMOCRACY AS CREATIVE PRACTICE

Democracy as Creative Practice: Weaving a Culture of Civic Life offers arts-based solutions to the threats to democracies around the world, practices that can foster more just and equitable societies. Chapter authors are artists, activists, curators, and teachers applying creative and cultural practices in deliberate efforts to build democratic ways of working and interacting in their communities in a range of countries including the United States, Australia, Portugal, Nepal, the United Kingdom, and Canada. The book demonstrates how creativity is integrated in place-based actions, aesthetic strategies, learning environments, and civic processes. As long-time champions and observers of community-based creative and cultural practices, editors Tom Borrup and Andrew Zitcer elucidate work that not only responds to sociopolitical conditions but advances practice. They call on artists, funders, cultural organizations, community groups, educational institutions, government, and others to engage in and support this work that fosters a culture of democracy.

This book is intended for undergraduate and graduate students in the humanities and social sciences, activists, funders, and artists who seek to understand and effect change on local and global scales to preserve, extend, and improve practices of democracy.

Tom Borrup is Senior Lecturer and Director of Graduate Studies for the Arts and Cultural Leadership and Civic Engagement Programs at the University of Minnesota and a community and cultural planning consultant.

Andrew Zitcer is an associate professor at Drexel University in Philadelphia, Pennsylvania, USA, where he directs the Urban Strategy graduate program.

The Community Development Research and Practice Series

Other books in the series:

Rural Areas in Transition
Meeting Challenges & Making Opportunities
Norman Walzer

Community Development for Times of Crisis
Creating Caring Communities
Mark A. Brennan, Rhonda Phillips, Norman Walzer, and Brent D. Hales

Democracy as Creative Practice
Weaving a Culture of Civic Life
Tom Borrup and Andrew Zitcer

For more information about this series, please visit: https://www.routledge.com/Community-Development-Research-and-Practice-Series/book-series/CDRP

DEMOCRACY AS CREATIVE PRACTICE

Weaving a Culture of Civic Life

Edited by Tom Borrup and Andrew Zitcer

Routledge
Taylor & Francis Group
NEW YORK AND LONDON

First published 2025
by Routledge
605 Third Avenue, New York, NY 10158

and by Routledge
4 Park Square, Milton Park, Abingdon, Oxon, OX14 4RN

Routledge is an imprint of the Taylor & Francis Group, an informa business

ISBN: 978-1-032-75873-2 (hbk)
ISBN: 978-1-032-75872-5 (pbk)
ISBN: 978-1-003-47599-6 (ebk)

DOI: 10.4324/9781003475996

Typeset in Times New Roman
by Apex CoVantage, LLC

CONTENTS

CONTRIBUTORS

Artists 4 Democracy is an all-volunteer group that promotes democratic and civic engagement by mobilizing artists and art students to get involved in political action: artists4democracy.com.

Maria Asp is the Director of Community Outreach and Education with the Speaking Out Collective in Minneapolis, Minnesota, USA.

Andrea Assaf, founding Artistic Director of Art2Action based in the United States, is a writer, theatre-maker, and cultural organizer. She has a master's in performance studies from New York University. Recognitions include: 2021 Best Experimental Feature, Silk Road Film Awards Cannes; 2017 Freedom Plow Poetry & Activism Finalist; and 2010 Princess Grace Award: Directing.

Marnie Badham is an artist-researcher focused on socially engaged art, participatory methodologies, and the politics of cultural measurement. She is Associate Professor at RMIT University, Australia.

Roberto Bedoya is the Cultural Affairs Manager for the City of Oakland, California, USA.

Susan Badger Booth is a professor and program director of Arts Management and Administration at Eastern Michigan University, USA. She serves on the editorial board of the journal Artivate. As a Fulbright Scholar, Professor Booth taught at Hongik University in Seoul South Korea.

Tom Borrup is Senior Lecturer and Director of Graduate Studies for the Arts and Cultural Leadership and Civic Engagement Programs at the University of Minnesota (USA) and a community and cultural planning consultant.

Penny Brandt (she/they) is Assistant Professor and Director of Arts Administration at Wagner College, New York City, New York, USA and has previously written for the *American Journal of Arts Management* and *A Cultural History of Western Music*.

Rui Gonçalves Cepeda is an art critic, curator, manager, and cultural researcher. His expertise crosses the fields occupied by arts and cultural management and production, the market for and contemporary art theory, as well as social criticism and participation, democracy, and epicure He is based in London (England).

Sagar Chhetri is a photographer and educator living and working in Kathmandu, Nepal. He is affiliated with photo.circle as the head of learning programs.

Elizabeth Cho is a cultural worker, artist, and current Partnerships Program Manager at LA Commons, where she fosters partnerships to uplift local artists and creative community engagement in Los Angeles, USA. Elizabeth received her BA from Wellesley College, majoring in cinema and media studies and minoring in education.

Lisa Jo Epstein is Principal Artist-Facilitator-Educator and Consultant as well as Presence-Based Leadership Coach at Just Act in Philadelphia, Pennsylvania, USA.

Maryo Gard Ewell, arts administrator and community arts development specialist in Colorado (USA), is deeply interested in the patterns of community-based arts in the United States, especially in rural communities.

Alan Hill is a photographer and lecturer in photography at the RMIT School of Art, Melbourne, Australia, where he is Program Manager of the Bachelor of Arts (Photography).

Alika Hope is the founder and CEO of The Ray of Hope Project based in Hartford, Connecticut, USA. She has degrees from the University of Notre Dame (BA), Columbia University (MA), and Cornell University (post-grad). She has won a Gold Global Music Award and a Gold Presidential Volunteer Award. But her favorite was receiving the Supermom Award from her children.

Kelly Hussey-Smith is Senior Lecturer in Photography in the RMIT School of Art and co-lead of the Social Practice theme of Contemporary Art and Social Transformation (CAST) Research Group.

Katya Johanson is Professor of Audience Research and Associate Dean, Creative Humanities at Edith Cowan University, Perth, Australia. She is a co-editor of the *Routledge Companion to Audiences and the Performing Arts*.

Kirsten Kaschock has been a member of Writers Room in Philadelphia, Pennsylvania, USA, since 2015 and is the author of five poetry books and a novel.

Anna Kennedy-Borissow is an early career researcher at the University of Melbourne, Australia, with a background in arts management and theater practice.

Sonja Kuftinec is Professor of Theater at the University of Minnesota and Board President of Speaking Out Collective, Minneapolis, Minnesota, USA.

Shannon Litzenberger (MA, Toronto, Canada) is an award-winning dance artist, embodiment facilitator, and experienced cultural leader working at the intersection of art, ideas, and transformational change. She works frequently across corporate, academic, and social benefit spaces, animating embodied practices of ensemble creation toward aims of relational leadership, collective wellbeing, and inclusive culture-making.

Jeremy Liu is a US-based artist, community builder, and real estate developer investing in transformative projects, places, people, and ideas through Creative Development Partners. He co-edited the *Federal Reserve Bank of San Francisco Community Development Innovation Review* journal issue, "Transforming Community Development Through Arts and Culture," and is a contributing author to the *Routledge Handbook of Placemaking*.

John K. C. Liu is an architect and community planner based in Taiwan, teaching and practicing participatory design and planning with over 40 years of working experience in Asia and the United States.

Amanda Lovelee is a civic artist, government change-maker and co-founder of CAIR Lab (USA).

Karen Mack founded LA Commons in 2003 to leverage the power of arts and culture to empower individuals, build connections and develop communities. The South LA–based nonprofit implements a range of programs from murals to festivals to tours and beyond, reflecting the unique character of LA's diverse neighborhoods (USA).

Bronwyn Mauldin is Los Angeles, California, USA based a writer, zine maker, arts researcher, and founding editor of the Artists 4 Democracy newsletter.

Heather McLean (she/her) is Assistant Professor in Environmental Studies and Human Geography at Athabasca University. As an intersectional feminist scholar, she is currently practicing community engaged arts-based research to investigate climate crisis and mutual aid in so-called rural British Columbia.

D'Arcy Molan is an artist from Natimuk, Australia, and works as a Research Assistant at Deakin University, Melbourne, Australia.

Meena Natarajan is Co-Artistic and Executive Director of Pangea World Theater in Minneapolis, Minnesota, USA. She is a playwright and director.

Emily Potter is Professor of Writing and Literature at Deakin University in Victoria, Australia. Her most recent book is *Writing Belonging at the Millennium: Notes from the Field of Settler Colonial Place*. She is co-convenor of the Shadow Places Network and co-editor of the *Journal of Australian Studies*.

Mallory Rukhsana Nezam is a co-founder of CAIR Lab & Founding Principal at Justice + Joy based in St. Louis, MO.

Diane Ragsdale, MFA, is Director of the MA Creative Leadership at Minneapolis College of Art and Design in Minnesota, USA and Coeditor of *Artivate: A Journal of Entrepreneurship in the Arts*. She held previous appointments in academia, philanthropy, and as a leader of two arts organizations, and she does freelance work as a speaker, writer, consultant, and, early in her career, theatermaker.

Vincent Russell is Assistant Professor in the Department of Communication at Western Carolina University, USA.

Kiyoko Motoyama Sims is an Adjunct Faculty member at Augsburg University and College of Continuing and Professional Studies at the University of Minnesota (USA) as well as a teaching artist at Upstream Arts.

Johanna K. Taylor is a cultural policy researcher, arts administrator, and co-founder of CAIR Lab based at Arizona State University, Phoenix, Arizona, USA.

Shehab Uddin is a visual artist, educator, and documentary photographer. He is Programme Director, Higher Degree Research, at Pathshala South Asian Media Institute in Dhaka, Bangladesh.

Rachel Wenrick is the founding director of Writers Room and executive director for arts and civic innovation at Drexel University, Philadelphia, Pennsylvania, USA.

Andrew Zitcer is Associate Professor at Drexel University in Philadelphia, Pennsylvania, USA, where he directs the Urban Strategy graduate program.

ACKNOWLEDGEMENTS, EDITORS' NOTES, AND POSITIONALITY

The editors would first like to acknowledge that, as cisgender white men and citizens of the United States, we have benefited from the theft of lands from Indigenous peoples and the genocidal and exploitative policies of colonial and US governments and other actors. Further, we acknowledge the taking of people from Africa by these same actors; people forced into brutal slavery for over 200 years to build the economy and infrastructure of the United States upon which our comfortable lives, livelihoods, and communities now stand. Extraction and misuse of natural resources from these lands and others around the world – from which we have also benefited – have led to untold natural disasters and human strife still unfolding across the globe in new and devastating ways.

Motivated by the higher ideals of democracy and human rights, and by a multitude of threats against those ideals, this book turns to hopeful progressive practices that we argue can improve and sustain daily lives and build more just and inclusive institutions of democracy.

We'd like to thank those most responsible for this book: the authors of the chapters, foreword, and section introductions. Not only have they shared intelligent and compelling reflections, but in their careers have devised, championed, studied, and participated in creative cultural practices that address social and community healing and contribute to practices of democracy in daily life as well as in explicitly political arenas. Without their generous contributions of time and experience, this book would not exist. We also acknowledge their work is built on decades and more of similar practices that have been under-recognized. This is partly because they challenge institutions of white privilege, hierarchical structures, and extractive economies and cultural practices. We celebrate enduring contributions to the advancement of this work, not only by artists, but by colleagues including Don Adams, Caron Atlas, Dudley Cocke, Jan Cohen-Cruz, Arlene Goldbard, Pam Korza, Barbara Schaffer Bacon, and others.

A special note of remembrance for Diane Ragsdale, whose elegant words grace these pages. She died suddenly and unexpectedly in her home at age 57 during the final preparation of this manuscript. Her long and enduring contributions to the field are valued.

The book contains the voices of 37 individual writers and, while diverse and from multiple countries, many voices are not included. Limitations of space and, in some cases, lack of compensation available for artists and independent writers made it impossible for some potential authors to devote the time. We regret these limitations while taking pride in the voices and ideas we are able to bring forward.

As you will read in our individual discussions of our backgrounds and motivations, the ideas in this book come from decades of experiences working with, observing, and valuing the work of artist-activists, artist-teachers, artist-leaders, artist-thinkers, artist-scholars, and other artists who not only generate light from darkness but do so together with others to illuminate and spread joy, honesty, beauty, understanding, empathy, and action.

In addition to the writers, we also acknowledge the contributions of many who gave support, ideas, and encouragement, including: Kiley Arroyo, Caron Atlas, Barbara Schaffer Bacon, Melissa Bond, Anuja Bose, Aaron Javsicas, Theresa Jordan, Pam Korza, David O'Fallon, Gyonggu Shin; with Routledge, Kate Schell, Francesca Ford, Adhilakshmi Parasuraman, and Selena Hostetler; and numerous anonymous reviewers who provided critical feedback and encouragement.

Throughout this book, the terms "citizen" and "citizenship" occasionally appear generally referring to the empowered and active roles people take in their communities. Given long histories of disenfranchisement in various countries, growing numbers of migrants – including those fleeing climate and political crises, searching for safe havens and new homes – lack the legal status of "citizen" in most countries where they seek refuge. The word "citizen" can thus exclude many people. That is certainly not the intent of the authors or editors.

Andrew's Positionality

A longtime resident of West Philadelphia, I take inspiration from the neighborhoods' unique geography, renowned for artistic and cultural expression, racial and economic diversity, and a progressive political orientation. The presence of wealthy residents also means ongoing gentrification and studentification. At the same time, West Philadelphia struggles with urban problems, including educational inequality, access to quality jobs, gun violence, housing instability, and income inequality.

My personal and intellectual history is inseparable from the story of these neighborhoods. As an undergraduate at the University of Pennsylvania, I helped conceive of the Rotunda, a community arts center designed to bring together campus and community. Housed in a former church at the western edge of Penn's campus, the Rotunda hosts thousands of patrons per year and serves as a community gathering place for the promotion of arts and culture. The Rotunda hosts important community meetings, film festivals, folkloric performance series, free jazz improvisation, hip-hop open mics, puppetry, and so much more. Penn subsidizes the Rotunda out of its real estate budget (it is the equivalent of a rounding error in a very large pot of money), so virtually all of the events are free to the public. For several years, I oversaw the work of the Rotunda from its first live events. Working for Penn after graduating with a bachelor's degree, I took on the title of Cultural Asset Manager, and in this capacity helped expand community cultural offerings along the 40th Street corridor, including an art gallery and an artist in residency program, through 2008. These programs have proven durable; all of them still exist in some form today.

In the early 2000s, I began to study urban planning, curious about the intersections between arts and community development. This academic trajectory ultimately led to a PhD in urban planning and public policy from Rutgers University, and a faculty position at West Philadelphia's own Drexel University, where I presently direct the Urban Strategy masters program, which I helped to found and for which I helped write the curriculum.

Over the years, I have benefited richly from my work with Philadelphia cultural institutions, including the Paul Robeson House (Robeson's last residence before his death), Headlong Dance Theater, the Calvary Center for Culture and Community, and Kol Tzedek Synagogue. These organizations and the other projects I have undertaken have taught me the value of cooperation, culture, community, and democracy, for which I am so grateful.

Tom's Positionality

Many threads throughout my life have led me to the ideas and the work described in this book. A distinct turn took place in 2017, when I was invited to give a keynote address at an Urban Design Forum in Gwangju, South Korea. The forum's theme was *Putting Culture and Humanity in Urban Design*. Prior to this time, I knew nothing of the tragic and powerful history of Gwangju in the movement for democracy in South Korea. As I learned more, it seemed fitting to integrate democracy into my talk. I had been working with ideas around *aesthetic justice* in urban design and thought I might incorporate ideas around *aesthetic democracy* as an approach to working toward aesthetic justice, leading me to think more about how practices of democracy manifest in many professional arenas.

Social activism and creative expression were intuitive for me from a young age. During political turbulence in the United States in the late 1960s, I rallied friends in high school to publish "underground newspapers." My 1970s college experiences involved social activist video, film, and radio at Goddard College, a small nontraditional school inspired by the ideas of John Dewey. Subsequently, I involved myself in public access television, food cooperatives, and experimenting as editor of a weekly small-town newspaper as a platform for community engagement. Beginning in 1980, and for 22 years, I led a nonprofit community arts center in Minneapolis focused initially on media arts. As it grew, Intermedia Arts took on a wide range of cultural and creative forms. During this time ideas around *cultural democracy* caught my interest as I actively participated in national networks of media and social change artists and organizations, including the work of Animating Democracy. From the mid-1980s I was active in city politics and neighborhood organizing through asset-based community development practices.

During the 20 years since leaving Intermedia Arts, I worked in community and cultural planning often with artists to facilitate dialogue and engage people in co-creation activities. While straddling the arts and community development worlds, I found an enormous gulf between these professions regardless of how much they shared similar values and goals. In response, and to try to build greater collaboration and synergy, in 2006 I published *The Creative Community Builder's Handbook: How to Transform Communities Using Local Assets, Arts, and Culture*. Seeing a lack of deep understanding and appreciation of the varieties and nuances of human cultures in city planning practices, I published *The Power of Culture in City Planning in 2021*. Similarly, as motivation for this book, it was clear that creative and cultural practices are not often aligned with other efforts to build more robust and equitable democracies, and I believe greater synergy can and must be built to benefit from the valuable contributions artists can bring.

FOREWORD: FAST FORWARD FROM 1914 – A HISTORICAL PERSPECTIVE

I'm writing this during my annual visit to Sauk City, Wisconsin, a community important to the book you're about to read. It's a village of some 3,500 people in the southwestern part of the state, politically "leaning conservative," the oldest incorporated village in the state, and home of a German Freethinkers Society founded in 1852. It looks like one of any number of small midwestern communities. You'd never guess that George Creel, a writer for *Harper's Weekly*, in 1914 proclaimed it to be "America's Foremost City."

Creel came from New York to attend a community pageant, and began his article thus:

> On October 3rd, 1914, about four thousand men, women, and children in the town of Sauk City, Wisconsin, gave over the whole sunny day to a pageant interpretation of events as richly significant as the rifle shot at Concord or the signing of the Declaration of Independence.
>
> *(Creel, 1914, p. 495)*

Perhaps I should back up a little. No doubt, in every era there is creative ferment, and I've had special interest in that ferment in the United States in the early part of the 20th century. Let's take a look at some of the things happening then, ideas that, to me, came together in the Sauk City pageant.

America was trying to figure out who it was. What democracy was all about. The Statue of Liberty was dedicated in 1886; its words, so stirring to many – "Give me your tired, your poor, your huddled masses yearning to breathe free" – were starkly contrasted with opinions such as that expressed in the *African American Cleveland Gazette:*

> Liberty enlightening the world, indeed! The expression makes us sick. This government is a howling farce. It can not or rather does not protect its citizens within its own borders. Shove the Bartholdi statue, torch and all, into the ocean until the "liberty" of this country is such as to make it possible for an inoffensive and industrious colored man to earn a respectable living for himself and family, without being ku-kluxed, perhaps murdered, his daughter and wife outraged, and his property destroyed.
>
> (*Postponing Bertholdi's statue . . ., 1886*)

As immigrants flooded into the United States, the Settlement House movement was a response, a way of helping immigrants gain a foothold and become active citizens. Initially articulated in Great Britain, the first Settlement House was in New York, though the most famous was Chicago's Hull House where its founder, Jane Addams, according to Jeffrey Scheuer, added democracy to its core functions,

> extending democratic principles beyond the political sphere and into other aspects of society. Addams . . . saw that political democracy had failed to eliminate poverty and class distinctions; workers had no place to congregate, to organize, to enjoy cultural or social activities, or to learn. The settlement was conceived as such a place.
>
> (*Scheuer, 1985*)

At the same time, at Harvard, George Pierce Baker was urging his students to inspire people locally to write and produce their own plays – a revolutionary idea at the time. One of his students was Frederick Koch, whose "folk plays" movement in North Carolina encouraged people to write the real story of community life: the result was plays about workers' strikes, life in African American communities, life in Mexican communities, and life in rural North Carolina, all written by people of these communities. Another student was dramatist Alexander Drummond of Cornell University, who believed that as an employee of a land grant institution, he had a responsibility to help rural people write and produce plays about their lives. Drummond, in turn, influenced his graduate student, Robert E. Gard, who took this idea to Wisconsin in 1945. Another student was Hallie Flanagan, head of Franklin D. Roosevelt's Federal Theatre Project, which included "living newspapers" about issues of the day, from housing to race, as well as new plays that challenged old ideas, and a host of plays in various languages that toured to rural areas.

Meanwhile, pageantry was being employed as an urban planning tool. Chapters in *American Historical Pageantry* (Glassberg, 1990) include "The Place Is the Hero," "Community Development Is the Plot," and "To Explain the City to Itself." Percy MacKaye was a playwright who was also a passionate champion of the democratic ideal. In 1912 he said, "True democracy is vitally concerned with beauty, and true art is vitally concerned with citizenship" (MacKaye, 1909).

He was hired by several cities to produce pageants to help citizens look ahead. I'd thought that pageantry was an urban phenomenon; but one day I was browsing in the Sauk City public library, saw photos of their pageant, and realized it was a rural phenomenon, too.

Then there's the theme of Progressive politics in the upper Midwest. In Wisconsin, the "Wisconsin Idea" represented a collaboration between State and University, a path to helping make Governor "Fighting Bob" LaFollette's vision that Wisconsin should become the most democratic state in America. University Extension arts played a part early in the century. The Bureau of Community Drama was headed by Ethel Rockwell, director of the Sauk City pageant. The Bureau of Community Music was headed by "Pop" Gordon, who believed that bringing different groups together to form community singing societies would help bridge cultural and political differences. The "Insurgent Theater" was conceived by Professor Thomas Dickenson in the 1910s. Reflecting on his work decades later, he wrote, "there is absolutely no question of the organic association of the spirit of our work with LaFollette progressivism. My chief interest was in the outworking of democracy, of which I considered the theatre the workshop" (Gard, 1955). This work was so successful that in 1945 Robert E. Gard, playwright (and – full disclosure – my father) was hired to help people uncover their creativity through writing and drama; he called this work the Wisconsin Idea Theatre. All this work laid the foundation for Gard's groundbreaking view of the role of the arts in broader, values-based community development (Gard et al., 1969).

Edward J. Ward, active in the Social Center Movement, recorded the discussion of the Center idea at the National Municipal League's conference in Buffalo (Ward, 1915). My historian friend, Gwen Drury, wrote in a personal communication to me:

> The motto of the Social Center Movement was "From the corners to the center." Proponents wanted people from opposite political views and social statuses, and even racial groups, to have a place where they could get to know each other face to face and use that diversity of viewpoints to discuss the issues and build the best self-governing democracy possible. Theirs was one of the first uses of the term "social capital."

Ward was brought to the University of Wisconsin in 1909 to create the Bureau of Civic and Social Development in the Extension division. In nearby Sauk City, a couple of years before the pageant, Ward led a four-day Community Institute to explore how people of all ages, backgrounds, and perspectives could together create a great community. One of the outcomes of this Institute was the decision to transform Sauk City's school building "into a headquarters of the Whole People where men, women, and children may come to talk, think, act, play, laugh, dance, and deliberate" (Creel, 1914). The village government conferred the title of Village Social Secretary on the principal of the school.

Which brings us back to the "Social Center Pageant" of 1914. The cover page of the script, written by Zona Gale (later a Pulitzer Prize–winning playwright) says:

> A Social Center Pageant and Processional: Celebrating the Transfer of the Ballot Box from the Town Hall to the Public Schoolhouse
>
> An Event which definitely Signalizes the Perception that Government is no longer merely the Selection of Agents for Repression But is the All-Inclusive and Living Fellowship of Citizens in a Creative Process of Self-Education.
>
> *(Gale, 1914)*

The show began with a glimpse at how the Indigenous Sac and Fox tribal groups had found common ground to defuse conflict. Then scenes – taking place in various parts of town as the audience moved along with the show – traced the community's history from tribal days to the appearance of French and then Germans who settled quickly into conflict based on culture and politics. The character of Nobody appeared:

> Into the turmoil slunk a . . . gloomy figure who announced: "Nobody is to blame. I am Nobody. The town, you say, is dead; no welcome is there here; your lives, you say are bleak . . . the things that should be done are left undone. Why? Because what's everybody's business is mine. I am Nobody."
>
> *(Gale, 1914)*

In the final scene of the show, played in front of the village hall, the door of the hall burst open and the principal, carrying the village ballot box, led the children of the school in a procession – followed by the cast and audience – to the school building where the ballot box would be installed as a symbol that the school was to be the crucible of democracy, not only as a place for voting, but also a place where the next generation of voters would learn about democratic participation in both political and social life. The building would become a setting for community social gatherings, discussion, music, the public library, an employment bureau, and more – it would become the place of "Whole People," a place where "The immigrant group can be tapped for its rich [culture] . . . so that not only the native-born be enriched and broadened, but the alien given that absolutely essential sense of belonging" (Creel, 1914).

While there's no evidence of voter intimication in Sauk City, the pageant took place during a time of threats against voters in the United States. Guards were posted at ballot boxes in some cities, as there were brawls at some polling places, and the invention of the voting machine around 1910 brought anxiety.

I see many ideas and ideals swirling around in the United States during the early part of the 20th century, as well as parallels to today. These came together in the Sauk City pageant. I see the struggle to articulate what democracy really means, what "liberty and justice for all" means. The struggle to create a meaningful life for everyone – rich or poor; elderly or young; Indigenous, long-time families or newcomers. The struggle to create truly representative government in which participation by anyone was welcomed. The understanding of the purpose of education. The dawning recognition that everyone had important stories and creativity and yearned to have a voice. The wrestling with ways that divisiveness could be addressed. The need for physical spaces in which people could speak and listen, work and play together, and come to understand what fellowship in community can mean. The valuing of "whole people." And the role the arts could play in all this.

These are questions facing communities and democratic institutions around the world today. There may be a different vocabulary and new questions raised by technology, immigration, globalization, family fragmentation, genetic modification, mobility, climate change, and personal identity. However, ongoing struggles around race, civil rights, justice, authoritarianism, and social inequity continue.

Artist-activist Judith Malina (1990) wrote that the role of the artist follows the needs of changing times:

- In time of social stasis: to activate
- In time of germination: to invent fertile new forms
- In time of revolution: to extend the possibilities of peace and liberty
- In time of violence: to make peace
- In time of despair: to give hope
- In time of silence: to sing out

In the pages that follow, you'll explore the roles of creativity and big ideas and big ideals. You'll read powerful stories.

Can we harness these in our communities? Of course we can. The artist-activists in the pages to follow challenge us to unleash creativity and access courage to make the promise of democracy real and meaningful for everyone.

Maryo Gard Ewell
Gunnison, Colorada, USA

References

Creel, G. (1914, November 14). America's foremost city. *Harper's Weekly,* 495–497.

Gale, Z. (1914). *The social center pageant and processional*. Typescript at Park Hall, Sauk City, WI, and Tripp Heritage Museum, Prairie du Sac, WI.

Gard, R. E. (1955). *Grassroots theater: A search for regional arts in America* (p. 86). University of Wisconsin Press.

Gard, R. E., Warlum, M., Kohlhoff, R., Friou, K., & Temkin, P. (1969). *The arts in the small community: A national plan*. University of Wisconsin Extension Printing. www.gardfoundation.org.

Glassberg, D. (1990). *American historical pageantry: The uses of tradition in the early twentieth century*. University of North Carolina Press.

MacKaye, P. (1909). *The playhouse and the play* (pp. 190, 191). MacMillan Company.

Malina, J. (1990). The work of an anarchist theater. In M. O'Brien & C. Little (Eds.), *Reimaging America: The arts of social change* (p. 40). New Society Publishers.

Postponing Bartholdi's statue until there is liberty for colored as well. (1886, November 27). *The Cleveland Gazette*, 2. https://en.wikipedia.org/wiki/Statue_of_Liberty#cite_note-Cleveland-117

Scheuer, J. (1985). *Legacy of light: University Settlement's first century*. University Settlement Society of New York. https://socialwelfare.library.vcu.edu/settlement-houses/origins-of-the-settlement-house-movement/

Ward, E. J. (1915). *The social center, from the national municipal league series*. Appleton & Company. Reprinted by BiblioLife (no date).

INTRODUCTION

The Unraveling of Democracy and Reweaving Civic Life

Modern liberal democracies around the globe are fragile, as many, including in the United States, are now learning firsthand. This prompts us to ask, what strategies and practices can help weave a stronger civic fabric – to build a *culture of democracy*? Observers over the past two centuries have articulated that this fabric must be much thicker than occasional visits to the ballot box; that democracy builds from daily individual and interpersonal actions. In other words, the strongest democracies grow from personal behaviors that are interwoven in community and organizational life and ways of working together.

Nearly a century ago, pragmatist social philosopher John Dewey warned that regardless of adherence to the ideals of democracy, without active participation and the practice of its norms, democratic systems and ways of life unravel. Dewey wrote, "for a long period we acted as if our democracy were something that perpetuated itself automatically; as if our ancestors had succeeded in setting up a machine that solved the problem of perpetual motion in politics" (1939, p. 1). Dewey was writing during the rise of Nazism in Europe and went on to warn of forces, "breeding hate, suspicion, intolerance in the minds of individual human beings" (p. 3) that mere guarantees of liberties will not protect. The political winds of that time are, sadly, resurfacing and resurging.

The stories and analysis in this book highlight creative and cultural practices that seed and foster norms and practices that promote a culture of democracy as well as action in support of its institutions at a critical time. *Democracy as Creative Practice: Weaving a Culture of Civic Life* showcases contributions made by artists and others to strengthen and forge more just, equitable, and sustainable democracies. The 16 stories that follow range from public artists in Australia and creative youth workers in Los Angeles, to teaching artists in Minnesota, to a public spectacle curator in Portugal, and many others. All point to the same conclusion: creative and

DOI: 10.4324/9781003475996-1

cultural practices have taken, and *can* take, even more substantive roles to enhance civic life and critical practices of democracy. As Maryo Gard Ewell described in the Foreword, these efforts are not new but have been marginalized in favor of aesthetic and cultural practices that reinforce dominant economic and social interests. They have not been provided the attention and support they deserve, and they are now so desperately needed.

In this Introduction, we explore some of the broader threats to democracy, look at relationships between democracy and creative practices, elaborate on what we mean by practices of democracy, examine how democracies can be enhanced through creative artistic practices, and introduce the contents of the book. Questions we explore include: What is a *culture of democracy*, and how does it become part of daily life and routine activities? What contributions are culture bearers and artists making to build more robust and equitable democracies? How can the work of these artists and culture bearers be better recognized, understood, enhanced, and supported?

Social policy scholar Paul Spicker (2008) distills democracy into three major elements. The first is the *ideal* of democracy, "such as the sovereignty of the people, the popular will and individual consent" (p. 251). The second addresses *norms* or everyday social practices and approaches to decision-making, including practices of deliberative democracy, cooperation, equity, and inclusion. His third category includes *systems* of government, legal structures including electoral models, "in which people choose representatives who are accountable to them" (p. 252). Recognizing that these three elements are interconnected and cannot exist independently, political scientist Richard Kimber (1989) describes the importance of "a requirement to behave democratically" He goes on to write, "Of course, the only way of institutionalizing this [behavior] is through the legal system of the regime; but the legal system itself is not enough. There must also exist accepted norms" (pp. 210, 211). As Kimber points out, the *ideal* alone does not ensure rights, and *systems* without *norms* are not on solid ground. Reflecting on what has become known as the January 6 Insurrection in Washington, D.C. – an event that nearly toppled democracy in the United States – it is evident that the actions of, or norms adhered to by, a relatively small number of people held the system together.

Working in community settings the past few decades has led us to appreciate multiple ways creative practices contribute to community and civic life, fertilizing the soil in which robust local democracies take root and flourish. In fact, such work goes beyond preparing the soil to fully engaging people in meaningful activities that constitute daily practices of democracy. Some artists and culture bearers, through their individual or organizational work – as well as some community activists who employ creative and culturally based practices – articulate their work with the intention of strengthening democracy to make it more just and inclusive. Others do not describe their work as such, but know they are adding critical threads that build on participation in democratic community life and helping people become potent actors in civic arenas.

Threats to Democracy

That democracies around the world are under threat is not news. Recent events, however, are but a symptom of a longer-term assault by authoritarian movements and antidemocratic global capital. It is important to explore the contours of these threats to remain attuned to their ever-evolving character.

Democracies failed in Europe during the 1920s, 1930s, and 1940s, and there is evidence some may do so again, according to Timothy Snyder, Yale historian of German, Eastern European, and Russian histories. In his 2017 book, *On Tyranny*, Snyder warns, "the bad news is that the history of modern democracy is also one of decline and fall" (p. 10). He points out that fascism in Europe came about in the last century in response to real and perceived inequalities created by globalization, "and the apparent helplessness of the democracies in addressing them" (p. 12). Rising inequalities and fears of globalization are again afoot, and Snyder goes on to warn that Americans in the 21st century, "are no wiser than the Europeans who saw democracy yield to fascism, Nazism, or communism" during the 20th century (p. 13). Until recently, many in the United States dismissed such concerns, believing that history moves only in one direction – towards liberal democracy. This opens the way, writes Snyder (2017), "for precisely the kinds of regimes we told ourselves could never return" (p. 118).

Most commonly, democracy is thought of in the limited aspect of voting for representatives or ballot initiatives, and as functions of governmental institutions designed to enact laws, allocate resources, regulate activities, and dispense justice. "Because democracy is so commonly identified in procedural terms," writes Spicker (2008), "Voting is a symbol, not the thing itself" (pp. 257–258). We do not, in the least, suggest diminishing critical functions of electoral choices through voting (see Chapter 5 by Andrea Assaf, Chapter 13 by Karen Mack with Elizabeth Cho, and Chapter 16 by Bronwyn Mauldin and Artists 4 Democracy in this volume). Rather, we hope to expand thinking on multiple ways in which democracy shows up in daily practices, and in doing so, to strengthen its institutional forms while simultaneously providing the essential fuel democracies need to evolve and function more equitably. It is through everyday lived experience that we encounter social and civic practices of democracy that build up communities – or, in the lack of such practices, that allow them to fall apart.

There are too many individual instances of threats to democracy to catalog here, so we examine some of the broader trends operating in service of a composite picture that help comprehend what is going wrong and what is at stake.

In the United States, recent public opinion speaks to the fragility of the democratic idea. According to the Pew Research Center, democracy is still a popular form of government that people generally favor. But some respondents lacked a full-throated commitment to democracy because of their frustrations with the way it functions in their particular context. These frustrations have been exploited by those who seek power in antidemocratic ways. Pew's researchers found that the strongest predictor of dissatisfaction with democracy was unhappiness with the state of the economy (Wike & Fetterolf, 2021). This finding is not surprising given the alignment between economic and political life, particularly under neoliberal capitalism dominant in Western countries.

One of the most salient threats to democracy globally is the resurgence of populism. By populism, we mean a constellation of political behaviors with several features. First, populist leaders appeal to "the people," posing them in opposition to intellectuals, scientists, public servants, journalists, and other experts, as well as established systems of laws and government. Second, populism responds to a sense of crisis for which political institutions and arrangements are deemed insufficient (Rivero et al., 2022). This may be caused by a number of factors, but the crisis is made to seem urgent and existential. Third, populists tinker with an outsider political style that disregards or engenders mistrust of traditional forms of evidence or facts, thus promoting ignorance of all that does not interest the populist actor (Moffitt & Tormey, 2014). In this post-truth trap, common evidentiary standards cannot be reached, and the nature of what is real (or scientifically valid) is continually contested and mediated through political rhetoric (Rivero et al., 2022). As Snyder (2017) warns, "Post-truth is pre-fascism" (p. 71).

Populist thinking includes the re-articulation of "freedom" as the absence of civic or social responsibility, and even gives permission to abandon civil behaviors or to observe laws. Finally, the construction of a favored "people" depends on an imaginary of an "other" that is outside the bounds of the body politic, such as immigrants, the undeserving poor, and gender minorities (Rivero et al., 2022, p. 103). This "other" is often the target of scorn, harmful policies, and acts of hate and violence. These cultural divisions are fed by social and popular media that reinforce polarization through disagreements about collective shared history (think of Holocaust denial, rebranding slavery as a "controversial labor practice," and more).

As a propellent of populism around the globe, economic inequality looms large. According to the international Organisation for Economic Co-operation and Development (OECD), income inequality in rich and poor countries is at its highest level in a century, with the richest 10% earning nearly 10 times the income of the bottom 10% across several nations (OECD, 2015). In the United States, the top 1% of the population control as much wealth as the bottom 90% (Smith et al., 2021). Economic inequality this severe has negative consequences for overall economic growth as well as immiserating the lives of the poor, who are left out of the benefits when economic times are good, while suffering the consequences when times are tough. But not all economic inequality or dislocation is real: some is perceived. Some economic anxiety is rooted in racial concerns tied to fears of white people losing their economic and dominant cultural status (Ehrenfreund & Clement, 2016).

A related and less visible global force threatening democracy is neoliberalism. Wendy Brown in *Undoing the Demos* (2015) describes neoliberalism as "a peculiar form of reason that configures all aspects of existence in economic terms [that] is quietly undoing basic elements of democracy" (p. 17). Geographer David Harvey, in *A Brief History of Neoliberalism* (2005), traces its origins to labor unrest of 100 years ago and efforts by large corporate entities to enlist governments in suppression of workers. Corporations largely succeeded, going on to pit governments (local and national) against one another in competition to attract capital to places with more docile labor pools as well as looser (if any) health, safety, and environmental regulations. Global capital, in general, endeavors to operate outside national borders and democratic governments while seeking to enlist their compliance. According to Brown, legal structures unfriendly to capital are

> identified in neoliberal reason as unacceptable blockades in a (mythical) free market, parallel to the ways that welfare provisions such as health care and social security, and even public services and public institutions come to be coded as socialist and cast as market democracy's antithesis.
>
> *(pp. 153–154)*

Brown (2015) recounts an early articulation of neoliberal philosophy promoted by British Prime Minister Margaret Thatcher in the 1980s. Thatcher declared, "There is no such thing as society. There are only individual men and women . . . and their families" (p. 100). With this subtle but profound cultural shift, the social compact dissolves, with everyone encouraged to act only on their own behalf. As a result, Brown argues, governments no longer serve the public, but act on behalf of the market. She writes, "Citizens, meanwhile, are rendered as investors or consumers, not as members of a democratic polity who share power and certain common goods, spaces, and experiences" (p. 176). French social philosopher Michel Foucault characterizes the difference between liberalism and neoliberalism in that, in the latter, the state must "govern for the market, not because of the market" (1979, p. 121, *The Birth of Biopolitics*).

Another assault on democracy in the United States comes ironically through its Supreme Court. An activist conservative majority has rendered decisions gutting civil liberties, reproductive rights, and voting rights – to the delight of the right – as the rest of the nation wonders what denigrations are yet to come. In 2010, the court issued a ruling (*Citizens United v. Federal Election Commission*) permitting unlimited corporate money in political campaigns. These and other actions are the result of a decades-long political and economic project to reshape the courts, led by conservative thinkers such as James Buchanan and funded by the right-wing billionaire Koch brothers, among others, as detailed in Nancy MacLean's chilling book, *Democracy in Chains* (MacLean, 2017).

Rampant misinformation and willful denial about the legitimacy of elections in the United States and beyond is fueled by Donald Trump and his allies, who continue to promote the "Big Lie" that the presidential election was stolen from him in 2020. In the 2022 midterm elections, an overwhelming majority of Republican candidates actively sowed doubt about the trustworthiness of electoral systems. These behaviors are not confined to the United States.

Liberal democracy in America was founded on the enslavement of Africans, the removal and decimation of Indigenous people, and disenfranchisement of women. No narrative of American history is complete without recognition of these facts (Mills, 2017). Nevertheless, there has been a massive backlash against discussion of racial equity, reparations, and historic injustices. Widespread legislative efforts have been undertaken to ban critical race theory in school curricula, defund or even prohibit diversity training, ban books that mention racial oppression and marginalization, and redefine slavery as a charitable job training program. Again, the United States is not alone in the maltreatment of Indigenous and non-dominant racial and ethnic groups. Alika Hope and Penny Brandt, in Chapter 10, describe their work with youth to explore slavery and other injustices through their performance and musical work. In turn, their practices are now guided by the youth who point out to them how similar conditions and treatment of people persist.

Cultural Sector Complicity?

We cannot say the formal creative and cultural sectors have directly contributed to the deterioration of democracies, but in some ways they have been complicit. Beginning in the 1980s, particularly in the United States and the United Kingdom, the arts and culture sectors were marketized in neoliberal fashion. The value of artists, arts organizations, and their activities began to be measured by their contributions to the economy, job creation, tourism, real estate development, and for their spillover impacts on restaurants and retail establishments. Arts agencies and advocacy groups across most Western countries have continued to bank on this rationale for support of the arts and culture sector. Participating as a consumer has taken the place of active engagement in cultural as well as civic arenas rather than sharing ones' stories and talents and deliberating concerns as citizens.

A study of philanthropic patterns by the National Committee for Responsive Philanthropy (Sidford, 2011) examined over $2 billion in annual grantmaking in the arts to find "the vast majority of that funding supports cultural organizations whose work is based in the elite segment of the Western European cultural tradition – commonly called the canon – and whose audiences are predominantly white and upper income" (p. 4). This study was reproduced in 2017 to find that the pattern had, in fact, become more inequitable (Sidford, 2017). After the racial reckoning in the aftermath of the George Floyd murder in 2020, some small shifts may have taken place. However, corporate-style institutional structures and curatorial processes and choices continue to reinforce long-standing patterns of a cultural sector largely supporting a status-quo vision of power and privilege. Top-down production and distribution models see art as product and the public as buyers. Only a miniscule portion of charitable resources have supported those artists and organizations challenging this status quo who promote equity and democratic practices.

In the face of this, and increasing threats to democratic ways of life, the arts and cultural sectors cannot go along or even stand on the sidelines as the advance of populism, neoliberalism, and growing inequities threaten the fabric of democracies.

We assert that a democratic corrective can and should come from every sector, and we have seen many examples of artists and creative cultural practices leading the way. We believe there is hope for equitable and inclusive democracies, and locate part of that hope in the work of artists and cultural workers. Examples in this book describe the vanguard of building more just cultures of democracy. In the sections that follow, we elaborate on what we mean when we talk about democracy and discuss how creative and cultural practices can and do make meaningful contributions to more equitable and inclusive forms and practices of both culture and democracy.

Democracy as Ways of Living Together

Democracy is an ideal and a set of practices made real through daily interactions as well as institutions established to carry out its functions that are designed to reflect the will of the people. In 1939, Dewey wrote that democracy succeeds,

> only as we realize in thought and act that democracy is a *personal* way of individual life; that it signifies the possession and continual use of certain attitudes, forming personal character and determining desire and purpose in all the relations of life.
>
> *(p. 2, emphasis original)*

Democratic ways of being and interacting begin with daily practices and, as such, succeed when they become part of the culture or cultures of communities. Dewey (1939) called for "creative democracy" to be practiced in everyday situations of human association, including the family, schools, the workplace, and religion. Using the anthropological definition of culture as "a way of life" (Williams, 1976), or as it has been extended to describe complex, diverse communities as "ways of living together" (Pérez de Cuéllar, 1996; Borrup, 2021), we argue in this book for the advancement of a *culture of democracy*, or in a pluralistic sense, *cultures of democracy* – ways of living and building communities around principles consistent with democratic ideals, norms, and systems – that strive to achieve more just and inclusive societies. "Creative democracy is more than a pipe dream," writes Andrew Zitcer (2021) in *Practicing Cooperation: Mutual Aid Beyond Capitalism*. "It is manifested by those courageous enough to enter into relationship with it as both a value and a practice" (p. 182).

A question that this book can only begin to explore is, what would a culture of democracy look like? Urban planning and civic engagement scholar and practitioner Patsy Healey (2012) sums up some of the practical aspects, writing:

> Formal government and accompanying political mechanisms to render government institutions accountable and hence legitimate are needed at federal, national, state/province/region and local levels, along with supra-national linkages and global arrangements. However, these exist within, and need to reflect and interact with a political culture in which multiple civil society voices and

> movements can find expression, and connect to the arenas of formal government. It is through this multiplicity that the hegemonies of dominant forces (such as those of corporate capitalism, or of a powerful political ideology) can be continually challenged. This implies that political cultures and the practices of government institutions co-evolve, shaped by complex processes of mobilization, networking and persuasion. It is through such interactions that the streets of daily life and the corridors of government activity move nearer together.
>
> *(p. 33)*

In addition to constituting a way of life, or the culture of a community, a critical tenet of democracy is that it is relational. Echoing Dewey, Richard Rorty, and others, Zitcer (2021) describes democracy as, "an ongoing relational process that needs to occur in our everyday interactions" (p. 216). One of the ways artists can make important contributions is in fostering relationship building that transcends cultures and differences, brings people together, and moves them to collective action.

Embracing cultural, political, racial, economic, and other forms of difference constitutes the work of building democracies. In her book *Deliberative Acts*, Arabella Lyon (2013) asks, "How do diverse peoples recognize and respond to each other while respecting differences of being and knowing?" (p. 8). She observes that "theories of deliberative democracy tend to omit the difficulties of engaging cross-cultural discourses and people" (p. 12). Who better, we argue, to help people engage in such discourses and experiences than artists? They elucidate cultural forms and involve people through creative expression to better understand and appreciate both similarities and differences to forge common ground. In this book, Alan Hill, Kelly Hussey-Smith, Marnie Badham, A. K. M. Uddin, and Sagar Chhetri, in Chapter 8, describe how their photography project that extends over several Asian-Pacific countries does just that.

This work helps people develop cultural competencies that extend to productive civic activities. Desirée Campagna (2022), in her book *Participatory Governance and Cultural Development*, writes, "Cultural participatory processes are opportunities for promoting 'inclusive cultural empowerment,' making individuals use their cultural competencies to develop cultural actions in their social context" (p. 3). Authors in the Learning Environments section of this book, Maria Asp, Sonja Kuftinec, and Kiyoko Motoyama Sims, describe building on those competencies in classrooms preparing young people for active democratic participation.

Distinguishing "Cultures of Democracy"

A lifetime of study is not sufficient to fully describe any culture, including one so complex that it embodies democracy. Social philosopher Charles Taylor (2007) in his article "Cultures of Democracy and Citizen Efficacy," writes:

> It may well be that the attempt to answer totally general questions – such as, what are the conditions of democracy? – is misguided. General questions

> assume that there is some recognizable political culture of democracy and a set of economic and social conditions that enable this. In fact, it would seem more sensible to start from another basic assumption: that there are culture*s* of democracy, in the plural. Just as we have (many of us) stopped talking about *modernity* and speak now of *multiple modernities*, so we will have to recognize different democratic forms.
>
> *(p. 118, emphasis original)*

We are not the first to employ the terms "culture" or "cultures of democracy" but hope to clearly illustrate ways creative work fosters such conditions. We distinguish cultures of democracy from related approaches such as *cultural democracy* and *democratization of culture* while building on these ideas in a continuum.

More widely used in Europe, the idea of the *democratization of culture* was initiated at the end of the 1950s, proposing that the masterpieces of humanity should be accessible to as many people as possible. In other words, "to bring cultural heritage closer to the public and to encourage the creation of works of art to enrich it" (Porto Santo Charter). Democratization of culture began as a top-down or colonialist vision in which one monolithic culture is to be "democratically" or more equally distributed. Recognizing the diversity of cultures, more recent iterations of democratization of culture in the European Union call on governments and cultural institutions to incorporate democratic practices within the mechanisms of funding, governance, and management of the field.

The movement and practice of promoting *cultural democracy* gained traction as a bottom-up or decolonizing approach in the United States in the 1980s. It is described in the Porto Santo Charter as an effort to build consensus around culture and democracy. According to the Charter, cultural democracy:

> advocates for the creation of conditions for a more active cultural participation, and the recognition of the cultural practices of different social groups. "Cultural Democracy" implies a new relational model between institutions and communities: culture becomes a platform where each person can participate and be responsible. This paradigm implies a change in attitude and a shift from the model of cultural consumption to a model of cultural commitment. It values what each one knows, their traditions, their voice. It does not "bring culture" into a territory, because culture already exists in every territory: it values local culture and complements it with other cultural expressions, opening up local experience to the universal, and stimulating this dialogue.
>
> *(Porto Santo Charter, n.d.)*

While perhaps two sides of a coin, these ideas are focused on building the ideals and practices of democracy in the cultural arena. They do not explicitly mobilize the cultural and arts sector to contribute to practices of democracy in the broader sociopolitical context, although many practitioners do just that and have built the foundation on which the work described in this book stands.

Recognizing activist approaches taken by many artists in the late 1990s, an effort was launched in the United States to support artists and arts organizations in social change work under a program called Animating Democracy. With Ford Foundation support, and housed within the Washington, D.C., arts advocacy organization Americans for the Arts, nonprofits across the United States were provided grants, networking opportunities, and support to engage communities in civic dialogue through topical artworks with artists and their work as catalysts. Artwork addressed local and global social issues, applying many strategies in public dialogue facilitation. Animating Democracy had a two-decade-long life building a legacy of practice among many artists and organizations.

Creative work that has come to be known as *civic* or *social practice*, or *socially engaged art*, often comes from schools of artists committed to employing their skills in progressive social change work. It aims directly at working in civic and political arenas generally focused around a specific social issue. Practices we include in this volume overlap with and draw from these concepts and practices. Andrea Assaf, in Chapter 5, traces her personal journey through these art practices evolving into ways of making theatre that employs and instills democratic practices with collaborators and audiences alike. Rui Gonçalves Cepeda, in Chapter 7, writes about an artist-designed public spectacle in Portugal that engages people as actors in a vernacular cultural practice. This work and ways of working, highlighted in these chapters and others, reverberate outwardly across the ideals, norms, and systems of democracy, fostering ongoing individual and social actions and ways of participating in everyday practices of democracy as well as in its institutions and systems.

Democracy as Practice

Echoing the work of moral philosopher Alasdair MacIntyre Zitcer (2021) writes, "ethical community life is based on sustained, complex forms of association known as practices. Practices are specific to a given time and place, derived from traditions, and based in shared narratives. Through practices, it is possible to pursue democratic, just, and inclusive ends" (p. 56). In a related idea, Zitcer goes on to assert that, "The work of securing the place of practices in the transformation of society is to emphasize that nothing is done in isolation from anything else or anyone else" (p. 67). Practices are inherently social and communal.

In a similar way of thinking, in a city planning context, Healey (2012) asserts the importance of a focus on what she calls *micro-practices of democracy-in-action*. These range from the day-to-day of accessing services, being recognized in the workplace, sharing public space in streets, parks, and playgrounds, to participating in neighborhood design, planning, or policy work. This involvement, she says, "points towards a 'culture of practice' (a way of being/doing; not just a way of saying)" (p. 34). It is in these micro-practices she asserts, "that people get to learn what building more people-centered, pluralistic and richly intelligent political cultures in which diverse voices get to be listened to respectfully can mean" (p. 30–31).

Healey's ideas are highly relevant to the community work of artists described in this book. In Chapters 2 and 12, Meena Natarajan and Lisa Jo Epstein, respectively, describe their work in the context of participatory community planning in Minneapolis and Philadelphia.

Rarely have just and humane societies come about through a focus on outcomes (or ends) while neglecting the ways of getting there (the means). Jane Addams, founder and long-time leader of Chicago's Hull House and the Settlement House Movement in the United States wrote, "Social advance depends as much upon the process through which it is secured as upon the result thereof" (cited in Serrat, 2017, p. 240). Australian contributors to this book, D'Arcy Molan, Katya Johanson and Emily Potter (Chapter 1 as well as Anna Kennedy-Borissow in Chapter 4) write about how community-led creative recovery addresses the integrity of cultural work that reflects community values while reinforcing democratic practices in rural communities.

From our studies of democracy and experiences with creative and cultural practices, we identified a set of six practices we find share common ground across democracy and ways artists and cultural organizations engage in community-building and social change practices. In summary, these are:

1. Storytelling and the construction of narratives that create empathy and increase levels of comfort with people and ideas that are different or unfamiliar. These are seen in this volume in chapters by Kiyoko Motoyama Sims, Maria Asp and Sonja Kuftinec, Alika Hope and Penny Brandt, Alan Hill et al., and Heather McLean.
2. Design of the built environment or creation of spaces and places that foster equitable interactions, relationship-building, and a sense of belonging. We see in the chapters by Rachel Wenrick and Kirsten Kaschock, Karen Mack and Elizabeth Cho, Rui Gonçalves Cepeda, as well as D'Arcy Molan, Katya Johanson, and Emily Potter.
3. Distribution of power and leadership that dissolves hierarchies, builds bridges, welcomes participation, and builds political agency among individuals and groups. These questions are addressed by Andrea Assaf, Lisa Jo Epstein, and Meena Natarajan, and Anna Kennedy-Borissow.
4. Discourse and deliberation that fosters learning and a sense of multiple possibilities while building capacities for collective problem-solving. More ideas on these practices can be found in the Learning Environments section, and in chapters by Vincent Russell, and Karen Mack with Elizabeth Cho.
5. Advocacy and organizing that generates greater understanding and provides inclusive vehicles for resistance and mobilizing change. These are addressed in chapters by Bronwyn Mauldin and Artists 4 Democracy, Meena Natarajan, and Andrea Assaf.
6. Engagement in governing and electoral processes to maintain accountability, legitimize, and formalize institutions of democracy. We learn more about this practice later in the book by Johanna K. Taylor, Amanda Lovelee, and Mallory Rukhsana Nezam (CAIR Lab), Bronwyn Mauldin and Artists 4 Democracy, as well as Vincent Russell.

In advancing these practices through their work, the artists, educators, and observers writing in this book illustrate what Healey (2012) describes as, "Small struggles which hardly seem to make a difference [that], if built on in the flow of time, lead to major changes in political cultures" (p. 20).

Learning "Democratic Dispositions"

Beyond the ideals and broad characteristics of democracy and its systems, establishing socio-political norms are central to successful democracies. How and where do people throughout life develop and practice democratic ways of living, gain practical skills, and build relationships to contribute as co-creators in their communities?

Democracy scholar, Mark E. Warren, looks at synergies between the norms and systems through his *self-transformation thesis*. He explores how participation in democratic processes and institutions alters attitudes and behaviors that in turn strengthen democracies. Warren (1993) speculates that, "increasing participation in a range of institutions – such as workplaces, schools, neighborhoods, and city organizations – is likely to produce individuals with democratic dispositions" (p. 209). The self, he claims, "is constituted through interactions with its social context" (p. 210). Campagna (2022) agrees, writing, "participation activates a virtuous cycle of capacity building, legitimacy, and social capital" (p. 32). People can be transformed through participation including discourse and deliberation in a variety of civic and social settings. Warm Cookies of the Revolution (Chapter 14), described by Vincent Russell, builds individual and community muscles for productive discourse, deliberation, and co-creation of solutions. Authors of all four chapters in the Learning Environments section illustrate how they employ creative tools for individual and collective transformation.

Warren goes on to say that individuals who participate in these social practices, "would be more tolerant of differences, more sensitive to reciprocity, better able to engage in moral discourse and judgment, and more prone to examine their own preferences – all qualities conducive to the success of democracy" (1993, p. 209). Ironically, one cannot assume that people in the professional arena who build and operate the systems and bureaucracies designed to carry out policies of democracy possess the qualities Warren describes. David E. Booher (2004) in his *National Civic Review* article, *Collaborative Governance Practices and Democracy*, finds that "Many public officials [as well as] members of the public are unfamiliar with such methods of collaborative governance practice as mediation and facilitation, process design, authentic public participation, cross-cultural communication, and reflective dialogue; nor do they have the skills to participate" (p. 42).

In his book *Democracy Administered: How Public Administration Shapes Representative Government* (2021), Anthony Bertelli describes how, "The project of public administration is to integrate policy work into representative government in theory and to ensure that the behavior of policy workers supports each theory of such integration in practice" (p. 174). Bertelli looks at the synergies and tensions between elected officials, policies they set, and policy workers who carry them out, pointing to the dilemma that "no structure is neutral to democratic values; each one enhances some values while compromising others" (p. 10). Interplay between ideals of democracy, administrative and policy structures, and norms practiced by people working within them are addressed in Chapter 15, by Johanna K. Taylor, Amanda Lovelee, and Mallory Rukhsana Nezam (CAIR Lab), who describe how artists-in-residence in municipal governments bring creativity and democracy closer together.

Public education has long been considered a critical space in which people early in life learn and hone citizenship skills. Civic education scholars Steven P. Camicia and Ryan Knowles (2021) write that while "supporting democracy comprises one of the most stated goals of public education" (p. 5), ". . . civic education has either fallen out of the public school curriculum or fails to address issues in our democracy" (p. vii). They are certainly not alone in this observation. Democracy scholar and activist, Harry Boyte (2018) came to the same conclusion in his book, *Awakening Democracy through Public Work*. Boyte works with schools to prepare students for active civic life while trying to create a more "democratic atmosphere" within educational institutions (p. 141). Boyte describes fostering young citizens-to-be, observing that, "people are not born knowing how to be citizen co-creators" (p. 107).

Personal transformation and the forming of cultures of democracy go hand in hand. Boyte's democracy-building work in educational settings prepares active citizens while bridging them with communities and the issues they face. He calls this, "an approach to citizenship in which citizens are co-creators, *builders of the common world, not simply voters and volunteers who fit into that world or protesters who oppose it*" (p. 5–6, emphasis in original). Although his book never mentions artists, he calls participants in his program "artisans of possibility" (p. 143).

The field of education since Dewey's advocacy in the late 19th century, and possibly before, has wrestled with ways of building individual and social capacities to bolster democracy. Planning and public policy scholar Robert W. Lake (2017) described Dewey's ideas in this arena:

> Education as preparation for participation in democratic reasoning represented a radical departure from the prevailing focus of education as preparation for participation in the industrial labor force. Dewey's views on education in this regard encountered vigorous opposition from corporate and government interests that sought to align the purpose of public education with the needs of a rapidly expanding industrial economy
>
> *(p. 487).*

Artists as Practitioners (and Teachers) of Democracy

Artists refract the world around them, breaking the light and re-assembling it differently. From this, we gain new perspectives and new ways of thinking. Artists in this book take their work further. They galvanize groups and communities to envision and build alternatives, mobilize movements through rehearsals, and move onto the public stage. In his 1939 charge to re-invigorate democracy, Dewey wrote, "The task can be accomplished only by inventive effort and creative activity." (p. 1). This is exactly what we see artists bringing. Writers in this book describe how public sentiment is moved, policies changed, political candidates rise and fall. Artists are in the thick of this work in more ways than is generally acknowledged.

Constitutional scholar Danielle Allen (2006) calls the American Civil Rights Movement a refounding of the United States that created an opportunity to reconstitute the social contract and build new democratic structures on the backs of the old, failed ones. In her book, *Our Declaration*, Allen wrote:

> The best way to avoid being dominated is to help build the world . . . to help, like an architect, determine its pattern and structure. The point of political equality is not merely to secure spaces free from domination but also to engage all members of a community equally in the work of creating and constantly recreating that community
>
> *(cited in Boyte, 2018, p. 8).*

Artists engage people to become architects and designers in ongoing processes of creation and re-creation. Meena Natarajan (Chapter 2) and Lisa Jo Epstein (Chapter 12) illustrate how practices of theater-making and the work of building and rebuilding communities can be one and the same. Kirsten Kaschock and Rachel Wenrick, writing about Philadelphia's Writers Room in Chapter 4, similarly reflect on collective processes to construct spaces for envisioning and building more equitable and engaged communities.

In an illuminating book, *Grassroots Leadership and the Arts for Social Change* (2017), contributing author Garth A. Ross asks, "since many of the problems our communities face are cultural, why do we invest so little in cultural tools for responding to cultural problems?" (in Erenrich & Wergin, 2017, p. 259). "Just as we turn to financial tools for responding to financial problems," Ross continues, "we must turn to cultural tools for responding to cultural problems" (p. 259).

Creative and cultural work needs to be recognized as a vastly underemployed vehicle for engaging people in stimulating imaginations, building relationships, and learning to work together in communities to define critical social issues, co-create new solutions, build power, and mobilize people to action.

This book is about doing just that, bringing more tools to the work of shaping more just and inclusive forms of democracy on the governmental level and in daily life, institutions, and professional practices. We need to turn to highly creative people who are available in every community: artists and arts and cultural workers and their organizations. And, while not all artists or organizations are inclined towards or prepared for this work, many are – and have been for more than 100 years, as described in the Foreword. "Artists and artistic leaders can be creative problem-posers who use the arts as a tool to galvanize communities into collective problem-solvers," asserts Ross (in Erenrich & Wergin, 2017, p. 260). They are at work in communities asking probing, challenging questions and leading processes in which people come together to learn and to devise unique solutions for social problems. Vincent Russell gives an inside view of Colorado's Warm Cookies of the Revolution in Chapter 14, and Karen Mack with Elizabeth Cho, in Chapter 13, illustrate how they engage residents in co-creating and deliberating solutions to sticky issues. This work brings people together and mobilizes them to address shared interests through co-created solutions and collective action as well as to press governmental bodies to do the right thing – or to change the players, as Bronwyn Mauldin and Artists 4 Democracy describes in Chapter 16.

The idea of the *citizen-artist* has been discussed by numerous scholars and practitioners (Burnham, 1998; Plessner, 2018, 2022; Green, 2011; Sturm, 2018), bridging the profession of artist with social responsibility and activism in the political world. James Baldwin was called a citizen-artist "who assumed the dual responsibilities of art practice and political activism" (Gehlawat, 2022, p. 108). Similarly, Leonard Bernstein, for his outspoken nature related to injustices he saw, has been called a citizen-artist (Bernstein, 2018). Artist collectives such as Group Material and Guerilla Girls, active in New York from the late 1970s through much of the 1990s, took more radical, activist roles largely to provoke debate and animate social issues. However, these kinds of efforts remain on the margins of cultural practice, or, as in the cases of Baldwin and Bernstein, the *citizen* part was considered a peculiar add-on to their central practice.

Artists, including Assaf, Epstein, Mauldin and Artists 4 Democracy, Natajaran, and others in this volume, take their role still further, fully blending artistic practices with social activism. Activism is their art. They apply creative methods to community organizing, group facilitation, formulating policy alternatives, and getting out the vote. Spaces and activities created by artists and other activists – whether they be mental, social, or physical spaces – can stimulate civic imaginations serving as models for new, more equitable ways of living together. Building civic imaginations and gathering tools to be agents of worldmaking (or remaking), as Dilip Parameshwar Gaonkar in *Public Culture* (2007) calls for, are other contributions these artists make along with inciting the "capacity to aspire" (Appadurai, 2007, p. 33). The work of artists and cultural organizations in this book illustrate this through ways they dissect stories, larger narratives, daily life patterns, and institutional behaviors. Heather McLean, in Western Canada (Chapter 6), with her collaborative satirical performances, inspires with humor and radical notions of addressing complex social issues.

Citing the transformative 1970s work of Paolo Friere, Jon Wergin (in Erenrich & Wergin, 2017) writes, "Friere's theory [is] that people undergo a shift in consciousness as they become aware of the limits that surround them, and require a 'dialogic process' for this to happen" (p. 317). Wergin goes on to highlight the critical role for the arts, "namely providing a forum for participation in a safe 'aesthetic space' and consolidation of energy" (p. 317). "Creating energy for social change," writes Wergin, "is not just about persuasion through rational arguments, as necessary as that might be; it is also about connecting to others in extra-rational ways, through the heart, which of course is what the arts do" (2017, p. xlii). We see artists moving not only hearts but mouths, feet, hands, the full action of bodies, and, most importantly, other people.

Structure of the Book

We hope you will be moved by the stories that follow. As editors, we employed our personal and professional networks to solicit writers for this book. We were moved by the large number of chapter proposals received, from which we selected 16 based on their mix of creative practices, writing quality, and connection with the practices of democracy. In this group we saw artists working in four distinct arenas around which we organized the book. We then invited writers who have recognized knowledge of each of these four arenas to compose introductions to these sections. Place-Based Work is introduced by Jeremy Liu and John K. C. Liu; Learning Environments, by Susan Badger Booth; Aesthetic Strategies, by Diane Ragsdale and Shannon Litzenberger; and Civic Processes, by Roberto Bedoya. While these are not the only arenas in which artists work, they encompass important sociopolitical settings and places to advance the conversation we hope this book contributes to.

References

Appadurai, A. (2007). Hope and democracy. In D. P. Gaonkar (Ed.), *Public culture, cultures of democracy*. Society of Transnational Cultural Studies.

Bernstein, J. (2018). Leonard Bernstein, citizen artist. *American Music Review, 48*(1).

Bertelli, A. M. (2021). *Democracy administered: How public administration shapes representative government*. Cambridge University Press.

Booher, D. E. (2004). Collaborative governance practices and democracy. *National Civic Review, 93*(4), 32–46.

Borrup, T. (2021). *The power of culture in city planning*. Routledge.

Boyte, H. C. (2018). *Awakening democracy through public work: Pedagogies of empowerment*. Vanderbilt University Press.

Brown, W. (2015). *Undoing the demos: Neoliberalism's stealth revolution*. Zone Books.

Burnham, L. F., & Durland, S. (1998). *The citizen artist: 20 years of art in the public arena: An anthology from high performance magazine 1978–1998 (Thinking Publicly)*. Critical Press.

Camicia, S. P., & Knowles, R. (2021). *Education for democracy: A renewed approach to civic inquiries for social justice*. Information Age Publishing.

Campagna, D. (2022). *Participatory governance and cultural development*. Palgrave McMillan.

Dewey, J. (1939). *Creative democracy: The task before us*. http://www.beloit.edu/~pbk/dewey.html

Ehrenfreund, M., & Clement, S. (2016, March 22). Economic and racial anxiety: Two separate forces driving support for Donald Trump. *Washington Post*. https://www.washingtonpost.com/news/wonk/wp/2016/03/22/economic-anxiety-and-racial-anxiety-two-separate-forces-driving-support-for-donald-trump/

Erenrich, S. J., & Wergin, J. F. (2017). *Grassroots leadership and the arts for social change*. Emerald Publishing.

Foucault, M. (1979). *Birth of biopolitics lectures*. University of Chicago Institute for Law & Economics.

Gaonkar, D. P. (Ed.). (2007). *Public culture, cultures of democracy*. Society of Transnational Cultural Studies.

Gehlawat, M. (2022). Baldwin and the role of the citizen artist. *James Baldwin Review, 8*(1). https://doi.org/10.7227/JBR.8.6

Green, A. (2011). Citizen artists: Group material. *Afterall: A Journal of Art, Context and Enquiry*, *26*, 17–25.

Harvey, D. (2005). *A brief history of neoliberalism*. Oxford University Press.

Healey, P. (2012). Re-enchanting democracy as a mode of governance. *Critical Policy Studies, 6*(1), 19–39. https://doi.org/10.1080/19460171.2012.659880

Kimber, R. (1989). On democracy. *Scandinavian Political Studies, 12*(3), 199–219.

Lake, R. W. (2017). On poetry, pragmatism and the urban possibility of creative democracy. *Urban Geography, 38*(4), 479–494. https://doi.org/10.1080/02723638.2016.1272195

Lyon, A. (2013). *Deliberative acts: Democracy, rhetoric, and rights*. Pennsylvania State University Press.

MacLean, N. (2017). *Democracy in chains: The deep history of the radical right's stealth plan for America*. Viking.

Mills, C. W. (2017). *Black rights/white wrongs the critique of racial liberalism*. Oxford University Press.

Moffitt, B., & Tormey, S. (2014). Rethinking populism: Politics, mediatisation and political style. *Political Studies, 62*(2), 381–397. https://doi.org/10.1111/1467-9248.12032

OECD. (2015). *In it together: Why less inequality benefits all (summary in English)*. Organisation for Economic Co-operation and Development. https://www.oecd-ilibrary.org/employment/in-it-together-why-less-inequality-benefits-all/summary/english_bc9f5d0b-en?parentId=http%3A%2F%2Finstance.metastore.ingenta.com%2Fcontent%2Fpublication%2F9789264235120-en

Pérez de Cuéllar, J. (1996, July). *Our creative diversity – Summary version (Report of the World Commission on Culture and Development)*. UNESCO.

Plessner, F. D. (2022). *Doing politics with citizen art*. Rowman & Littlefield.

Porto Santo Charter. (n.d.). *Preamble*. https://portosantocharter.eu/the-charter/#preamble

Rivero, J. J., Sotomayor, L., Zanotto, J. M., & Zitcer, A. (2022). Democratic public or populist rabble: Repositioning the city amidst social fracture. *International Journal of Urban and Regional Research, 46*(1), 101–114. https://doi.org/10.1111/1468-2427.12898

Serrat, O. (2017). *Knowledge solutions: Tools, methods, and approaches to drive organizational performance*. Asian Development Bank. https://doi.org/10.1007/978-981-10-0983-9_24

Sidford, H. (2011). *Fusing arts, culture and social change: High impact strategies for philanthropy*. National Committee for Responsive Philanthropy.

Sidford, H. (2017, July). *Not just money: Equity issues in cultural philanthropy*. Report for the Surdna Foundation, New York.

Smith, M., Zidar, O., & Zwick, E. (2021, October 18). Top wealth in America: New estimates and implications for taxing the rich. *Department of Economics – Princeton University*. https://economics.princeton.edu/working-papers/top-wealth-in-america-new-estimates-and-implications-for-taxing-the-rich/

Snyder, T. (2017). *On tyranny: Twenty lessons from the twentieth century*. Penguin Random House.

Spicker, P. (2008). Government for the people: The substantive elements of democracy. *International Journal of Social Welfare, 17*, 251–259.

Sturm, A. M. (2018). *Citizen artist*. UC San Diego Electronic Theses and Dissertations. https://escholarship.org/uc/item/28p659v3

Taylor, C. (2007). Cultures of democracy and citizen efficacy. *Public Culture, 19*(1). https://doi.org/10.1215/08992363-2006-027

Warren, M. E. (1993). Can participatory democracy produce better selves? Psychological dimensions of Habermas's discursive model of democracy. *Political Psychology, 14*(2), 209–234.

Wike, R., & Fetterolf, J. (2021, December 7). *Global public opinion in an era of democratic anxiety*. Pew Research Center's Global Attitudes Project. https://www.pewresearch.org/global/2021/12/07/global-public-opinion-in-an-era-of-democratic-anxiety/

Williams, R. (1976). *Keywords: A vocabulary of culture and society*. Oxford University Press.

Zitcer, A. (2021). *Practicing cooperation: Mutual aid beyond capitalism*. University of Minnesota Press.

PART ONE

Place-Based Actions

INTRODUCTION TO PLACE-BASED ACTIONS

Following the Thread of Place-Based Actions

Jeremy Liu and John K. C. Liu

Culture, unlike democracy, is self-propelled and self-propagating: it is persistent, in ways that democracy strives to be; it is effusive, in ways that democracy should be; it is practical, as democracy must always be; and it is critical, in ways democracy is too often not. In these ways, culture's strength and importance to civic life is that it runs through everything; it is the warp to democracy's weft. The growing recognition of Indigenous wisdom about place and its management are important to acknowledge in any discussion of place-based work. The "new" ideas of regenerative and permaculture agriculture can draw a lineage to Indigenous wisdom, for example. Regeneration of democracy, and permaculture-like practices in its stewardship, remind us that democracy has had an Indigenous lineage well before the misattribution of its birth date as the American Revolution or even 5th-century BCE Athens.

Democracy – the value and its practice – requires constant nurturing, widespread participation, regular renewal, visible processes, and meaningful outcomes. It is neither a given nor a natural state of human affairs. Creative practice is one mechanism for this social embodiment of democracy, just as its dark twin, civic deviousness, can be for society's authoritarian impulses.

Creative practice runs in our family and in our community along culture's warp, interwoven with democratic values manifest in community gardens, affordable housing, historic preservation, community organizing, economic development, sustainability, politics and policy, and arts such as performance, poetry, and film. This path guides us through the four chapters in Part One as they describe creative practices in four communities where democracy and culture are woven into beautiful tapestries.

DOI: 10.4324/9781003475996-3

These chapters, read together, reflect an important underlying truth: that culture is reflected in all democratic practices. Sometimes it manifests expressly as artistic practice that is a surrogate for a democratic one, as in the examples of the Lake Street Arts in Minneapolis (Minnesota, USA) and Creative Recovery in Australia, in which cases dramatic upheaval disrupted the routine functioning of democratic processes. The examples in West Philadelphia (Pennsylvania, USA) and in Northwest Victoria (AUS) highlight creative activity or culturally resonant symbols that anchor the gathering, aligning, and mobilizing effects necessary to a thriving democracy.

In Chapter 4, "Democracy as Demonstration: A Lifelong, Dreamed of, Home," we tap into the conversation that witnessed a patient insistence on widening the circle of influence around the idea for a Writers Room in West Philadelphia. As the initial project, the Writers Room, responded to the hopes and dreams of more and more people in the neighborhood, it evolved into the Second Story Collective, a working model for "shared living space and shared stories (that) can create a foundation for meaningful cohabitation and community-building and preservation – that the right housing innovations can address affordability and equity at the same time." Community-based creative practices that guided the evolution of the Writers Room into the Second Story Collective are powerful examples of persuasive democracy, where the work of dreaming and designing together persuades more to the causes of equity and justice in civic life.

Pangea World Theater and the community surrounding Lake Street in Minneapolis are located at the epicenter of the uprising in response to the George Floyd murder. In Chapter 2, "Lake Street Arts! – Creative Democracy in Practice," Meena Natarajan (co-artistic and executive director of Pangea World Theater) describes four dimensions of their creative practice and its influence on shaping a series of art interventions across from the police station that was the focal point of the 2020 uprising: collective power, preparing the ground, politics of space and time, and transformation. The core assertion is that "Art and performance that is rooted in these cross-cultural relationships can model pathways to strengthen the arts as a vital space for racial, gender based and economic equity." This effusive democracy claims space in race, gender, and economic life, pushing it well beyond its most common association with the political realm.

Democracy happens in all the places where ideas, beliefs, and values are manifested. The greatest triumphs and failures of democratic values have occurred over the contestation of power in place and over place. It is the link between who and what and for whom and for what we build and create. In north-west Victoria, abandoned grain silos are utilized to reflect a contemporary version of a town "commons" through "the combination of practice, process, and outcome that actively embraces large-scale community participation and co-creation, as well as smaller scale artistic interventions in community life" that the authors of Chapter 1, "Repurposing Agricultural Infrastructure to Build Cultures of Democracy in Rural Communities: A Case Study From North-West Victoria," call "democratic spectacle."

This case study describes a creative project in which the processes of its creation are designed to serve an artistic and democratic goal. This insistent democracy imagines a richly layered civic life where democratic processes are embedded and made visible throughout, including acknowledgement of the grain silos as symbols of a colonial and contemporary anti-Indigenous agenda.

Seeking resilience is a growing priority among communities and public and private institutions alike. Author Anna Kennedy-Borissow makes a compelling case for building in arts and cultural approaches to disaster and emergency response planning in Chapter 3, "How 'Creative Recovery' Stimulates a Culture of Democracy: Case Studies of Post-Disaster Creativity in Rural Australia." We are offered the possibility that creative recovery projects can directly inform and make more equitable and just "non-creative recovery" projects. Just as importantly, Kennedy-Borissow highlights the transformative and transformable nature of creative recovery efforts; indeed, the recovery efforts themselves are resilient!

The diverse perspectives of the four chapters only begin to touch on the range of diverse cultural practices found in different social contexts. These authors suggest that considering community in cultural terms makes it much easier to understand them. For example, in most Western contexts, the focus tends to be on the individual and/or individuals; an individual is the unit of analysis or concern. Whereas in large parts of non-Western societies, the community is most often considered as the basic social unit. In these divisive times, it is heartening to learn of the evolution towards recognizing and operationalizing the community as the basic social unit in these four examples.

For over two decades, in places as different and similar as Boston and Oakland, and as far-flung yet so close as Taiwan and Japan, we have practiced community development as a form of creative expression. Jeremy's experiences are grounded in a close and cultural reading of the practice of community development by and for the Asian American community in two different cultural and identity-based community development corporations, the Asian Community Development Corporation in Boston (Massachusetts, USA) and the East Bay Asian Local Development Corporation in Oakland (California, USA). But this could also be described as a myopia that helped him to recognize the cultural in every community's development.

Practices that are grounded in culture have a particular value in advancing an equitable and just democracy and resilient and regenerative civic life. For example, while it is common to equate democracy with the act of voting, simply adding up how many individuals prefer one solution over another often does achieve real workable solutions in a community setting. Countering this simplistic notion of democracy can be found in the story of a profound intergenerational community's self-help action that created the Siyuan Castle Story Hall, as documented by John, founder and chairperson of the the National Taiwan University Building and Planning Research Foundation, who writes: "we switched gears and relied on repetitive story-telling rather than counting individual heads to get closer to the whole picture, avoiding splitting the community into majority and minority voices, and thereby holding the community together" (NTU BPRF, 2023).

Place-based practices, learning environments, community-based aesthetic, and civic processes represent the fabric of civic life that artists, culture bearers, and community members weave. And this is related to how we understand democracy. By weaving culture and creativity into forms of social organization, i.e., a democracy, we come around to "community as the basic social unit," and "collective and creative actions" as the core necessary capabilities. And these address the rights of community members to participate in decision-making – that each has a voice and a role in contributing to decisions made.

The specific methods and procedures for this voice and role to take place require cultural input to be efficacious. In an urban diverse community, the procedures could be quite different from those of a rural tight-knit traditional community, or of a Native Indigenous community. None is more or less democratic than the others, but in order to move from participation to influence, the unique nature of these procedures must be grasped. Different forms of democratic participation around the world rely on storytelling as well; Town Hall meeting governance in Massachusetts (Commonwealth of Massachusetts, n.d.) and parliamentary government in the United Kingdom and Europe are two examples.

In our work, we have used role-playing, storytelling, scenario writing, collage making, spatial patterns, etc., as instruments in facilitating processes of participation. A longitudinal, randomized trial of storytelling and perspective-taking by researcher Ayesha McAdams-Mahmoud, ScD, MPH (McAdams-Mahmoud, n.d.) found that these practices generate statistically significantly steeper decreases in social prejudice, increased institutional trust, and more equitable and trusting conversations.

One of the enlightening aspects of community participation is the energizing effects of the process over the end result. And as important, this energizing effect can lead to more impactful end results even when the end result is unpredictable until it emerges. When a physical form finally emerges, it is a full representation of the collective efforts of the community. This is what we as designers have called "community aesthetics" or "Democratic aesthetics," which becomes distinctive and characteristic of the community.

The full integration of democracy and creative practice can lead to a weaving of culture into civic life at the most systematic levels of policy and social infrastructure. A Culture-in-All-Policies approach, akin to the "Health-in-All-Policies" movement, can provide a comprehensive approach that recognizes the cultural underpinnings of housing, education, economic development, and other sectors. Without creative practice, we are knitting a single strand of democracy with the very real risk of a small snag or catch turning into a catastrophic unraveling. When we weave culture and creative practice into civic life, we reinforce democracy like the strength, utility, and beauty of an expertly woven fabric.

References

Commonwealth of Massachusetts. (n.d.). *Forms of government in Massachusetts*. Retrieved December 5, 2023, from https://www.mma.org/wp-content/uploads/2018/07/forms_of_local_government_0.pdf.

McAdams-Mahmoud, A. (n.d.). *Portfolio of work*. https://scholar.harvard.edu/ayeshamm/portfolio-work

NTU BPRF. (2023, May 5). 思源機堡-從集體記憶到生活地景之共做. *變革：反思臺大城鄉基金會30年*. https://ntubprf30.online/siyuan/.

1

REPURPOSING AGRICULTURAL INFRASTRUCTURE TO BUILD CULTURES OF DEMOCRACY IN RURAL COMMUNITIES

A Case Study from North-West Victoria

D'Arcy Molan, Katya Johanson, and Emily Potter

Natimuk is a town of just over 500 people in the Wimmera region of Australia. A four-hour drive northwest of the Victorian capital city of Melbourne, and a four-and-a-half-hour drive from the South Australian capital city of Adelaide, it is officially considered "remote" (Australian Bureau of Statistics, 2023). Natimuk has developed a unique culture from a highly diverse collective of people: a culturally active and respected First Nations community; farming families with long historical landholdings; a network of rock climbers who choose to live in the town to access the nearby popular landmark Dyurrite/Mount Arapiles (which is eight kilometers west of Natimuk); and artists who – if they were not born into any of the groups already mentioned – are drawn to take up residence by the vibrancy of the community and the beauty of the environment. Local arts activities involve not only all of these groups, but also the physical landscape of the town as an active participant. These arts activities play a critical role in establishing, enacting, and celebrating democratic processes between the town's diverse people. They provide a means by which the town faces common challenges and manages potential tensions in a manner we call here a "democratic spectacle" (Molan, 2023).

The first author of this chapter, D'Arcy Molan, is a Natimuk musician and writer. A non-Indigenous man, D'Arcy has a matrilineal connection through his mother, Sherrin Molan (nee Huntly), to farming families in the Wimmera, who migrated from Scotland and England in the late 1840s and persisted until the death of D'Arcy's grandparents Audrey and Bill Huntly in the 2010s. Both grandparents were born and lived in the Edenhope/Apsley areas. D'Arcy's arts practice (tenor saxophone and piano) stems from Audrey, who was a well-known and loved pianist, jazz musician, and community arts organizer that D'Arcy grew up performing with (although he lived in Melbourne). As an adult, D'Arcy set up a home in Natimuk to pursue research on the Wimmera's cultural history and its current

DOI: 10.4324/9781003475996-4

artistic expression. This chapter is written with Katya Johanson, whose research focuses on the relationship between artistic practice and political or social objectives, and Emily Potter, who researches the cultural life of the Wimmera and neighbouring Mallee region.

Much has been written about the role that arts play in symbolically accompanying or supporting democratic movements (Kölbl & Trümpi, 2021). Arts are seen as providing people with critical social and life skills, such as resilience and social and civic participation skills (McHenry, 2011, p. 246). This chapter illustrates the ways in which in a regional community, the skills and social capital that arts help to build facilitate community-based democracy. Case studies of Natimuk's arts activities provide examples of the relationship between human creativity and the physical environment, and their ability to navigate complex place histories. We coined the term "democratic spectacle" to refer to the combination of practice, process, and outcome that actively embraces large-scale community participation and co-creation, as well as smaller-scale artistic interventions in community life, including installations, activities, and workshops that are more conversational in tone and content but still contain performative and collaborative aspects.

Rapid urbanization, globalization, and the shift first from community-based to state-based social services and then toward their privatization have challenged participatory forms of democracy by undermining the geographical stability of local economies and communities (Gallagher, 2021). They have replaced collective decision-making processes with government-determined and increasingly commercially driven processes (Basson et al., 2018). In small regional townships, democratic processes are often further challenged by the location of the towns, distant from metropolitan power bases, and the fact that they often bear the brunt of economic change and environmental degradation (McHenry, 2011; Sunderland et al., 2022).

In Australia, the rise of non-metropolitan communities since European colonization has been based on agricultural production and resource extraction, underscored by Indigenous dispossession. As these industries decline, region by region, local communities experience falling populations, which are in turn used to justify the withdrawal of local services. Without local banks, schools, and healthcare centers, residents lose informal opportunities to encounter one another, as well as opportunities to shape the purpose and outcomes of such services. These trends exacerbate challenges to participatory democracy.

Natimuk is one example of a community that has faced such challenges. In the nineteenth and twentieth centuries, European colonization forcibly displaced the Wimmera's Wotjobaluk (First Nations) community into missions, introduced lethal infectious diseases, and impacted much of its knowledge and decision-making structures. It also transformed the environment, destroying native ecosystems and establishing Natimuk as a service center for agriculture. Conflict over resources resulted in settlers massacring and displacing large numbers of Indigenous people, and Indigenous people retaliating by killing settlers. Eventually, settler family-owned grain and sheep farms dominated the local economy. These small farms are now increasingly replaced by large-scale commercial operations, which consume larger and larger areas as environmental degradation makes farming less sustainable.

Now home to farmers, Wotjobaluk families, and people attracted by a rural lifestyle, the Wimmera region's small population is diverse, with the potential to be less socially and politically cohesive than in past eras. Natimuk itself has lost public service, such as medical and financial services, and with them the opportunity for regular interaction in public spaces that can build community cohesion, shared values, and a sense of belonging (Balfour et al., 2016).

A potentially problematic issue in Natimuk is the integration of its rock-climbing population. Rock climbing is a highly contested recreation activity in contemporary Australia. An activity and identity that is growing in popularity, rock climbing can pit climbers against First Nations traditional custodians and conservationists, as many sites prime for rock climbing are also home to sacred sites and threatened animal and plant species. The extensive use that such areas receive as a result of their popularity can damage these sites and the environment around them. Both the development and the performance of arts activities discussed here play a role in mitigating the potential for tensions to emerge between Natimuk's different demographic groups, by facilitating democratic processes and expressions. An important contributor to these arts activities, perhaps unexpectedly, is Natimuk's grain silos. During the Second World War, the state government established a series of concrete wheat silos along railway lines throughout regional Victoria to provide collective storehouses for local harvests. Ranging from 10 to 90 meters tall, these imposing structures often serve as landmarks to passersby. They became important cultural sites as well as economic assets. Tsakonas (2019) states that the silos were an agricultural landmark with symbolic resonance, and "where farming communities came together during harvests to exchange news and stories and reconnect with old friends while the grain was unloaded" (p. 273).

Subsequently, larger and more flexible storage methods such as steel silos and tarpaulin covers have resulted in concrete silos becoming redundant. As concrete silos fell into disuse, their imposing presence on the landscape and importance in settler agriculture and ritual has sometimes been read as a sign of rural decay and the contraction of community, what Birch (1999) describes as the "landscape of abandonment" (p. 61). However, for some local agricultural families, silos (whether they are operational or not) are seen as a source of pride, hope, resilience, and sometimes beauty.

In Natimuk, the silos have become literal canvases for arts produced or commissioned by the local community, and have contributed to the development of a unique form of arts activity based around two of the town's assets – its familiarity with and appetite for grand-scale landmarks (including Dyurrite/Mt. Arapiles) and its rock climbers' advanced aerial skills. Settler descendants and other local individuals and groups have historical and cultural attachments to silos, so using them as a site to tell stories associated with the history of Natimuk and the people who live there can impact on different segments of the community, for multiple reasons. The case studies described in this chapter exemplify how the silos are deployed for this purpose and how they help to anchor and provide a focus for the community.

Before we discuss how this interaction between Natimuk's people and landmarks arose, we introduce three local organizations responsible for the works the case studies describe. The producer and performer Jillian Pearce (Y Space, 2023) established the Natimuk-based company Y Space in 1999 to work with rock climbers and dancers to create work on high and iconic structures. The structures Y Space works with and on include silos, large machinery, and large bamboo structures. Y Space uses physical theater, aerial dance, and an ethos of collaboration to empower artists and deeply engage with communities in the co-creation of large-scale, multimodal outdoor performance events (Y Space, 2023). In doing so, Y Space often collaborated with Bambuco, a Natimuk-based producer of temporary installations. Founded by Simon Barley in 1998, Bambuco made grand-scale structures using bamboo, which has the advantage of being flexible, lightweight, and cheap, and creates visually impressive installations when used on a large scale. Bambuco employed crew members from Natimuk's rock-climbing community to fulfill its largely international commissions.

The third organization is Arapiles Community Theatre Natimuk (ACT Natimuk), an incorporated arts organization that programs and facilitates arts and cultural work. Established in 1979 as an amateur theater company, during the early 21st century, ACT Natimuk shifted its focus and programming to reflect contemporary art forms and the multidisciplinary practice of local artists. The ACT Natimuk activity with the largest profile and involving the most work is the Nati Frinj, a biennial festival showcasing a wide range of art forms, including theater, dance, visual and sound art. D'Arcy has been a member of ACT Natimuk since 2019, served as Vice-Chair in 2021–2022, and became Chair in 2023.

ACT Natimuk is itself a significant contributor to democratic processes in the town, in the way that it practices and facilitates collaboration. Membership of ACT Natimuk is open to anyone in the world and is conferred by a low-cost yearly fee. ACT Natimuk has three paid positions, and its governance is guided by a volunteer committee. Committee meetings are open for any member to attend and contribute. Participating in ACT Natimuk, as an employee or volunteer, provides an opportunity to work with others to shape the organization's activities. Volunteer labor acts as a form of alternative economy, determined not just by traditional economics of supply and demand, "but also the social interests and needs of individuals" (Edwards, 2012, p. 519). Now with a 2022 income of A$440,000, ACT Natimuk remains an artist-led organization that is founded on democratic principles and community arts approaches. This approach to decision-making is not unique to ACT Natimuk, but is a common local approach to ensuring that decisions serve the community's interests. In lieu of government-provided social services, well-established community-run committees such as the Agricultural and Pastoral Society, the Arapiles Art and Craft Centre committee, and the Natimuk Soldiers

Memorial Hall Committee are responsible for collective decision-making in their area of purview for both the town and surrounding region.

Since 2000, ACT Natimuk has produced the Nati Frinj Festival and has supported Goatfest Film Festival, Palais de Pixel, and the on-selling of arts activity through Made in Natimuk. These arts activities provide avenues for employment, expression, and social inclusion to disadvantaged and marginalized socioeconomic groups underpinned by democratic participation. Using democratic political theory, Kidd (2009) compares three levels of democratic practices in arts organizations, and their wider implications for communities and society:

> When art is treated as an elite status good, it is likely to have antidemocratic effects that largely reproduce status hierarchies. When art is treated as an exclusive group identity good, as in the case of identity politics, it is likely to contribute to democracy by giving voice to marginalized groups. Finally, when art is treated as an inclusive social good, it is likely to contribute to democracy by producing solidarity and encouraging commonality.
>
> *(p. 296)*

The aim of the democratic processes informing Natimuk arts production is to "normalize" arts participation because of its effects/affect as an inclusive social good and its contribution to democracy. ACT Natimuk aims to produce solidarity and commonality amongst the community, whilst not homogenizing the diverse storytelling possibilities in Natimuk.

If collective decision-making is the first way in which ACT Natimuk provides a democratic model and opportunity for locals, it also does so through the production of arts events that create a democratic spectacle. These events have included aerial and shadow performances that draw on the skills of Natimuk's rock climbers, as well as those of dancers and choreographers and backstage contributors. The silo provides a canvas for projected animations, paintings, drawings, folk music, opera, and orchestral works (Figure 1.1). These activities often encourage reflection on the town's colonial history by subverting (sometimes whimsically, sometimes seriously) the grain silo as a symbol of settler agricultural society. In a small community with few resources, these activities have relied on the input of locals by mobilizing a network of volunteers, and so have required the building of community skills. They have also provided employment opportunities, and allowed a range of experiences and inputs (for and from) nonartists. Two case studies of Natimuk's arts events – *Space and Place* and *Vault* – demonstrate these arguments.

Space and Place Case Study: Background and Precedent for Natimuk Community Arts

The original large-scale community arts project produced and performed on the Natimuk silo was *Space and Place* in 2003. Directed by Jillian Pearce from Y Space and developed by local artists, *Space and Place* included a range of mediums,

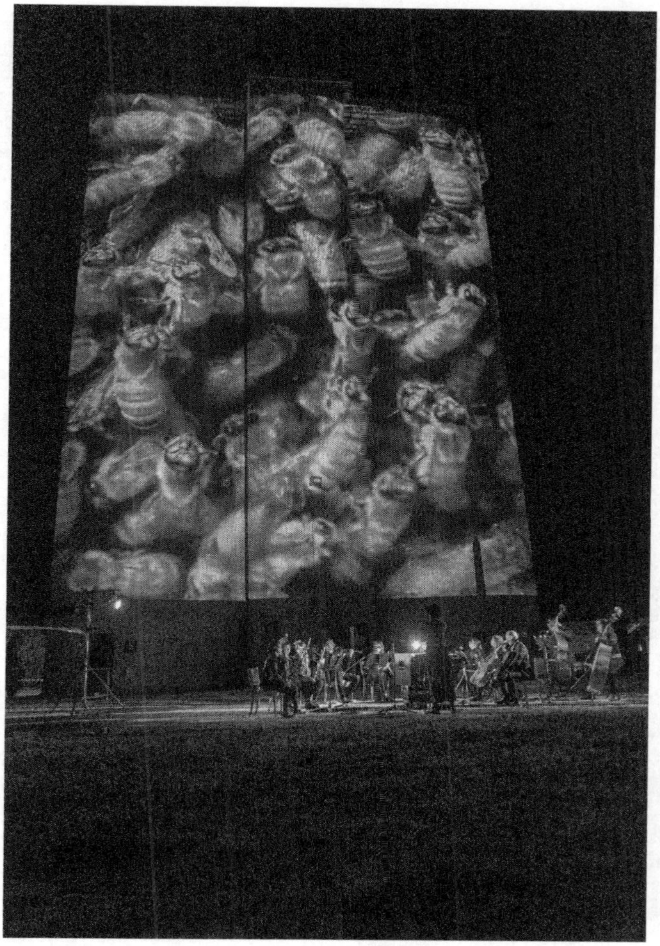

FIGURE 1.1 Natimuk Silo, performance of Rae Howell's Bee-Sharp Honeybee at Nati Frinj Festival 2019. Photo: Michelle McFarlane Photography.

including aerial performance, animation, shadow puppetry, shadow sculpture, and music – including a choir. Each part of the production was created through community consultation, input, and workshops, including with local First Nations people, and was regarded as "a collection of poetic images that explore a community's unique relationship to land, space and what gives them their sense of place" (Made In Natimuk, 2021, para. 1). Due to critical demand, *Space and Place* was recommissioned on the Natimuk silo in 2004 as part of a national conference on regional arts (Made In Natimuk, 2021, para. 5).

A democratic spectacle is one that not only enacts democratic processes, but also showcases and celebrates those processes and their outcomes. Resulting from a consultative and collaborative process and showcasing the artistic results of that process, *Space and Place* provided a democratic spectacle. This spectacle was oriented around what was common to all of the people who participated, namely their local environment, and was displayed on and around the silo as a symbolic landmark of that common environment. It also drew on, leveraged, and fostered the unique sets of skills of participants and encouraged skill-sharing. Perhaps most importantly, as a spectacular display on the silo, it provided both the local community and cultural tourists with an example of an ambitious project made achievable by the democratic involvement of a small community. This early experimentation into how unique aerial skills of Natimuk's rock climbers, coupled with the existing industrial infrastructure of the silo and willing community participants, led to the generation of further arts activities that built on the town's artistic reputation for grand-scale aerial work. The next case study, *Vault*, provides an example.

Vault Case Study

The concept of the Third Space used by Homi Bhabha (2008) relates to the hybrid nature of identity and cultural forms due to the process of colonization, with its power dynamics and violence, inequities, entanglements, and cross-cultural exchange that occur in a postcolonial society. Bhabha (2008) argues that the Third Space heralds:

> the emergence of a dialogical site – a moment of enunciation, identification, negotiation – that was suddenly divested of its mastery or sovereignty in the midst of a markedly asymmetrical and unequal engagement of forces. In an intercultural site of enunciation, at the intersection of different languages jousting for authority, a translational space of negotiation opens up through the process of dialogue.
>
> (p. 5)

An example of Bhabha's Third Space dialogue through community arts programming is the collaboration *Vault* (Figure 1.2), which premiered at the 2019 Nati Frinj Festival as a 30-minute development performance. *Vault* was a community collaboration which was spearheaded by Black Hole Theatre (BHT) and its artistic director Nancy Black. Jillian Pearce from Y Space choreographed *Vault*, commissioning Styckx Bamboo Theatre – a large, visually striking performance space made from bamboo and designed by the Bambuco company – as the performance site. *Vault* was the product of collaboration between a range of artists and community members. These included Wotjobaluk Elder Uncle Ron Marks as a consultant and collaborator, Vietnamese-Australian writer and director Chi Vu, and three performers: actor, circus performer, and Indigenous man Jack Sheppard, of the Kutjar clan in north Queensland; local rock climber and aerialist Abby Watkins; and American actor John Pyburn. Natimuk locals rigged the lines that the performers attached to as they moved and climbed.

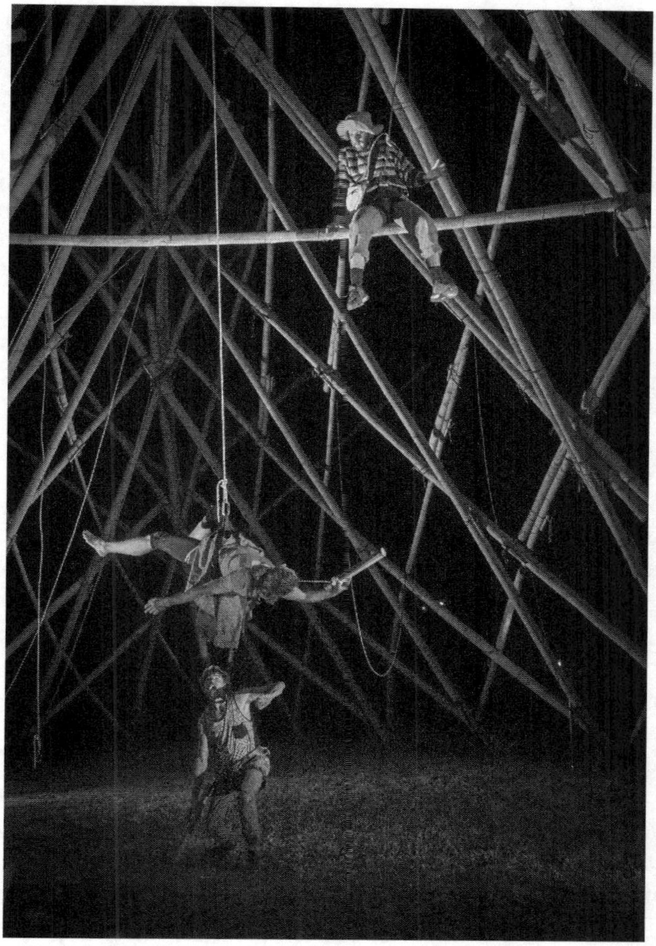

FIGURE 1.2 Styckx Theatre (Y Space), performance of *Vault* at Nati Frinj Festival 2019, Black Hole Theatre. Performers (bottom to top): Jack Sheppard, Abby Watkins, John Pyburn. Photo: Michelle McFarlane Photography.

The process of making and performing *Vault* involved consultation and collaboration from local Traditional Owners through the Barengi Gadjin Land Council (who were represented by Uncle Ron) and a series of closed and open workshops used to gather stories from the local Indigenous and non-Indigenous community. I was involved in one of the story-gathering sessions, a community meeting and research event at the Natimuk Soldiers Memorial Hall, where there was a discussion between all the available Vault collaborators and any other local people wanting to pass on stories or listen. This intercultural space of Indigenous and non-Indigenous stories allowed the director, consultant, writer, and all other collaborators and participants associated with the project to offer their perspectives to help create and shape the story of *Vault*. What emerged was a highly localized story that tapped into the cultural, social, political, legal, and spiritual dimensions of placemaking in Natimuk and used Indigenous and non-Indigenous relationships to Dyurrite/Arapiles as a central theme.

The story of *Vault* is a fictionalized dystopia of post-apocalyptic Natimuk where rock-climbing survivors meet and argue about issues of sovereignty and belonging. These issues are dramatized and problematized in a performative style that directly speaks to community sentiments and anxieties from a future Natimuk ravaged by climate change. Telling this story from an imagined future, at a safer distance from the volatility of the present, is a way to grapple with these issues seriously but in a less confrontational style than a contemporary realist depiction. In the Nati Frinj (2019) program, the synopsis of *Vault* reads:

> In a post-apocalyptic Natimuk, all knowledge has been lost and the land is ravaged by drought. Survivors share stories and fragments of history to explain their world, and shape a future. But they don't all agree! Using Y Space Theatre's soaring bamboo structure, three quarrelling climbers swing toward the sky, hoping to get rain either from the Creator (definition disputed) or with a drill.
> *(p. 14)*

This overview not only outlines the story and performance with the underlying issues, but its tone hints at a whimsy and playfulness that accompany the serious and vexed subject matter.

As an audience member on opening night, D'Arcy noted the humorous and snappy dialogue used to draw the crowd in, from characters who represent Indigenous Australia (Jack), non-Indigenous Australia (Abby), and America (John). *Vault* covered issues including Indigenous language and deep history, spiritual beliefs, non-Indigenous belonging, and arguments about the environmental and cultural costs of rock climbing, with a smattering of pop culture references. The audience was free to move within and around the structure during the live show, and this created a palpable closeness and three-dimensionality to the performance and the ability to change one's angle of perception. All performances in 2019 began after sunset between 8:00 and 9:45 p.m., with modest lighting, and because the Styckx theatre has no cover, the night sky was a prominent feature. The word "vault" has many literal and figurative connotations that include leaping, movement, a burial site, a room or object for safekeeping, and an arched structure (Merriam-Webster Online Dictionary, 2023). The *Vault* project engaged with these literal and metaphoric strands to reflect, shape, and transform the discourses connected to placemaking in Natimuk and the broader Wimmera region.

Vault was planned for expansion for the 2021 Nati Frinj Festival. It did not, however, continue to full realization. The COVID-19 pandemic postponed the festival until 2022, but even without this disruption, the partners involved chose to discontinue it due to polarized community views, expressed over time in public meetings and social media posts within the Natimuk community and broader area. The closure of once-open rock-climbing areas in 2019 – due to the rediscovery of Wotjobaluk cultural heritage, including rock art – strained local relationships. It created distrust and animosity between layers of government bureaucracy (state government, Parks Victoria), various climbing advocacy groups, the three Aboriginal Land Councils in the Gariwerd Wimmera area that were impacted (the Barengi Gadjin Land Council Aboriginal Corporation, the Eastern Maar Aboriginal Corporation, and the Gunditj Mirring Traditional Owners Aboriginal Corporation), and the general public. The story that *Vault* tells speaks to sensitive and unresolved issues around perceived (and actual) rights. These include general access to areas in Dyurrite/Mount Arapiles and nearby mountain range Gariwerd/Grampians for climbing and recreation, the ongoing cultural heritage assessments in the region, cultural sovereignty and agency, and cultural safety. It is also worth noting that democratic processes, consultation, and building trust between Traditional Owner Land Councils, state government agencies, and groups such as the Gariwerd Wimmera Reconciliation Network has led to the reopening of sites such as the northern section of Gunigalg/Taipan Wall in Gariwerd in December 2022, where Traditional Owners are comfortable that there can be a coexistence of rock climbing and cultural heritage protections.

The fact of *Vault*'s discontinuation – as a decision determined collaboratively by the community – is as much a testament to Natimuk's democratic practice as its completion might have been. The negotiation that led to this decision reflects the fact that community sensitivities were aired, heard, understood, and responded to.

Conclusion

These two case studies provide points along a roadmap in the development of Natimuk's production of democratic spectacle. *Space and Place* brought Natimuk's diverse community together around the silo, inclusively soliciting, telling, and celebrating their different stories and the multiple histories of place made visible through these, refusing a monolithic account of a place. These stories, coming from community participation, allow for agency and inclusivity in how Natimuk and the wider Wimmera are known and narrated. *Space and Place* made use of the silo as a physical asset for the work's display, but it also highlighted and celebrated the silo as a symbol of the town's uneasy past that continues to have effects: the displacement of the Wotjobaluk people by European colonization and the subsequent economic and social challenge to the farming community that took its place. *Space and Place* also provided an opportunity to investigate the outcomes of genuinely inclusive collaboration. One of the side-products of this collaboration was experimentation with the aerial skills of rock climbers and the integration of local stories of Indigenous and non-Indigenous people. *Vault* continued this experimentation, advancing the *Space and Place* theme of diverse local stories told against grand-scale (though temporary) architecture, using skills unique to the region.

The outcome of *Space and Place* and the 2019 performance of *Vault* both provide a democratic spectacle, in that they communicated and celebrated not just the artistic fruits of a collaborative process, but also the process that created them, and the collective histories that continue to produce place. Their use of large-scale infrastructure, beginning with the silo and ending with a locally made and vast bamboo installation, provided the opportunity for these endeavors to be spectacular. The decision not to continue *Vault* into 2021 is a more modest but no less important point in this roadmap, because it demonstrates the community's commitment to justice and its respect for the cultural sensitivities that characterize its township.

References

Australian Bureau of Statistics. (2023). *Remoteness areas: Australian statistical geography*. Standard Edition 3. Retrieved March 21, 2023, from https://www.abs.gov.au/statistics/standards/australian-statistical-geography-standard-asgs-edition-3/jul2021-jun2026/remoteness-structure/remoteness-areas

Balfour, B., Fortunato, M., & Alter, T. (2016). The creative fire: An interactional framework for rural arts-based development. *Journal of Rural Studies, 63*, 229–239.

Basson, M., van Rensburg, H., Cuthill, M., & Erdiaw-Kwasie, M. O. (2018). Is regional government-governance nexus delivering on social sustainability promises? Empirical evidence from Moranbah in Australia. *Local Government Studies, 44*(6), 826–847. Retrieved December 17, 2023, https://research.ebsco.com/linkprocessor/plink?id=70b46078-e676–3c18-bae3-fe2778a546d5.

Bhabha, H. (2008). Cited in Ikas, K., *Communicating in the third space*. Taylor & Francis. Retrieved December 10, 2023, from https://research.ebsco.com/linkprocessor/plink?id=71ffcb26-ba9d-3b69-af09-74b55c014824

Birch, T. (1999). Come see the giant koala: Inscription and landscape in western Victoria. *Meanjin, 58*(3), 60–72.

Edwards, R. (2012). Gympie's Country Music Muster: Creating a cultural economy from a local tradition. *Journal of Rural Studies, 28*, 517–527.

Gallagher, B. K. (2021). Death and life: The promise and problems of the arts in rural communities. *International Journal of Arts Management, 23*(2), 30–42.

Kidd, D. (2009). Democratic practices in arts organizations. *Journal of Arts Management, Law and Society, 38*(4), 296–309.

Kölbl, M., & Trümpi, F. (2021). *Music and democracy: Participatory approaches*. MDW Press.

Made In Natimuk. (2021). *Space and place*. Retrieved October 10, 2021, from https://madeinnatimuk.com/space-and-place/

McHenry, A. J. (2011). Rural empowerment through the arts: The role of arts in civic and social participation in the mid west region of Western Australia. *Journal of Rural Studies, 27*, 245–253.

Merriam-Webster Online Dictionary. (2023). *Vault*. Retrieved December 11, 2023, from https://www.merriam-webster.com/dictionary/vault.

Molan, D. (2023). *The Wimmera speaks: Adaptive work, poetic histories, and place-based arts* [PhD thesis, Deakin University].

Nati Frinj, N. (2019). *Nati Frinj Biennale 2019 programme*. Shelton and Lane.

Space, Y. (2023). *Jillian Pearce – Y Space director*. Y Space, Natimuk. https://www.yspace.com.au/jillian-pearce

Sunderland, N., Woodland, S., O'Sullivan, S., & Bartleet, B-L. (2022). The role of Australian first nations knowledges and the arts in 'inclusive' regional and remote development: A narrative review. *Journal of Rural Studies, 89,* 423–436.

Tsakonas, A. (2019). Victoria's silo art trail. *Fabrications: The Journal of the Society of Architectural Historians, Australia and New Zealand, 29*(2), 273–276.

2

LAKE STREET ARTS! – CREATIVE DEMOCRACY IN PRACTICE

Meena Natarajan

The murder of George Floyd in Minneapolis was a watershed moment for the Twin Cities and beyond. The wounds in American cities have created broad recognition that racism is a public health epidemic impacting everyone. The City of Minneapolis passed a resolution in 2020 declaring racism a public health emergency (City of Minneapolis, 2020). According to the resolution, racism in all its forms causes persistent discrimination and disparate outcomes in many areas of life, including housing, education, health, employment, public safety, and criminal justice, exacerbated further by the COVID-19 pandemic crisis. Even before the pandemic and the murder of Mr. Floyd, racial and gender disparities, historical trauma, and the ongoing over-policing and police brutality directed at Indigenous and communities of color have left many vulnerable to mental and other health disparities, addiction, and housing instability – all exacerbated by loss of connection to land and cultural connections that root people to place and each other. In the wake of George Floyd's death, individuals and communities came out in protest and defiance at the brutal murder of yet another Black man at the hands of the police. Protests broke out all over Minneapolis and St. Paul, and in a matter of days, the area outside the police Third Precinct became the site of a major uprising. The precinct was located in a neighborhood area known as downtown Longfellow. As a result of public anger and resentment, the Third Precinct was set on fire along with other buildings in the area. Many businesses of downtown Longfellow, such as Gandhi Mahal, Minnehaha Lake Wine and Spirits, Migizi, and El Nuevo Rodeo were destroyed in the fire. The majority of the businesses destroyed were BIPOC-owned. Pangea World Theater has collaborated with many of these spaces since then, hosting conversations, gatherings, and events.[1]

Pangea World Theater was founded in 1995 to bring diverse artists and community members together through theater and the arts. Pangea strives to build a

DOI: 10.4324/9781003475996-5

just world by creating multidisciplinary theater that embodies decolonizing practices of solidarity, sustainability, and equity. Over its 28-year history, Pangea has created programs and performances that consistently center Immigrant, Dakota, Ojibwe, Indigenous, Asian, Black, East African, and Latinx artists, stories, and communities along Lake Street. In addition, since the mid-2010s, Pangea has been involved in Creative Placekeeping work, keeping and maintaining a sense of place and belonging that is generated and owned by the people who live and work in the neighborhood. This sense of democracy and sovereignty is maintained through a project called Lake Street Arts!, bringing public art, performances, gatherings, and conversations along the length and breadth of Lake Street, a vital corridor that connects the Mississippi River to Bde Maka Ska Lake.

In the years since the murder of George Floyd and the uprising, Pangea has embarked on several projects that have embraced public participation and created a vehicle in which the public can express their grief and sorrow, their resistance to injustice, as well as what they wish for their neighborhood in the future. This chapter will explore one such project – Pangea World Theater's collaboration with Holy Trinity Lutheran Church to commission Dakota artist Angela Two Stars in spring and summer 2021. *The Transition Stage*, as the project came to be called, was imagined as a space for community members, especially the residents of Longfellow, to express their laments, hopes, and reflections for a just future. This project consisted of a temporary public outdoor art installation where community members were invited to add their laments and hopes for transformation to the artwork as it was being created.

We are exploring how this work aligns with movements toward community-directed development, mutual aid, and racial justice in placekeeping. One question we are asking as we create projects like this are: How can art projects such as this one become part of a systemic shift so that arts and culture play a catalytic role in the way we steward our neighborhoods, always taking into consideration and the politics (and power dynamics) of space, belonging, and (re)development? At Pangea, we have observed how art and artist-based strategies and processes can identify creative solutions to some of the most dire challenges of our times. It can energize communities, organizations, and institutions and foster a sense of belonging, healing, and relationship building. Artistic work that comes from an ecology of interdependence can shift white centered diversity models into actual space for cross-cultural relationships. Art and performance that is rooted in cross-cultural relationships can model pathways to strengthen the arts as a vital space for racial, gender-based and economic equity.

Because of our deep connection to place and our history of creating in this corridor, the artistic leaders of Pangea World Theater, Dipankar Mukherjee and I, joined business leaders, church leaders, community builders, and activists in the area of 27th Avenue, Lake Street, and Minnehaha Avenue. We have met every week beginning in July 2020. This coalition led to the creation of an organization called Longfellow Rising, with the intention of rebuilding the neighborhood in an equitable and just way with a focus on BIPOC ownership, strengthened social fabric infrastructure, and redesigned buildings that facilitate community gathering and belonging for all.

The Twin Cities' seven-county area has seen increasing racial diversity and continued economic and population growth. In 2010, people of color comprised 24% of the regional population. By 2040, projections suggest that 43% of the residents in the region will be persons of color. Youth violence and poverty are a challenge for communities of color in the Minneapolis/St. Paul area. The McKnight Foundation's report, "Unrealized Potential: East Lake Street Perceptions," recommends an "an economic development plan that builds on the multicultural community" (Waters, 2014).

Pangea World Theater is located on West Lake Street, and the artistic leaders of Pangea live in the Longfellow neighborhood on East Lake Street and a mile from the police Third Precinct. Lake Street is a five-mile stretch that has long been a landing place for new immigrant and Indigenous communities, boasting a diversity of culture and small businesses despite deep disparities in employment, income, and education. Lake Street straddles the Longfellow neighborhood, dividing commercially owned buildings to the north and more locally owned businesses to the south, many of whom are BIPOC. The area that Longfellow Rising was seeking to redevelop were the businesses and lots to the south of Lake Street, many of which had been reduced to rubble by the fires caused by either white supremacists or the uprising that took place.

Pangea World Theater's Lake Street Arts! (LSA!), is a multiyear initiative, involving eight neighborhoods, focusing on cultural asset mapping, leadership, and community development through the arts, shaping plans towards a more equitable and sustainable model of growth for an evolving blueprint for Minneapolis. This blueprint uses intergenerational community engagement, building artists' professional, artistic, and organizing capacity as a tool to produce outcomes that represent the communities we serve. Through teams of artists, volunteers, interns, and community organizers, it is a strategy to involve the business corridor, the social service sector, and neighborhood organizations and build our case for an arts corridor.

Using culturally relevant place keeping strategies, LSA! engaged residents that are historically difficult to reach in developing a vision for East Lake that informed the 2040 Minneapolis' Comprehensive Plan.[2] Projects included a ceramic pillar created by renowned Colombian artist Hana Bibliowicz called the Colors of Lake Street, located inside the Global Market in Minneapolis in the heart of Lake Street, and that still generates conversations about racism and colorism. Pangea ran an Art Organizing Institute, a yearlong, applied learning intensive initiative with the goal to train artists in community organizing, community planning, and placemaking techniques with a lens of racial justice. The cohort partnered with GoodSpace Murals to create a Lake Street Loves Murals at the Plaza Centenario on Lake Street and 12th Avenue.

Since the murder of Mr. Floyd and the Uprising, Pangea has been engaged in neighborhood building practices as well as art and theater-making practices that promote collective healing, belonging, participation, and transformation, especially in the communities most affected down the length of Lake Street. We are working on ways that we can carry the stories, concerns, and visions of Longfellow neighbors and business owners to the City of Minneapolis to ensure that our diverse communities have a voice in shaping the planning and development of our neighborhood.

Collective Power

In the days following the murder and the uprising, the pandemic of racism deepened the grief felt by the community already affected by the isolation of COVID. The group of business owners in the neighborhood expanded to include multiple stakeholders from beyond the immediate community. What started as a place to share our stories and support one another with navigating insurance and demolition transitioned in the fall to work on rebuilding downtown Longfellow. This involved connecting business owners, residents, individuals from the local community councils, the local community development organizations, artists, and the broader community. It also involved convening one-on-one and small-group discussions about the possibilities of what the neighborhood could become. We work with others who also live and work here, as well as organizations and city departments who are involved in the rebuilding of downtown Longfellow, and along Lake Street. The creation of Longfellow Rising (LR) provided residents and stakeholders with a channel to create a shared vision of our neighborhood. Nearly all the board members of LR are owners of the buildings where they operate their businesses.

In order to increase democratic engagement, LR held listening sessions with neighbors and community members in the area, building participation through a grassroots approach, soliciting and compiling feedback about the neighborhood regarding what was needed, how to proceed, and more. These sessions were conducted in a way that dissolved hierarchies and welcomed participation from all stakeholders. LR members made an effort to bring both BIPOC owners of homes as well as BIPOC artists who lived in the area to the table. The values of Longfellow Rising that we agreed to were: general long-term, sustainable wealth through deep, meaningful relationships and diverse ownership; prioritizing people over profit; actively centering marginalized voices and communities in decision-making, planning, and actions; promoting the role of the arts and culture in creating and sustaining justice for all; and prioritizing long-term planning over short-term gains.

In Longfellow Rising's listening sessions with the community, it emerged that prior to the destruction, other challenges endemic to the area were safety, city negligence, and an unresponsive police force. We committed to healing the ruptures that caused the uprising, and to forging healthy, cross-cultural, and cross-sector collaborations. This could provide a model for rebuilding the community along Lake Street and beyond. As we built a vision for equity, justice, and belonging, we also built deep relationality and intentional listening in the neighborhood. The Holy Trinity Lutheran Church on 31st Avenue offered their space as a medic center during the uprising, and the artists and leaders of Pangea built a deep relationship with Senior Pastor Ingrid Rasmussen. Pastor Rasmussen and the congregation of Holy Trinity were interested in building a giant cocoon that community members could slide their laments/hopes into during the seasons of Lent (which in 2021 began on February 17) and then the laments/hopes would be used to create a giant butterfly at Easter (in April), which that year also aligned with Passover. As Pastor Rasmussen expressed it, it wouldn't be explicitly religious. They wanted a community engagement project that would allow the neighborhood to talk about "emerging anew."

As February 2021 began, Pastor Rasmussen called me and asked if we knew of a visual artist who would build a cocoon that would act as a vessel for community laments and hopes as the neighborhood and city attempt to move towards growth, redevelopment, and healing. We spoke about the grief that our community was still experiencing and the need for them to express this sorrow and confusion, exacerbated by the isolation caused by COVID. As we expressed our willingness to collaborate more fully during this project, Indigenous artist Angela Two Stars's name emerged as we spoke to other artists in the community. Angela Two Stars is a member of the Sisseton Wahpeton Oyate, works as a public artist in the Twin Cities, and is a curator in All My Relations Gallery at the Native American Community Development Institute. She is experienced in community engaged art practice and has created several public sculptures that serve the intention of both building participation as well as healing this land that has been stolen from the Dakota people.

As we spoke about the form this would take, the idea of a cocoon or chrysalis emerged, a form that is a protective covering that occurs during one stage of growth of the pupa of a butterfly. As the community leaves their laments at the site, their words would be woven into the chrysalis, eventually filling the entire vessel. The central idea, according to Angela Two Stars, was that "the weaved material was meant to represent the community of individuals, woven together in mutual experiences, collectively coming together to reflect, heal, and grow." This ephemeral monument was dreamed of as a transformative space for our collective memory. The idea of art itself and the form of the pupa inherently metaphorized transformation as a central theme of the project. As Angela designed the cocoon, more and more partners came on board. Thanks to Mary Margaret Zindren, Executive Director of the American Association of Architects Minnesota, we put out an RFP to our community in general for how we could realize the physical structure for the cocoon. As Angela began to design the project, it began to attract partners who wanted to be a part of the healing process, including architects from local firm BKV and individuals from construction company J. E. Dunn, who came forward and helped us visualize and implement the installation.

Preparing the Ground

As a Native American, we hold pow wows which is like a community gathering and prior to the pow wow, our grass dancers would come to the arena and stomp it down to prepare it for the dancers that would be coming in during the pow wow. So for me, that was a significant tie in, a connection to my culture as a Dakota artist from this land.

(Angela Two Stars, Artist of The Transition Stage, *quoted in Pangea World Theater, 2022).*

On May 25 and 27, 2021, the project launched with an invitation to prepare the soil and plant flowers into the ground in the shape of a butterfly. Staff of Pangea, members of the congregation of Holy Trinity, Board members of LR, people associated with the project, and community members came with shovels and gardening tools to dig and put their hands into the earth to plant flowers and seeds. Passersby who had not heard of the project stopped and helped dig earth and plant flowers into the soil. One of those passersby, longtime Longfellow resident Betsy Altheimer, expressed, "I didn't know how much I needed to be part of rebuilding and collective healing with my work and my organizing but also, I needed to put plants into the ground." This process served to prepare the ground for the cocoon. Our intention was to create a sacred space for the next few months and provide a space for histories, memories, and hopes to be gathered to provide a vision for a more just and sustainable ecosystem in the area.

Pangea and Holy Trinity organized five gatherings through the summer, timing a few of them with the Farmers Market on Saturday mornings just up the road from the cocoon. Materials used included a wooden frame structure and vinyl strips that were available during the gatherings. The aptly named *The Transition Stage* was dreamt of as a participatory, temporary installation, approximately 10 feet high, that acted as a vessel for community laments and hopes as the neighborhood and city moved towards growth, redevelopment, and healing. The shape of the vessel was designed to be a chrysalis. Community members wrote on the strips with a permanent marker, and Angela Two Stars then wove these strips into the wooden frame. During this time, we hosted a series of artistic events and community conversations open and free to the public at the site of the installation. At these events, Angela Two Stars along with Pangea artists and staff facilitated more than 250 community members to make their contributions to the sculpture.

The year 2021 ended up being a drought year, and the land surrounding the cocoon became arid. No water was available because all the buildings surrounding the area had been burnt down. We managed to innovate and bring water from a fire hydrant nearby. Our Production Coordinator, Suzanne Cross, watered the site every other day to make sure the plants were watered; she often encountered nearby residents sitting on concrete benches that we had in the area, reading the messages that community members wrote during the gatherings. Community members and residents in the area often brought contributions to the space – one young African American woman brought seed bombs that we planted. Each gathering included Dakota and Ojibwe youth from Ikidowin Youth Theatre who served as crew, and at the end of the last gathering, as our staff were cleaning and clearing the area, our three youth danced a grass dance spontaneously as if to close out this part of the project.

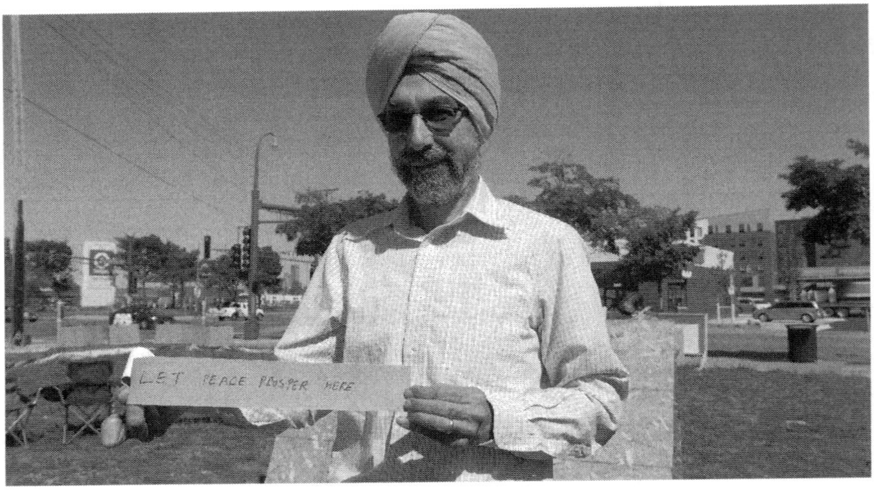

FIGURE 2.1 Charanjeet Singh holding a sign created for *The Transition Stage* cocoon. Photo by Jenny Zander.

The Politics of Space and Time

According to Ingrid Rasmussen of Longfellow Rising and the Holy Trinity Lutheran Church (Pangea World Theater, 2022):

> This community is filled with hopes and laments, yet there are few places where we can share them with one another. This project seeks to till the soil, so to speak, so that the seeds of equity and belonging can take root in the Downtown Longfellow rebuild.

The project took place at the site of the now-destroyed Minnehaha-Lake Wine and Spirits located just opposite the former Third Precinct. The owner, Steve Krause, planned to begin rebuilding his store as soon as possible. He welcomed the opportunity to have a healing sculpture in his lot until he began rebuilding. We had a relatively short window of time to facilitate the project. The project remained on the site until the fall of 2021, at which time rebuilding of Minnehaha-Lake Wine and Spirits was set to begin.[3]

This way of approaching public art as a participatory project that foregrounds social justice and holding it in a site that is trauma infused, a site that has been through a major crisis, provided an opportunity for mitigating the grief that many of us in the neighborhood felt at witnessing what happened in the area. Being right opposite the Third Precinct with 10,000 cars passing by every day, the team of *The Transition Stage* boldly asks people to remember what happened in the city, that this area was the epicenter of something violent. *The Transition Stage* turned our organizations and the artist into frontline responders through the art, using creative practice as methodology. As we rebuild the Longfellow downtown neighborhood, this project helps us reimagine a future in which the community can come together. This project memorialized the site and reminded us why it's important to remember collectively. All the more valued because of its temporality, this sculpture became a monument and a place of solace for the community to gather. Most visual arts monuments memorialize individuals; but, isolated as we were in the summer and fall of 2021, this act of coming together in this particular place and time is core to how we work with community, as we believe that artists and projects such as this assists our community to process and integrate the multiple forms of information, emotion, and conflict affecting them.

Transformation

> Metamorphosis: change of physical form, structure, or substance especially by supernatural means.
>
> *(Merriam-Webster Dictionary, n.d.)*

Metamorphosis acted as phase II of *The Transition Stage* (2021). In the summer and early fall of 2023, the cocoon morphed into a mural of a butterfly with the written contributions of the community still able to be viewed. The long-term vision is for this resulting artwork to become a permanent part of our new Pangea World Theater space at an adjacent lot as an archive of the dreams of the community as it metamorphoses in a rapidly shifting political and cultural landscape. This is also planned as a collaboration between Holy Trinity Lutheran Church and Pangea World Theater and was produced by the Wakpa Triennial. Wakpa, meaning "River," spanned over 12 weeks and provided an opportunity to experience new public art commissions, other projects, and exhibitions by Minnesota-based artists installed in a network of locations across St Paul and Minneapolis through a festival produced by Public Art St. Paul. Metamorphosis was in one of the Minneapolis sites of Wakpa.

Metamorphosis was planned as a two-sided mural. One side features the compilation of written community contributions, a reminder of the losses experienced after the uprisings of 2020, but also a reminder of the resilience and hope of the Longfellow neighborhood and how, together, we can rebuild. The other side of the artwork shows a butterfly pollinator garden, the representation of the transformation, rebuilding, and strength of the community. Materials used include a wooden frame structure and vinyl and polytab applied to plywood. Interactive chrysalis sculptural art forms invite audience participation to enter and emerge from the discarded chrysalis "transformed," a metaphor of the rebuilt neighborhood. Community engagement activities held in June invited the audience to create their own butterfly designs to add to the artwork. These butterfly designs were then transformed into decals by Angela Two Stars, who invited community participants to stick the final butterfly design into a place of their choosing on the mural. The mural was therefore community-created.

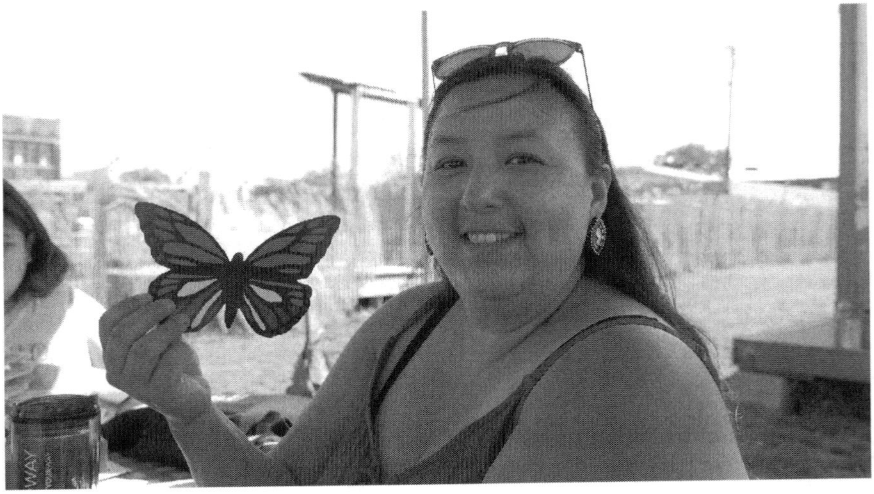

FIGURE 2.2 Visual Artist Angela Two Stars holding up a decal of a butterfly created by community members. Photo by Jenny Zander.

This mural has been installed in a space on 27th Avenue that has been purchased by Holy Trinity Lutheran Church and will be donated to Pangea World Theater in the near future. This land was owned by a Native American organization, Migizi, whose offices were destroyed (they did not wish to rebuild and moved to a new space) and the first public art piece on this land is Metamorphosis, a sculpture by a Dakota artist whose family was displaced from this region. This was an intentional choice, since we work with an awareness of the land and First Nations Peoples, the Dakota and Ojibwe, who stewarded this land before colonization. We honor our partnership with First Nations, and we stand for Indigenous sovereignty. Again, the implications for healing are not lost on us. This will be a space where Pangea World Theater will build an outdoor amphitheater, create a rain garden, and grow food in the future. We plan to bring visibility and vitality in the area by bringing artists and culture bearers who have a solid foundation in place and story, sharing a multi-ethnic vision for what is possible and creating a sense of belonging for our various communities.

Questions Remaining

We believe that community wealth includes relationships, culture, and a deep sense of belonging. We hope this intentional programming of public space creates a sense of belonging for *everyone* and supports community healing. Pangea's ensemble building is guided by daily decolonizing practices of solidarity, sustainability, and equity and contributes to societal transformations. We value relationship building and reciprocity and seek to decenter Western mainstream practices so as to create a

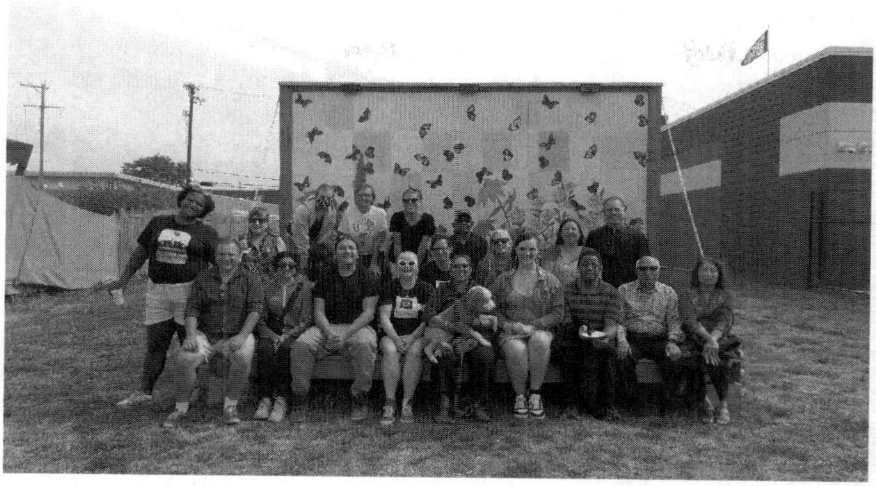

FIGURE 2.3 Community members in front of the completed mural at the closing celebration of Metamorphosis. Photo by Jenny Zander.

circle with all perspectives with equity and justice. Part of the decolonizing methodology that we employ is to ask questions. How do the methods and protocols that were activated reflect the community we are part of? Did we achieve what we set out to in our ways of working with everyone, our commitment to uplift the voices of BIPOC community members? Does this project allow people to take action based on what they expressed, or does it merely diffuse the anger? How does it collectively address and challenge power? What does it actually change? Does it actually shift power, which was its intention? How is democracy uplifted and encouraged by this way of engagement? How does creative practice act like a collective energy release? Whose evaluative framework are we using? What criteria are we using? How do we measure impact in a way that is not Eurocentric?

Most public art does not consider the audience deeply. We hope that this public art, being participatory and for the people in our neighborhood, was an exercise in democracy, in having people see themselves both in the cocoon and the butterfly. We believe artists like Angela Two Stars create a context for the community to express themselves and see themselves within the art. As we reflect on the fact that we witnessed a moment in which the cocoon created by a Dakota artist caused three Indigenous youth to perform a grass dance before we took the structure down, it was a transformative moment for the youth and the people witnessing. We dropped a stone in the water with this project, and we know the first ripples that it caused. What are the second and third ripples? We do this work because we want to see actual change, we want justice, and this is what moves us to create. Do projects like this cause that needle to shift? We hope so. We are instinctively and organically creating a different kind of public space, one that is community driven and something that is for the common good, a kind of direct democracy in which people participate. Decolonizing our world requires us to recognize the ways in which we have centered arts and art practices that are Eurocentric and build value for art and artists who remind us of our relationship to land, people, and history through their rituals and ways of being and knowing. We maintain and keep place through the healing practices of community-centered art projects that celebrate and build a collective sense of democratic participation in the many phases of this project, starting with the cocoon and ending with the butterfly. As we look at this fragile monument to temporality that Angela Two Stars created, we know that art and artists are crucial to community rebuilding processes and can help create and model a process that is truly transformational.

Notes

1 Thanks to France Trepanier, Chris Creighton-Kelly, and Dipankar Mukherjee who helped me think through the implications and nuances of creating an art project opposite the precinct.
2 As of this writing, the 2040 Comprehensive Plan was on hold due to a legal challenge.
3 As of this writing, the liquor store still had not begun rebuilding for many reasons, one of which is current city building regulations that would make it cost much more than the original projection.

References

City of Minneapolis. *2020–00717 – Racism as a public health emergency – Minneapolis*. Minneapolis Legislative Information Management System. Retrieved December 4, 2023, from https://lims.minneapolismn.gov/File/2020-00717.

Merriam-Webster. (n.d.). Metamorphosis. In *Merriam-Webster.com dictionary*. Retrieved January 23, 2024, from https://www.merriam-webster.com/dictionary/metamorphosis

Pangea World Theater (Director). (2022, July 13). *The transition stage documentary*. https://www.youtube.com/watch?v=rOabdUtSaME

Waters, E. (2014, October 1). *Unrealized potential: East lake street perceptions*. Search Issue Lab. https://search.issuelab.org/resource/unrealized-potential-east-lake-street-perceptions.html.

3

HOW "CREATIVE RECOVERY" STIMULATES A CULTURE OF DEMOCRACY

Case Studies of Post-Disaster Creativity in Rural Australia

Anna Kennedy-Borissow

The state of Victoria in Australia is one of the most wildfire-prone regions in the world. This reputation was cemented internationally during the Black Saturday bushfires, which is widely regarded as the worst disaster in Australia's history (National Geographic Society, 2022). In 2009, on Saturday, February 7, up to 400 individual fires broke out across Victoria, burning more than 1,737 square miles, destroying over 2,000 homes, and killing 173 people (National Geographic Society, 2022). Lesser known is that following this catastrophic event, multiple creative projects were instigated by artists, community members, and community groups throughout the state. These projects stimulated the social recovery of the communities in which they took place and helped re-establish a culture of democracy.

This chapter explores two case studies of creative projects that were produced in affected townships that demonstrate links between creativity, disaster recovery, and democracy: (1) the Blacksmiths' Tree in Strathewen, a life-sized metal tree sculpture; and (2) a series of live performances, arts and crafts workshops, and exhibitions facilitated by the Kinglake Ranges Visual and Performing Arts Alliance. Discussion of these case studies is complemented with findings from interviews on the role of the arts in emergency management. With more frequent and intense disasters occurring globally due to climate change, it is imperative that the creative sector considers their role in sustaining democracy and supporting communities to prepare, respond, and recover from disasters.

Democracy and Disaster Recovery

Democratic principles are difficult to uphold during disasters as government and emergency services often need to act quickly to protect lives and properties

DOI: 10.4324/9781003475996-6

(Hayward & Johnson, 2022). However, emergency management processes that neglect democratic principles of equity, inclusivity, and transparency can lead to maladaptation in disaster recovery, making affected communities more vulnerable to exploitation (Hayward & Johnson, 2022). For these reasons, community-led recovery is increasingly recognized as best practice by the emergency management sector. Community-led recovery is a strengths-based and collaborative approach to recovery that empowers "individuals, families and the community to actively participate in their own recovery" and "is guided by the communities' priorities" (Australian Institute of Disaster Resilience, 2018, p. 31). However, community-led recovery requires a high level of awareness and structural support, which is not always available (Dibley et al., 2019, p. 10). This makes community-led principles difficult to realize on the ground.

Within disaster-affected communities there are also social factors that influence a communities' ability to recover. Psychologist Rob Gordon (2004) explains that following disasters, communities may experience a period of intense bonding or "social fusion" as they collectively respond to their community's most pressing needs. After the initial period of "high arousal" has subsided, the sense of community can be eroded by unhelpful comparisons between community members: who is the worst affected, who is receiving the most support, and so on (Gordon, 2004). When the "social fabric" of a community is ruptured, democratic processes face erosion from within the community itself. Therefore, it is crucially important to embed approaches that strengthen democracy within disaster-prone and disaster-affected communities.

Creative recovery is one potential mode for embedding democratic principles in communities that have been affected by disasters. Gordon (2004) explains that the "social fabric" of communities can be repaired by establishing communication channels and networks, providing opportunities for communities to gather, and stimulating shared meaning-making processes through representations or reflections on disaster events. Community participation in creative activities can produce these conditions. Additionally, democratic processes are characterized by inclusivity, transparency, and accountability (Hayward & Johnson, 2022), which can also be seen in creative recovery processes in Australia and internationally.

Characteristics of Creative Recovery

In Australia, the term "creative recovery" is used to describe a framework and process of embedding creativity and the arts in disaster recovery. It is often a community-led or community-engaged process that emerges following disasters such as wildfires, floods, cyclones, and storms. In the United States, the term "creative recovery" is more commonly used to describe the recovery of the creative sector following COVID-19. However, this chapter will focus on Australian examples following so-called "natural disasters." To date, very little literature has been produced in this field, but government project reports and industry case studies show that participating in arts projects across a range of artforms can help individuals and communities make meaning from their experiences, and help re-establish trusting relationships and connections *within* communities, as well as *between* communities and outsiders.

International examples of arts-based recovery can be seen following Hurricane Katrina in the United States (2005), Tōhoku earthquake and tsunami in Japan (2011), the Christchurch earthquakes in New Zealand (2011), and elsewhere. There are hundreds of Australian examples of community-led or engaged creative projects that have been initiated following natural disasters. Current creative recovery projects can be found in the northern rivers of New South Wales, which was heavily impacted by flooding throughout 2022, and in the states of Queensland, New South Wales, Victoria, and South Australia in response to the 2019–2020 Black Summer fires. These projects range in scale from discrete visual arts exhibitions, to choir rehearsals, to 50-day-long festivals. Creative recovery projects traverse a broad range of art forms, including visual arts and sculpture; blacksmithing and jewelry-making; mosaic, clay, felting, lantern-making, and other crafts; theater, dance, and music; poetry, creative writing, and storytelling. There are too many art forms represented to name them all. Yet despite the proliferation of post-disaster creativity in Australia, creative recovery continues to be woefully under-resourced by government.

It is challenging to isolate the reasons for continued under-resourcing of creative recovery in Australia, as there is a lack of research in the field. Documentation of creative recovery projects is often limited to what project facilitators and communities themselves produce – memorials, publications, webpages, funding acquittals, photographs – or to government reports on funding initiatives. One such report by NSF Consulting (2011) on behalf of the Victorian state government identified that arts projects following Black Saturday produced positive social and psychological outcomes in disaster-affected communities. Some of their findings align with key mass trauma intervention principles established by Hobfoll and colleagues (2007): creative projects appeared to promote a sense of safety, calm, self- and collective efficacy, connectedness, and hope. These principles can help guide best practice in a wide range of disaster recovery interventions, including creative recovery (Korndörffer et al., 2023).

Interviews that I conducted with artists, arts leaders, and emergency services workers in 2020 revealed that creative recovery can also contribute to a culture of democracy in disaster-affected communities. Interviewees identified barriers to including and sustaining creative processes in disaster recovery. By addressing these challenges, creative recovery could become an even more effective avenue for maintaining democratic processes and principles in an age that will be defined by climate-related disruptions. The following case studies and interviews reflect the aforementioned principles and explore the ways in which creative recovery processes can stimulate a culture of democracy.

Australian Case Studies

One better-known example of creative recovery in Australia is The Blacksmiths' Tree: a life-sized, metal eucalyptus tree sculpture that weighs over three tons and is situated in the small town of Strathewen (Garton, 2020; Korndörffer et al., 2023). The Blacksmiths' Tree is one of several creative recovery initiatives in Strathewen following Black Saturday, many of which were community led. I interviewed project manager Amanda Grant about her experience leading The Tree Project. She explained that the project began as a series of leaf-forging workshops with fire-affected communities:

> We [the Australian Blacksmiths Association (Victoria)] were thinking it would be a six-month project that would result in a small little sculpture as a gift to a fire-affected community and now . . . this is our eleventh year where . . . we're still in contact with the fire affected community from 2009.

The Tree was constructed and installed over a period of five years, with community members and recovery workers contributing over 1,500 names and personal messages to be stamped on steel and copper leaves for the canopy. Altogether, 3,500 leaves were made, with approximately 1,000 of these donated by blacksmiths from 28 different countries.

Amanda and her team quickly realized that they would need to expand their vision beyond a small sculpture, and instead set out to construct a life-sized stainless steel tree sculpture that could support the weight of all the leaves. Amanda and the Blacksmiths Association raised further funds – attracting sponsorship and donations from multiple private companies and nonprofit organizations – to pay for the materials and installation. They also formed welding groups to upskill local community members to weld the leaves onto the branches and the branches onto the tree. Five years from inception, The Blacksmiths' Tree was installed in Strathewen; the site was selected in consultation with fire-affected communities.

Community members and other supporters of the project noted The Tree's importance to those affected by Black Saturday, both directly and indirectly (Garton, 2020). The Tree Project helped develop networks within the fire-affected region and increased feelings of belonging for community members who came together to participate in creative group activities. The project also established relationships between community members, recovery organizations, and government. Amanda said that at last count, The Tree Project team had worked with 100 different organizations across sectors. The Tree continues to inspire sister projects today, with a Community Tree Project underway in Cobargo, New South Wales, in response to the 2019–2020 Black Summer wildfires.

While Amanda was working on The Tree Project, visual artist Michelle Bolmat was coordinating a series of workshops, exhibitions, and live performance events

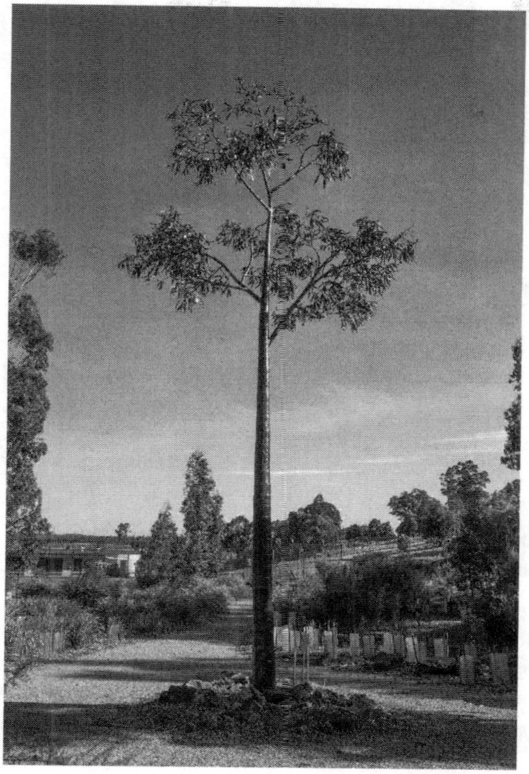

FIGURE 3.1 The Blacksmiths' Tree, Strathewen, Australia. Photograph by Amanda Grant.

in the neighboring district of Kinglake Ranges. This township is where the highest level of fatalities occurred, with 120 lives lost in the Black Saturday fires; Kinglake Ranges has a population of only 1,500 people. I spoke with Michelle about her experiences as artistic director of the then newly formed Kinglake Ranges Visual and Performing Arts Alliance. Immediately after the fires, she described the town as "a community of lost souls who don't know what to do, how to act, how to protect their families." In these early stages post-fires, Michelle explained that local artists would simply set up art materials in emergency services marquees for children to play with. Initially, no one would touch them.

> Then this one little boy came along, and he very tentatively reached out for paper and pencil and crayons, and he started to draw, silently, with very subdued, controlled strokes, structured, and then after a while, he changed his colors from cool blues and greens to vibrant reds and oranges. His strokes got wilder and larger and we saw that he was recreating the fires. His mother was standing behind him and her eyes filled with tears, and she said, "I've been trying to talk

> to him about the fires, . . . and he won't to talk to me. I can't get him to share his feelings." And we just stood there and watched him. This continued on for nearly an hour and then he finished, and he packed up his paintings to take with him. His mother gently put her arms around him and simply led him away through the crowd of people. And then the other children started to join in. And the parents started to join in. And then people started to talk about the artworks. And that's how it all started.

Michelle explained that when the artists saw the effect they were having on the wider community, they started to believe that the arts could make a meaningful contribution to their community's recovery. And they did.

In the three years following the 2009 fires, the Arts Alliance supported approximately 30 projects across a wide range of art forms: multiple music festivals and visual arts exhibitions, arts and crafts workshops, a local choir, a community publication, and even a new local radio station. This provided a range of accessible entry points for community participants. Like Amanda, Michelle highlighted the broad range of partnerships that were founded between the Arts Alliance, community groups, local businesses, schools, emergency services agencies, and arts funding bodies. She echoed Amanda's reflections that arts projects contributed to a sense of belonging within fire-affected communities. Both Amanda and Michelle noted that their respective projects established avenues for outsiders to engage with fire-affected communities in a respectful and appropriate way.

Interviews on Creativity, Disasters, and Democracy

Alongside my conversations with creative recovery facilitators Amanda and Michelle, I also interviewed two arts leaders working in this space: Liz Zito from the nonprofit Regional Arts Victoria (RAV), and Scotia Monkivitch, Executive Officer of the Creative Recovery Network, an advocacy and development organization. In addition, I spoke with two emergency services professionals – Bruce Esplin AM, former Emergency Services Commissioner of Victoria and former Chair of RAV, and Cecily Fletcher from the Victorian state government's Department of Health and Human Services – about the role of the arts in emergency management. They all described positive impacts to individual and community well-being, explaining that creative recovery projects can help people make meaning from their experiences, contribute to a sense of belonging, inspire agency, and give voice to underrepresented community members. These factors also indicate that creative recovery can stimulate a culture of democracy in disaster-affected communities. The following explores this in detail by reflecting on themes from interviews and building on Hobfoll and colleagues' (2007) principles. These principles have also been explored by psychologists Korndörffer et al. (2023) in a case study of The Blacksmiths' Tree.

Catharsis and Collective Efficacy

The cathartic effect of creative expression for trauma-affected individuals has been long recognized. This was supported by interviewees with respect to both individuals and communities more broadly. Scotia Monkivitch from the Creative Recovery Network explained that the arts help people "come to terms with the unimaginable" and move beyond the physical and emotional impact of disasters. By processing the emotional impacts of disasters, Scotia explained that individuals are then empowered to engage with the wider community to make decisions. Former Commissioner Bruce Esplin concurred, adding that participating in art-making can help affected community members regain confidence in their abilities, as well as offer a mental reprieve from the demands of rebuilding, managing insurance claims, and so on. Bruce explained that moments of respite can help people think more clearly overall. What Scotia and Bruce described relates to Hobfoll and colleagues' (2007) principles of self-efficacy and collective efficacy. Safely expressing and learning to regulate emotions following disasters can lead to an increased sense of competency and control. As Scotia argued, this can lead to increased participation in community-led recovery: a core tenet of best practice in disaster recovery that aligns with democratic principles.

Connectedness and Social Support

Promoting a sense of safety, calm, and connectedness are trauma intervention principles (Hobfoll et al., 2007) that can be seen in creative recovery projects. Bruce and Michelle from Kinglake Ranges both advocated for "nonthreatening" creative spaces that help disaster-affected community members express themselves both verbally and nonverbally. Michelle articulated the value of nonjudgmental and inclusive creative spaces, saying that they promote "an atmosphere of relaxation and the ability to release inner emotions." Bruce explained that nonverbal, task-based engagement can lead to talking, which he argued is critical to recovery. The creative processes described by Bruce, Michelle, and other interviewees also link to Gordon's (2004) strategies for recovery. They do so by strengthening a sense of individual identity, promoting social bonding, normalizing communication about the personal impacts of disasters, and showing a breadth of possible individual experiences while constructing shared realities. Both *expressing* and *witnessing* the expression of disaster-affected individuals can help repair the social fabric of communities and increase feelings of connectedness.

Hope and Transformation

Creative projects also foster a sense of hope for the future. Amanda explained that:

> this sort of work proves that there's life beyond the fires. It's not just about survival. It's not about replacing what was lost. It's about moving into life beyond

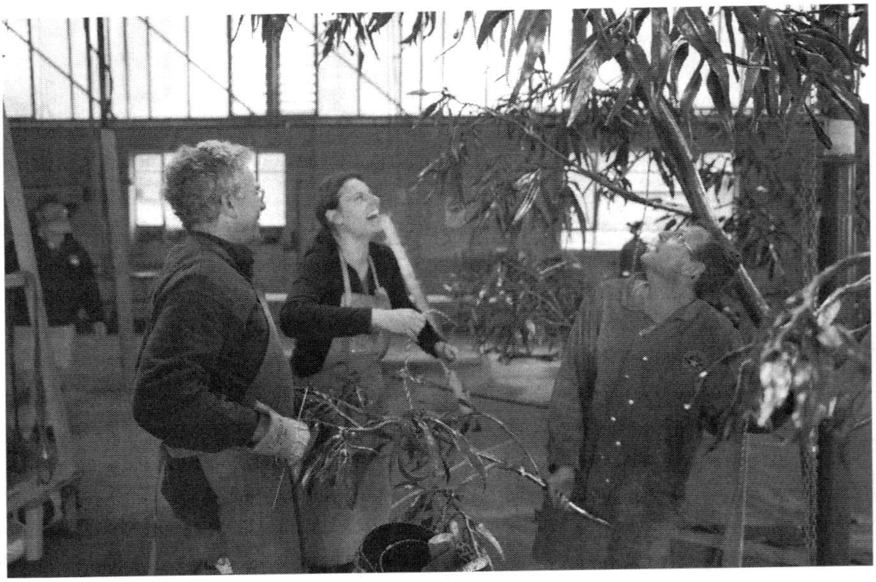

FIGURE 3.2 Assembling The Blacksmiths' Tree. Photograph by Neil Grant.

> the fires, and [creative recovery] creates the environment where that sort of transformation can take place. That's both on the personal level and it's on a community level.

Scotia agreed, adding that the arts and creativity stimulates imagination. She said that:

> recovery is about being able to re-dream and to come together around this common vision, which is about sustainable, safe and open, accessible futures.

These observations align with Hobfoll and colleagues' (2007) note that hope can be instilled through storytelling and positive goal-setting. Michelle stressed the adaptability of creative processes, which can facilitate grieving and the acknowledgement of loss through memorial and ritual; provide opportunities for respite, pleasure, and play; and contribute to individual healing processes through creative expression, and to community connections through shared meaning-making processes (NSF Consulting, 2011). Michelle also described the *aesthetic transformation* of harsh recovery infrastructure such as temporary fencing and marquees, explaining that Kinglake artists turned wire fences into gallery walls and marquees into live music venues. While Amanda and Scotia explained that creative processes are *transformative* for individuals and communities by fostering hope for the future and cultivating a sense of agency and purpose, creative processes are also *transformable*: they are adaptable to the needs of individuals and communities

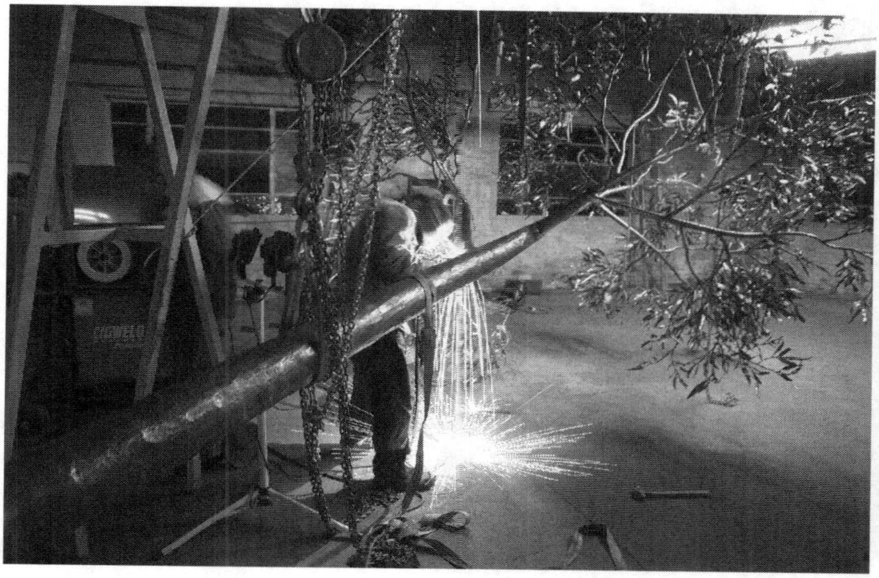

FIGURE 3.3 Welding the trunk of The Blacksmiths' Tree. Photograph by Amanda Grant.

and provide a range of accessible entry points that promote participation and inclusion. These qualities all contribute to a culture of democracy in disaster-affected communities.

Partnerships and Generosity

Amanda noted that the transformative nature of creativity can support non-arts organizations to connect with communities in a meaningful and empathic way:

> Creative recovery gives people on the outside a way of connecting to those communities in a very gentle, very positive, very uplifting way.

Michelle agreed, adding that creative projects also helped service providers and other nonlocal agencies to connect with affected community members, as well as to stay abreast of rapidly evolving community recovery needs. She explained that service providers met the Arts Alliance's requests for resources like marquees, tables, and chairs for events in a "behind-the-scenes way." This built trust between local and nonlocal organizations, as well as contributing to what NSF Consulting (2011) described as "a culture of giving," both *to* and *within* disaster-affected communities. Additionally, Scotia and Liz Zito from Regional Arts Victoria stressed the importance of ongoing collaboration between arts organizations and the recovery sector, which is an example of adaptive cross-sector collaboration that strengthens recovery outcomes (Dibley et al., 2019, p. 21).

Listening and Adaptation

One of the strengths (and challenges) of creative recovery projects is the capacity for projects to adapt to the needs of the community as those needs evolve. Scotia emphasized the importance of building trust by spending time with communities and being responsive to their needs. Liz concurred, adding that:

> communities that have workers on the ground in those regions, or really good arts officers, are more resilient because they know how to come together, to express, to share, to gather, to make work, to tell stories, all of those things.

This strengthens the case for long-term relationship building between creative workers and local communities to improve outcomes of creative projects following disasters. Amanda concurred with Liz and Scotia's points, adding that direct connections with communities that are not constrained by government funding arrangements and other bureaucratic structures are especially beneficial. This adds a further benefit to including creative projects in cross-sector recovery initiatives: they may have capacity to be more flexible and responsive to community needs than many non-arts initiatives.

Self-Determination and Civic Engagement

Hobfoll and colleagues' (2007) assertion that self-efficacy and collective efficacy are protective against trauma aligns with emergency management principles of community-led recovery, as well as democratic principles of participation and agency. It also relates to Scotia's description of the training that the Creative Recovery Network provides to artists, which positions them as "active citizens" that:

> help communities to be self-determined in their own recovery. So that means that culture and the arts can be used as a way to articulate and to drive and to demand what they wish to see as their support.

Liz added that generally, strong creative communities produce spontaneous community responses that address gaps in formal disaster recovery arrangements. Liz offered an example from the small town of Cudgewa, Victoria, which was impacted by the 2019–2020 Black Summer fires. She said that a local artist recognized that he didn't have the skills to fight the fires, but that he was a great organizer from having worked in the arts:

> So he started a Facebook page, he started getting people to run fuel and volunteering and they were getting into places that Council couldn't get into. It was quite extraordinary. . . . Artists and people who work in the creative industries are able to think outside the box and are able to look at all the different

> possibilities . . . so when a disaster happens, they are more freely able to come up with ways to survive or to help look after each other.

This example shows that creativity can empower individuals to respond spontaneously and effectively to disasters, complementing the work of agencies and government. As Scotia explained, creative recovery is about self-determination: promoting agency within communities so that they can lead their own recovery and develop a shared vision for the future.

Barriers to Incorporating Creativity in Recovery

While creative recovery is recognized for its contribution to social recovery following major disruptions, there are significant barriers to embedding the arts and creativity in disaster recovery long term. Amanda, Michelle, Bruce, Cecily, Liz, and Scotia spoke at length about these challenges, offering suggestions for improvement to planning and collaboration within and between the arts and other sectors. Their suggestions would enable creative approaches to recovery to be more effective in the future by protecting arts workers from burnout and increasing the sustainability of projects within communities.

Tensions Between "Top-Down" and "Bottom-Up" Responses

Cecily and Bruce reflected on the tensions between "top-down" government responses and "bottom-up" community leadership following disasters. Cecily acknowledged that commitments from government, such as funding or recovery workers, often come before local needs are ascertained. Scotia explained that these "top-down" imperatives can be seen in creative recovery projects, too, despite the good intentions of government and agencies funding them. She argued that creative projects are unsuccessful when they fail to respond to a community's self-determined needs. Bruce agreed, warning that governments need to be facilitators, not leaders of recovery projects. He said that poorly facilitated projects can leave a "legacy of mistrust" in the creative recovery process, and that in the past, some local governments have been too involved or brought in outsiders to facilitate projects that inevitably collapsed. Liz stressed that communities don't respond to "fly in, fly out" projects. Rather, they need workers supporting them on the ground.

Amanda said she has witnessed governments invest in projects led by outsiders or consultants who are not embedded in the community, explaining that communities have become angered by creative outcomes because they didn't reflect their wants and needs. However, Liz and Amanda both suggested that there are some benefits to communities working with outsider-artists to lead projects. Outsiders can be seen as impartial by community members, which minimizes actual or perceived bias regarding the distribution of funding and administrative support, and reduces the possibility of exacerbating existing social fractures within the community. This *outside-in* approach was seen in Amanda's leadership on The Tree

Project, which is often held up as an exemplar of best practice in creative recovery with respect to community engagement. However, there are benefits to local creative leadership – such as Michelle's *inside-out* approach in Kinglake – that are equally important to acknowledge. Scotia argued that, overall, facilitators should either be locals or invited by locals for their skillset or ability to coordinate across a range of complex needs. Ultimately, these two approaches, *outside-in* – where nonlocal facilitators become embedded in the community – and *inside-out* – where local leaders initiate projects and can access support as needed – may offer equally effective frameworks for creative recovery.

The Seeming Irrelevance of Creativity After Disasters

A significant barrier to garnering support to incorporate the arts and creativity into disaster recovery is that it is not always perceived as relevant or useful to community, agencies, and government. Scotia proposed that this could be due to sociopolitical perceptions of arts and culture more broadly because "currently in Australia, we're not seen to be intrinsically of value." She stated that these attitudes – from government and agencies especially – can make it difficult to get projects off the ground. Not only this, but Amanda explained that creative recovery projects can be seen as an added burden to emotionally exhausted recovery workers. Disaster-affected individuals may also struggle to perceive the value of creative projects because, as Amanda noted, when relief support is being withdrawn, they may feel that their immediate needs are no longer being met. This may cause people to view arts-related expenditure as frivolous or insensitive. She and Bruce pointed out that having creative recovery facilitators on the ground before immediate relief is withdrawn mitigates this potential conflict and its impact on creative project development.

Bruce and Amanda stressed that when creative projects are introduced later in the recovery process when funding finally becomes available, the level of community trauma and hostility can be difficult to navigate. Scotia, Bruce, Liz, and Amanda all advocated for the inclusion of creative recovery in emergency planning prior to disasters to address this challenge. Liz and Amanda suggested that creative recovery should be written into local government plans prior to disasters because government and agencies can be difficult to connect with when they are focused on responding to immediate community needs. Scotia and Bruce also proposed that embedding creative recovery in state and local emergency management arrangements would help organizations like Regional Arts Victoria and Creative Recovery Network to dispense funding and on-the-ground arts workers earlier in the recovery process.

Lack of Funding and Coordination Leads to Facilitator Burnout

Amanda explained that when creative recovery isn't embedded in government plans, it becomes difficult to access funding for projects. Without funding, Scotia said that it takes longer for communities to experience the positive impacts of creative recovery. Compounding this is the impact that a lack of funding can have on the well-being of creative recovery facilitators. Amanda said that despite positive feedback from the community, she wouldn't work on another project like The Blacksmiths' Tree due to burnout from working for free for a long time on a highly complex and demanding project:

> I don't usually talk about this with a lot of people, but the lack of funding was brutal. Like the blacksmiths used to repair my car so I could keep it on the road. . . . I was so freaking broke.

This raises issues about managing expectations from communities and funders that creative recovery facilitators will work for free or next to nothing. This links to sociopolitical perceptions of the arts not being of value, as expressed by Scotia. Alongside the risk of burnout due to low or no pay, there is also a risk of vicarious trauma for creative recovery workers. Facilitator burnout not only harms individual workers but can also limit the effectiveness and long-term sustainability of creative recovery projects.

Liz identified another funding-related issue, which is a lack of coordination on creative recovery initiatives within the arts sector. Scotia thought that this might be compounded by the highly competitive nature of arts funding. This is worsened by arts sector grant guidelines that sometimes exclude creative recovery projects from being eligible. Amanda explained that for this reason, creative recovery typically receives funding from outside the arts sector, such as from mental health or community resilience funds, causing applicants to retrofit their projects to grant criteria in order to maintain project viability. This emphasizes that the arts and cultural sector needs to consider its role in disaster recovery prior to disasters occurring. This would help establish a wider range of arts-appropriate funding pathways for facilitators to access as their projects develop in response to community interest and needs.

Valuing and Resourcing Creative Recovery

Interviews with artists, arts leaders, and emergency services experts revealed that creative processes can stimulate a culture of democracy in disaster-affected communities. This occurs when individuals engage in creative expression, which can lead to greater understanding between affected community members. By creating safe spaces for expression, creative recovery fosters connectedness and belonging. This promotes participation and inclusion within disaster-affected communities more broadly. Further, creative recovery inspires hope and future planning, cultivating a sense of agency and purpose. Creative recovery can be flexible in response to the needs of disaster-affected individuals and communities where government and other service-providers may not be able to. Additionally, creative projects can strengthen networks within communities, as well as with external organizations and agencies. This contributes to trust and a sense of generosity toward and within disaster-affected regions, strengthening collaboration and self-determination.

However, tensions between "top-down" and "bottom-up" imperatives can doom creative recovery projects to fail. This can be compounded by poor timing of projects due to creative recovery not being considered in pre-disaster planning. The arts and cultural sector could address this by considering their role in responding to the impacts of the climate crisis. Climate change has increased the risk and impact of disasters worldwide, and this erodes the social, physical, and financial health of affected individuals and communities. This makes communities vulnerable to exploitation through the weakening of democratic processes following disasters. By presenting case studies of best practice in creative recovery, these Australian examples may inform international approaches to community empowerment.

Creative recovery can address the impact of disasters on democracy by promoting empathy, connection, trust, and agency in affected communities. But for this to occur, it is essential that both the arts and emergency management sectors recognize the value of these initiatives and resource creative recovery projects and facilitators accordingly.

References

Australian Institute for Disaster Resilience. (2018). *Australian disaster resilience community recovery handbook*. Commonwealth of Australia. https://knowledge.aidr.org.au/media/5634/community-recovery-handbook.pdf

Dibley, G., Mitchell, L., Ireton, G., Gordon, R., & Gordon, M. (2019). *Government's role in supporting community–led approaches to recovery*. Department of Health and Human Services. https://knowledge.aidr.org.au/media/6916/srrg-community_led_literature_review.pdf

Garton, A. (Director). (2020, July 6). *Forged from fire – The making of the Blacksmiths Tree Online* [Vimeo Video]. https://vimeo.com/ondemand/forgedfromfire

Gordon, R. (2004). The social system as site of disaster impact and resource for recovery. *The Australian Journal of Emergency Management, 19*(4), 16–22.

Hayward, B., & Johnson, S. (2022). Lessons for democracy from a decade of disasters. In S. Uekusa, S. Matthewman, & B. C. Glavovic (Eds.), *A decade of disaster experiences in Ōtautahi Christchurch: Critical disaster studies perspectives* (pp. 335–351). Springer Nature. https://doi.org/10.1007/978-981-16-6863-0_16

Hobfoll, S. E., Watson, P., Bell, C. C., Bryant, R. A., Brymer, M. J., Friedman, M. J., Friedman, M., Gersons, B. P. R., de Jong, J. T. V. M., Layne, C. M., Maguen, S., Neria, Y., Norwood, A. E., Pynoos, R. S., Reissman, D., Ruzek, J. I., Shalev, A. Y., Solomon, Z., Steinberg, A. M., & Ursano, R. J. (2007). Five essential elements of immediate and mid–term mass trauma intervention: Empirical evidence. *Psychiatry, 70*(4), 283–315. https://doi.org/10.1521/psyc.2007.70.4.283

Korndörffer, L., White, C., & Mackelprang, J. L. (2023). Psychological first aid principles within a community-led arts initiative: Lessons from the Blacksmiths' Tree. *Disasters, 47*(3), 806–829. https://doi.org/10.1111/disa.12564

National Geographic Society. (2022, May 20). *Black Saturday bushfires in Australia*. https://education.nationalgeographic.org/resource/black-saturday-bushfires-australia/

NSF Consulting. (2011). *The role of the arts in rebuilding community: An evaluation of arts Victoria's and regional arts Victoria's bushfire initiatives*. Arts Victoria. https://victoriancollections.net.au/media/collectors/52f0757e9821f40464f73ecb/items/565d25642162f10ac4046b0f/item-media/57668ab7d0cdd12538731aa4/original.pdf

4

DEMOCRACY AS DEMONSTRATION

A Lifelong, Dreamed of, Home

Kirsten Kaschock and Rachel Wenrick

> Yes, there are obstacles. Unwillingness [of] individuals to work together in harmony to produce a unified community; lack of patience, lack of unconditional love, lack of time set aside to get to know people and work with people . . .
>
> – Anonymous Writers Room participant

> Imagine a home . . . on the inside there are potted plants and flowers . . . rooms for Artistic Expressions of all kinds . . rooms that could be used by any tenant that has scheduled an appointment . . on the rooftop there are four huge rooms for social gatherings for all kinds of events . . . [downstairs] a fully equipped and stocked kitchen is broken off in sections where we can cook, cater, and teach cooking classes . . . the beauty of it all is when things are over and done with, we can return to our personal domiciles . . . SWEET!
>
> – Rosalyn Cliett (Writers Room participant and West Philadelphia resident)

#

What follows is the story of how Writers Room, a university-community literary arts program at Drexel University in Philadelphia, Pennsylvania, found itself involved in the research and design of affordable housing. The story will be told – as most Writers Room stories are told – polyvocally, setting the voices of the community in direct conversation with professional artists and academics, real estate developers, and university administrators. A collage of episodes, dialogues, and reflections will offer a sense of the process through which this evolution occurred and is still unfolding. In other words, this narrative will attempt – no doubt imperfectly – to model both democratic and artistic practices (and show how deeply

DOI: 10.4324/9781003475996-7

related they are) even as it tries to convey the history of an organization founded in response to a single question:

What if?

#

In July 2014, a group gathered at the inauguration of a university-owned community center in West Philadelphia was asked to imagine a writers' house centered in the neighborhood. If that could be – what might it be?

Then a non-tenure-track teaching faculty of Drexel University's English and Philosophy Department, Rachel Wenrick was at the Dornsife Center that late summer afternoon. Located on a 1.3-acre property between tree-lined avenues of occasionally dilapidated Victorian houses and narrower rowhouse-filled streets, Dornsife is Drexel's "urban extension center," straddling the Powelton Village and Mantua neighborhoods of West Philadelphia. The area had just that year been named by the US Department of Housing and Urban Development (HUD) as a Promise Zone – an area of high poverty (nearly twice the ~24% Philadelphia average) but also of potential opportunity, with universities and health centers within walking distance – and the designation was being seized upon as an imperative for renewed civic engagement by local anchor institutions, the University of Pennsylvania and Drexel among them.

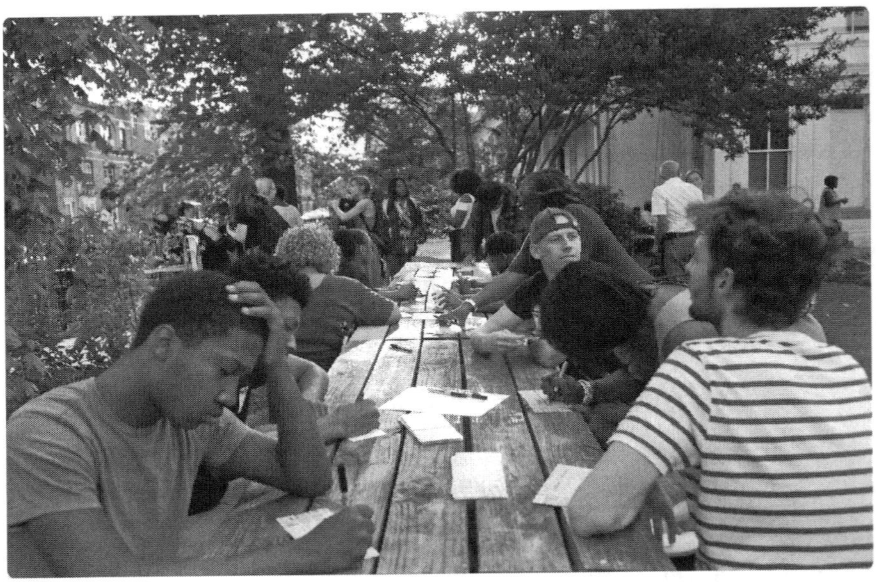

FIGURE 4.1 Writers Room participants in thought and writing at an outdoor workshop prior to community dinner. Photograph by Devin Welsh.

Not a Writers' House – Writers Room

When Wenrick heard the term "writers' house," she first flashed to the historic liberal arts campus model, a place where literary luminaries are invited to give readings to undergraduates, where English professors hold high-level seminars and graduate students discuss theory. The concept is attractive, but it isn't inherently community-centered or inclusive. Cloistered inside their ivory towers, such spaces – even when they invite the public in – are not largely designed with those outside the university in mind. Imagining something different, Wenrick did as Wenrick does and turned to those around her. The people she met that day, people who eventually would become the founding members of Writers Room, did not want the house on the hill. They did not dream of resume-writing sessions and grammar tutorials. Given access to university resources and faculty, they wanted to learn how to better tell their own stories, to archive their family histories, and to express themselves as the artists they knew they were.

> *I know there are endless ways to share creativity. I love sharing my creativity in two ways those being physically and verbally. Physically I create art and put it all over my room. Not just art but everything that is important to me. The drawing me and my little sister did. The drawings I did when I was in a dark place . . . Verbally I share my ideas. Like how I want to make a space for people who've experienced abuse. Or how I don't understand how we can't just make more money to get out of debt. And the poem I wrote when I was crying, or the poem I wrote when I was happy.*
>
> – Amina Mosley (Writers Room participant, graduate of Paul Robeson High School)

A writer herself, Wenrick got to work and called the project, simply, Writers Room. (There's no apostrophe – it's not a place writers own, it's a place *they are*.) To explain the "room," she quotes the architect Louis Kahn, "[The room] is the place of the mind." But neither he nor Wenrick stops there. "The street," he continued, "is a room by agreement." These quotes are not offered up as some cryptic mantra: Writers Room began as a theoretical response, as an imagined space. In 2014, it began with First Tuesdays – free one-off writing workshops scheduled in the afternoon before the monthly community dinners at the Dornsife Center (Drexel's answer to an urban extension center) and held wherever space was available. The "room" of Writers Room is any place that its writers convened.

This may sound utopic, but these are the adjustments and reframings artists (and others) know how to make when they don't have a designated space to call home or enough funding to build one. Without foundational support from a university that prizes innovation, Writers Room began in the margins, and from there began to find its own way, to make its own spaces. This story will not be unfamiliar to those working at the intersection of art, higher education, and community.

At the end of its first year, Writers Room held a reading and *Anthology* release – which would become an annual event. The Dornsife Center was packed. Anyone who had participated in a First Tuesday or had work published in Writers Room's inclusive publication was invited to read, and they brought friends and family to listen. The work was real, it was powerful, it was shared and heard.

On the day after that event, a founding member of Writers Room, Carol Richardson McCullough, told Wenrick that she and her family had been evicted. The developer who'd recently bought their apartment building had decided to market its units to student renters. She explained:

> It was pressing on me. And in the writing I had done a lot of reflection and shared things about what had gone on in my life. I felt a connection with you, so I just mentioned it. Almost as a point of conversation. The Anthology reading was the first thing we did, and this was the next thing coming up in my life.

Undergraduate members of Writers Room, students who'd attended workshops with Carol and Jordan, her son, who has special needs and was 25 at the time, showed up that weekend with Wenrick's partner Cyrille to help the McCullough family move. It was in that whirlwind (Carol references the Tasmanian Devil as a visual) that the group began to understand how implicated they were in each other's stories. At the end of Writers Room's very first year, the seed for a different type of writers' house was planted. It sprouted out of adversity and necessity, but it suggested something different might be possible – maybe students and neighbors could do more than workshop together. *What if? What if a writers' house meant writers living together?*

Wenrick knew that the challenges of housing in West Philadelphia were manifold – not only for those seeking affordable living spaces, but also for anyone trying to understand and effect change in that landscape. And the reality of doing that from within an anchor institution with a complicated history in the neighborhood was even more daunting. One administrator, upon hearing that Writers Room had an idea for joint university-community housing, expressed excitement and trepidation. "I want so badly for this to work, but . . ." and then she shook her head, "Maybe I'm too institutionalized. I've forgotten how to dream." This was the type of disbelief the project was met with again and again. And this was only on the university side.

Neighbors were also skeptical. There is long-standing community distrust of the universities in West Philadelphia (Drexel's and the University of Pennsylvania's campuses are contiguous). Residents live in fear of displacement, have seen university interventions come and go, and have taken repeated surveys about their needs that led to no action. Drexel's administration is perceived to be non-transparent, promising unrealized prosperity for residents as it increases its footprint in the neighborhood, and its researchers can be viewed as self-interested (when offering inadequate compensation for community time and participation in academic studies). Additionally, Drexel's ten-week quarter system, with many students leaving campus for six-month co-op internships, makes it difficult for students to view themselves as part of West Philadelphia, and some don't treat it as if it is anyone's home. Finally, as with many urban universities, few Drexel faculty live in the neighborhoods surrounding the university.

> Looking back – I see the plan. Gentrification for the so-called Gentry but not my people. Underserved, unwanted, are marched to the hinterlands, the facilities, the shelters, the jails. And the powers, the Med's and Ed's, can reclaim their city – Temple to U of P.
>
> – *Elizabeth Abrams (Writers Room participant, West Philadelphia resident)*

#

In 2016, the day after Donald Trump's presidential election victory, the sky over Philadelphia was charcoal-colored. Wenrick, at a loss and feeling the sense of loss so many were feeling, decided to attend an informational meeting for ArtPlace America, a ten-year collaboration among foundations, federal agencies, and financial institutions to support and strengthen the field of creative placemaking. Javier Torres-Campos, Director of National Grantmaking, was there, and he complimented her skirt – a small human moment that marked that morning as something other than dark. To a packed room, he presented a vision for positioning "arts and culture as a core sector of equitable community planning and development." For many of us, it seemed like time to start engaging in local action with whatever tools we had. Sitting back waiting for others to do the work no longer seemed like a viable option.

A few months later, February 2017, Writers Room submitted a first-round application to ArtPlace America's National Creative Placemaking Fund with the idea for an anti-displacement project. McCullough's illegal eviction had been the seed, but since that moment, more and more members had shared their concerns about the changing face of West Philadelphia, their fears of displacement, and their desire not to be complicit in the devastating effects of rapid gentrification. Keyssh Datts, Writers Room member and founder of Decolonizing Philadelphia, describes the situation this way: "I stand here in a city undergoing a community memory amputation as its members are at a cry-for-help to save the last of what's left of a dying city currently being brought up by developers" (McCullough, 2022, p. 35). Since its inception, Writers Room had been flipping the script of a typical writers house by treating all comers as potential artists and teachers – but this application put forth a house that was not only community-centered but also residential.

The application process consisted of a year of working with residents and civic groups, building partnerships, and co-designing the concept for a house where students and community members could live together and learn from one another.

When the project was named a finalist for ArtPlace, one of 70 out of a field of 1,000, we spent the summer refining the idea, planning a site visit, dreaming. Much of this work was happening while our civic partners were negotiating a community benefits agreement with the developer of Schuylkill Yards, a $3.5 billion innovation district created in partnership with Drexel. It was apparent that one house wasn't enough, that the writers house we had initially envisioned could be the first stage of a much-longer-term project. In a meeting with Wenrick and McCullough at the Dornsife Center, Gwen Morris, Secretary of the Mantua Civic Association and a neighborhood resident since the 1970s, asked, "How are you going to scale it up?" They began imagining a constellation of homesharers, of residents renting to students, with arts programming cohering the whole and providing the feedback loop that would make the program responsive and, ultimately, successful and replicable. The work ahead was so big, but we felt energized, ready.

On the day the call came that ArtPlace had not funded the project, that the initial residential house would not be happening that year, Wenrick walked out of her office and said, "I feel like we're at the bottom of the mountain."

#

What follows is a small portion of a scored dialogue between four Writers Room members including Wenrick, founding member McCullough, then Drexel undergraduate Lauren Lowe, and Barbara Dale, who worked for a local housing collective. The form was adapted from the work of the late composer Pauline Oliveros. This writing experiment, which took place over email and in a roundtable discussion, used a collaborative, consensus-oriented practice to slow down conversation, giving participants time to deeply listen to one another and process their responses. The overarching question put before the group of four women of various ages, educations, races, religions, and identities was this: did they still think long-term West Philadelphia residents and more transient students could live together cooperatively, creating an alternative to displacement while also beginning to build a richer, more inclusive community – and more importantly, if so, should we continue to pursue this idea despite the recent setback that pushed the realization of home-sharing even further into the future?

Describe the Writers House Project as You Have Come to Understand It

Barbara Dale: The writers' house is a response to disconnect between a university and the community surrounding it . . . This collaboration came into existence because housing (a home) is both a necessary function of social and economic justice (a human right), and a space where life and creativity happens.

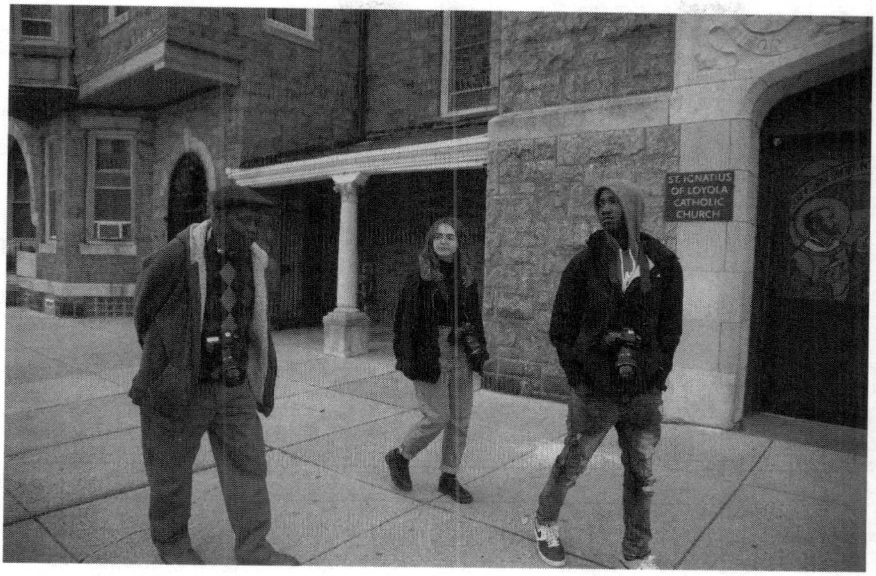

FIGURE 4.2 Norman Cain, Natasha Hajo, and Mark Dawkins talk and stroll around their shared neighborhood of West Philadelphia. Photograph by Lauren Lowe.

Carol McCullough: The writers' house, as I understand it, is to be a greater extension of the Writers Room concept, where select writers (students and community members) would not only come together and write, but also reside together.

Lauren Lowe: I always think of the project with this one particular idea in mind . . . instead of building "an enclave for the initiated" as Wenrick would probably say, our project recognizes that the talent is already here – and *has* been here.

Rachel Wenrick: Writers Room is the radical idea that people of different races, religions, genders, generations, orientations, cultures can live and create together. That we can support each other. Love each other. Recognize ourselves in each other. That we can be part of something bigger, make something bigger than just ourselves by being just ourselves.

How Did You Get Involved in the Project, and Why Did You?

McCullough: I got involved in the project as a result of my dedication to Writers Room, and, of course, my experience with being forced to move out of my apartment when my landlord (illegally) sold the property to a company which rehabbed and refurbished it, and then raised the rent and rented it out to students . . . The possibility of living in a super creative space at a price that I could afford I find very appealing.

Now, with word of the funding miss, it creates both the familiar sadness which follows rejection, as well as a feeling of determination and hopefulness at the prospect of refining the design . . . to make it happen anyway . . .

Dale: I became involved as a representative of Friends Rehabilitation Program (FRP), an affordable housing and social service nonprofit . . . The idea of this writers' house aligned with our Quaker values, and . . . reminded us of a housing cooperative our Quaker predecessors created in the 1950s – the first racially integrated housing cooperative in Philadelphia . . . I am interested in how cooperative communities can resist injustice.

If the Sky Were the Limit – What Would a House Created by Writers Room Look/Feel/Be Like?

Lowe: I'm learning . . . how important visibility is for our projects.

Dale: The [house] shines the light on tension, opens it up for discussion. Inside of the house, discussion happens. Students and community members talk about what it means to lead a life in this environment . . . How do we build an inclusive community that leaves no one behind? Out of this discussion, change happens.

What Communities Do You Carry Into This Room? Who Weighs In?

Lowe: Students, both undergraduate and, I also think about what the highschoolers would think in the area and how they might benefit . . . and grad students (maybe I will be one eventually). I also was thinking about families, and my dad – who would probably be like "This is like hippie bullshit." (laughter) He totally would. But also [his and my] larger community of Chinatown. I think about how similar the issues around housing can be in those two neighborhoods . . .

McCullough: One community that has not been mentioned yet but which is definitely there is the African American community . . . of which I am a part. And we'll be in the house, we're in the neighborhood . . . Rather than bulldozing through and pushing them aside, bring them in. And so I think of the communities of students, and learners. This is a university project, and so it's an opportunity for everybody to learn, to learn from each other . . . there are lifelong learners, different ages, they might not have a backpack on their back full of books, but they have things they carry with them.

#

As bell hooks reminds us, “to be truly visionary we have to root our imagination in our concrete reality while simultaneously imagining possibilities beyond that reality” (hooks, 2000).

> Thinking – through some weird cocktail of rugged individualism and ego – that I have to come up with my own answer when, of course, the answers [are] already stretching and yawning to life somewhere in the collective . . .
>
> – *Amy Gottsegen (Writers Room participant, Drexel graduate, community organizer)*

The last time democracy almost died –
we were not even thoughts yet.
But if you and I were able to materialize from the dust,
maybe we can turn back the clock.

Our aim: to illuminate and protect
as we gather, learn, see a future . . .

– Alex Wasalinko (Writers Room participant, ArtistYear AmeriCorps Resident Teaching Artist)

#

When Writers Room persevered, after an initial rejection, in developing that initial idea for a single residential home into a plan for sustained growth within a community, this was an artistic act. Enlisting a cross-sector, cross-disciplinary, diverse, intergenerational collective to lend their voices to the project, to be co-creators in every step of the process. This is self-determination. This is democracy.

We shouldn’t need permission to imagine – humans are born as dreaming beings. Children take their sensory experiences and transform them through play, often through collaborative play. But at some point during social development, the belief that the things we cultivate in the mind might then thrive in the world is challenged by circumstance. It is challenged by poverty, racism, sexism, homophobia, xenophobia, and by systems that claim to be meritocratic while hiding in plain sight entrenched hierarchy and its accompanying oppressions. People stop believing in the power of their imaginations – they forget how to dream. They doubt their ability to make change happen in their own lives, much less in the world.

Because artists make – because they create and repurpose and extrapolate – they can show the work of transforming the dreamt into the done. They show that it remains possible, even in difficult circumstances, even with materials others might dub *less than*. Writers Room honors the artist in us all. Making together helps us understand that creating something new is an inalienable right, that having others willing to truly hear and see our ideas, and committing to seeing and hearing their work in turn: that is democracy in its most basic form.

#

During the application process for ArtPlace, Writers Room established partnerships with the Mantua Civic Association, the Powelton Village Civic Association, and Drexel's Justice-oriented Youth (JoY) Education Lab led by Dr. Ayana Allen-Handy. Together we completed an AmeriCorps-funded community-driven participatory action research project to investigate the potential for cooperative living to combat displacement. This intergenerational research team found that the displacement of Black residents in West Philadelphia is happening at faster and higher rates than initially hypothesized, with a 73% increase in the white population in the neighborhood bordering Drexel – Mantua – over the past ten years. Further analysis of a sample block group revealed rental rates rose 44.33% with increases of 73.97% in rent-burdened households (paying more than 30% of income on rent) and 453.85% in those that are extremely rent-burdened (paying more than 50% of income).

During this period of investigation, Writers Room's housing work became its own strand of programming, Second Story Collective. This collaborative of artists and scholars, activists and architects, and West Philadelphia residents believe that shared living space and shared stories can create a foundation for meaningful cohabitation, community-building, and preservation – that the right housing innovations can address affordability and equity at the same time. In this model, older homeowners receive help renovating their homes for student tenants. Community-minded youth agree to provide needed practical help to the homeowners in exchange for lower rents. In addition to these aging-in-place homes – which are being piloted this year – in consultation with the group, local developer Charles Lomax is building 18 multi-family units as part of Village Square on Haverford, a mixed-use development in West Philadelphia. Lomax says, "This is an opportunity to change the narrative of university-adjacent development from one of displacement of long-term residents to engagement and community-building." The duplexes will create an extra rental income stream for first-time homebuyers, helping young families become homeowners. The model shows how alternative affordable housing options can benefit this university-adjacent area and its overlapping communities. In the words of Carol Richardson McCullough, "It would also be one instance of neighborhood placement rather than the dis-placement that has historically accompanied university expansion into neighborhoods" (Kaschock, 2023).

The dread of displacement and the lack of affordable housing again and again rose up through artmaking and storytelling as the most pressing concerns of Writers Room members. Although these problems predate both the election of Trump and the onset of COVID, during the past eight years they have been compounded, revealing the entangled nature of social issues and the need for locally imagined and voiced solutions. Writers Room members have listened to one another's concerns

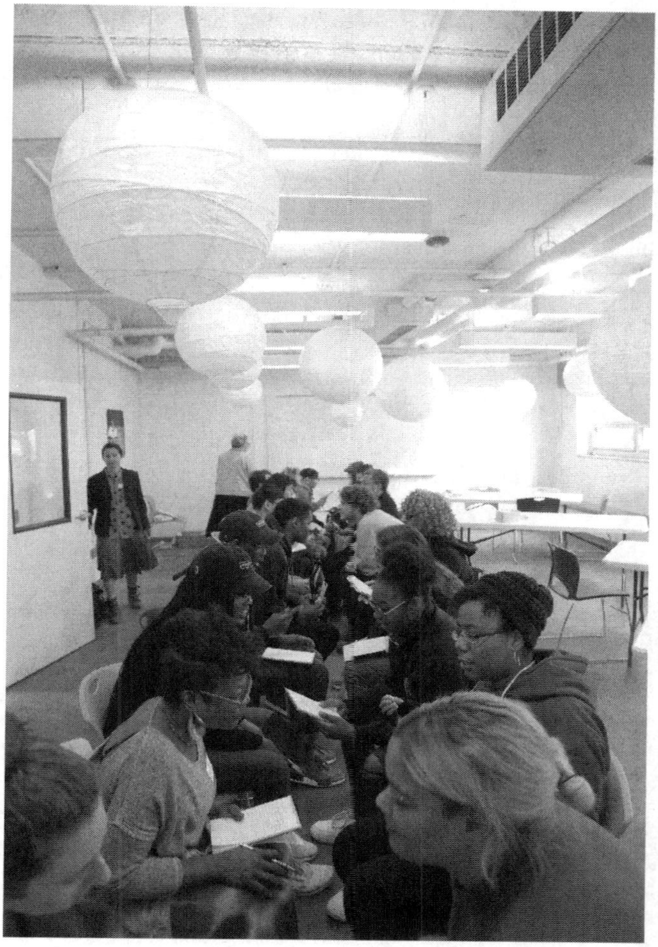

FIGURE 4.3 Attendants at a housing symposium sharing ideas of home. Photograph by Lauren Lowe.

and together decided to act, to take what they've imagined – sharing stories and lives beyond the workshop space – and make it an actual thing in the world. It has been a long road, but we are on the brink of finally seeing the residential homes that we dreamt of together.

From Writers Room's inception, our participants have been co-designers of our programming, and they use the tools they bring from their lives and the ones they find in workshops to expand all our thinking about what a community is and what it can do. The stories our members tell, their desires for new ways to discuss issues that matter, and the resultant dialogue – these all determine the direction of our work and bolster resolve when it gets hard, which it does, frequently.

Andrea Walls, a Philadelphia multidisciplinary artist/activist and founder of the Museum of Black Joy, runs a weekly photography and writing program at Writers Room. In summer 2023, that program's work was featured in conversation with images of historic Philadelphia at the Pennsylvania Academy of the Fine Arts. This installation, "Seeing Philadelphia," spurred dialogue about the changing face of the city, a city sometimes known as the cradle of American democracy. The power of the work's placement, and how these images and words share space with more traditionally elevated images, has been a powerful reminder of how infrequently the voices and the ways of seeing evidenced in the work (BIPOC, elderly, youthful, queer) have been promoted as representative of America. Walls introduced the group's work this way: "The first question that comes to mind: what is a city? Is it the buildings, the land, the history, the way it feels to be a citizen? Who is the city for? Who serves? Who is served? Which aspects of city life are upheld and which are invisible – then and now? Who decides? Who disrupts?"

Writers Room has, in nine years, moved beyond its given frame as an imagined site for arts programming to become a force for social change. It is impossible not to notice, here in Philadelphia, that this same work has been performed by citizens (and those wrongly excluded from citizenry) since this country began: continually enacting what is necessary to remake the dream, to be in a state of doing democracy rather than thinking it ever already done.

References

hooks, b. (2000). *Feminism is for everybody: Passionate politics*. South End Press.

Kaschock, K., Allen-Handy, A., Dale, B., Lowe, L., McCullough, C. R., & Wenrick, R. (2023, April 25). How a university-community home-sharing collective is creating a new model for affordable housing in West Philadelphia. *Brookings*. www.brookings.edu/blog/the-avenue/2023/04/25/how-a-university-community-home-sharing-collective-is-creating-a-new-model-for-affordable-housing-in-west-philadelphia/.

McCullough, C. R., Datts, K., Allen-Handy, A., Sterin, K., & Escalante, K. (2022). Zip code colonization: Counter-narratives of gentrification's traumatic impact on Philadelphia's Black educational communities. *Journal of Trauma Studies in Education*, *1*(3), 23–44.

PART TWO
Aesthetic Strategies

INTRODUCTION TO AESTHETIC STRATEGIES

Remaking Worlds and Ourselves: Aesthetic Strategies for a Culture of Democracy

Diane Ragsdale and Shannon Litzenberger

Part Two of this book explores the way aesthetic practices and experiences help humans develop a range of relational capacities essential to making more inclusive, pluralistic democracies. The authors in Part Two are arts practitioners who use satiric webinars, collaborative art projects, ensemble-building strategies, and embodied community co-creation processes to advance a culture of democracy. One way of interpreting the aims of their aesthetic strategies is as a form of intentional worldmaking through collective practice – that is, a means of co-creating environments in which participants are enabled (required, even) to shift how they remake their relationships to themselves, others, "modernity/coloniality" (De Oliveira Andreotti, 2021), the natural world, and time.

This Introduction begins by problematizing a perceived state of "pernicious polarization" (McCoy & Somer, 2019) and, following political theorist William Connolly (2005), argues for "work on our relational selves" (p. 30) done by developing a set of virtues that need to be cultivated in individuals and communities in order to manifest pluralism. We explore how such virtues have come to be subordinated in this modern/colonial world and point to a fundamental shift in consciousness that is necessary not only for the realization of pluralism, but for future survival of the human species. We then seek to demonstrate ways in which projects and practices (i.e., aesthetic strategies), described in the chapters that follow, enable worldmaking and, in doing so, foster in participants a range of relational capacities essential to the practice of pluralism.

Rehearsal for Pluralism

Humanity has entered a period of reckoning. Complex interdependent systems are failing, and current ways of living are unsustainable. Transformational change is

DOI: 10.4324/9781003475996-9

needed, and for that we need the ability to collaborate across differences. Unfortunately, in the United States and elsewhere, the ability to coexist and converse across political or other cultural divides, much less collaborate, is in short supply. There is perhaps no more urgent question at this moment than "How can we live well together?"

The promise of pluralism in democracies in most parts of the world has proven elusive. Pluralism not only entails the peaceful coexistence of multiple perspectives and narratives, it requires sharing the power to shape the now and the future. A significant question is how we get *there* from a pernicious and polarized *here* (McCoy & Somer, 2019), as pluralism requires a fundamental shift in collective and enduring ways of relating.

Within a section titled "The Politics of Becoming" in his 2005 book, *Pluralism*, theorist William Connolly (2005) asserts that to increase our capacity to be pluralists, two cardinal virtues must be cultivated. The first is *agonistic respect*, by which Connolly means engaging forthrightly with those holding other views and values, but doing so with an ethos of respect. The second is *critical responsiveness*, which entails "careful listening and presumptive generosity," particularly vis-à-vis members of society struggling to achieve recognition, rights, justice, or legitimacy (pp. 124–125). Beyond these two cardinal virtues, Connolly (2005) argues for the development of other predicate virtues, including: "tolerance of ambiguity" (p. 4), "connection across multiple differences" (p. 66), "receptive listening" (p. 48), and having "a foot in two worlds" (p. 4).

Each of the chapters in Part Two utilizes artistic experiences and processes as a mechanism for bringing people together across divides around difficult or controversial issues. They intentionally engage historically unheard voices and encourage divergent perspectives to be expressed with the aim of fostering a more democratic culture, which we conceptualize here as "rehearsal for pluralism."

Remaking Relationships to Self, Others, Place, and History

How did we end up in a state of "pernicious polarization"? Why do many people seem to resist pluralism? Essentially, the humanmade modern/colonial world has, in turn, remade us. Research by psychiatrist, neuroscience researcher, and philosopher Iain McGilchrist, who studies the two hemispheres of the brain and their differences, demonstrates that the hemispheres differ not so much in what they do as in how they approach the world. The left brain understands component parts, while the right brain understands relationships that make up a whole. The left brain pays sharp attention to detail; it sorts and organizes and is concerned with order, control, categorization, manipulation, and bureaucracy (Rowson & McGilchrist, 2013, p. 17). While the right brain, more central to intelligence, understands our interconnected reality, sees movement and metaphor, discerns patterns and context, and is capable of reading humor, body language, and implied meaning (Ayed, 2021, 15:15). McGilchrist cautions that over the past 100 years, modern society has, more and more, begun to mirror the world of the left hemisphere, resulting in a distortion of experiences of reality (Ayed, 2021 15:45); he further argues that a rebalancing is critical and that, if anything, the right brain should be dominant in humans and the left its agent.

In much the same way that McGilchrist finds right-brain deficits, Potawatomi scholar Robin Wall Kimmerer speaks of the perils of the scientific process of rational inquiry that dominates the Western world. "The destructive lens is not science itself, but the lens of the scientific worldview, the illusion of dominance and control, the separation of knowledge from responsibility" (Kimmerer, 2015, p. 346). Like left- *and* right-brain ways of knowing, the Mi'kmaq practice of "two-eyed seeing," coined by Elder Albert Marshall, is a practice in which communities approach a question or problem by "seeing from one eye with the strengths of Indigenous ways of knowing and from the other eye with the strengths of Western ways of knowing and using both eyes together for a holistic and truly informed (depth) perspective" (Michie et al., 2018, p. 1207, as cited in McMillan, 2023, p. 150).

Likewise, cognitive scientist John Vervaeke, whose work is focused on questions of meaning-making, amplifies the notion that there are lost ways of knowing that humans imbued in Western cultures need to resurrect. Specifically, while modern humans are generally effective with *propositional* knowing (knowing that something is the case, or *facts*) and *procedural* knowing (knowing how to do something, or *skills*), Vervaeke asserts that they have diminished capacities for *perspectival* knowing (sensing the world and one's place in it) and *participatory* knowing (knowing how to act in one's environment) (Vervaeke, 2020, 19:30). When not engaging with perspectival and participatory knowing, the world is reduced to facts and skills, and people ignore aspects of themselves that are integral to humanity. When we experience our bodies, minds, and spirits as independent entities – separate from the world as an integrated, interdependent system of life – we find ourselves "cut off from meaning-making" (Vervaeke, 2020, 31:30).

New research has also shown that "embodied self-awareness grows resilience, emotional regulation, adaptability, and flourishing, as well as empathy, connectedness, and the ability to de-escalate and manage conflict" (Blake, 2022, p. 8). These capacities are essential to the work of living well together in a pluralistic democracy. Thus, a shift away from the dominant, hyper-rational modalities of the modern/colonial world will be necessary to develop such capacities.

Collective, embodied practices of co-creation, such as those demonstrated in the contributions in Part Two, animate right-brain, perspectival, and participatory ways of knowing. Becoming conscious of how we "think" relationally with and through our bodies strengthens the connection between our felt sense experience of the world and how we interpret and make sense of it through concepts, metaphors, language, and story. It protects us from becoming manipulated by narratives, beliefs, and concepts incongruent with our felt experiences; and it supports our capacity to participate in co-creation of the world. Collectively, all three chapters highlight sensory and/or participatory approaches that bring participants into a new relationship to self, others, and community traumas, conflicts, or systemic harms.

Activating Collective Imaginaries

What we are describing is nothing short of an ontological shift, which Colombian American anthropologist Arturo Escobar characterizes as the "political activation of relationality" (Blaser et al., 2014, as cited in Escobar, 2018, p. 153). Escobar argues for a reorientation that would value and encourage the development of a range of human dimensions that, since the Enlightenment, have tended to be subordinated – e.g., emotions, the spiritual, nonscientific forms of knowledge, the body, and place – *so that we might collectively construct worlds that are healing, caring, and life-sustaining* (Escobar, 2018, p. 153).

How we see and sense the world is conditioned by past experiences and plays out like a predictable algorithm unless default attentional filters are consciously disrupted. Musician, composer, and visual artist Brian Eno describes the role that art can play in this disruption:

> What is possible in art becomes thinkable in life. We become our new selves first in a simulacrum, through style and fashion and art, our deliberate immersions in virtual worlds. Through them we sense what it would be like to be another kind of person with other kinds of values. We rehearse new feelings and sensitivities. Imagine other ways of thinking about our world and its future. We use art to model new worlds so that we can see how we might feel about them.
>
> *(Eno, 2022, p. 4)*

While many art forms create fictionalized worlds, some appear to have worldmaking as a goal – meaning, their practices, or aesthetic strategies, are a means to that end (DiGiovanna, 2007). The chapters in Part Two exemplify the latter, in the sense that they endeavor to create a transitional space in which people can engage in processes of resurrection, reorientation, reflection, and rebalancing vis-à-vis the worlds in which they find themselves, so that they might collectively experience and imagine "the worlds that could be" (Sarasvathy, 2012).

An Overview of Part Two

Andrea Assaf (Chapter 5) uses a range of community-based arts practices, characterized as "revolutionary aesthetics," to decenter professionalism and democratize the creative process in her chapter *Co-Creating Democracy: Aesthetics in Action.* Methodologies for collective surfacing, witnessing, and multi-perspective processing of (sometimes traumatic) experiences include: Story Circles (as designed and deployed by playwright and civil rights activist John O'Neal); Collective Poetry (from the poet, cultural organizer, and former Executive Director of Alternate ROOTS Alice Lovelace); Collective Dramaturgy (ordering and shaping "raw material – writings, poetry, dances, songs, stories, images, etc." – into work for an audience); and movement-based theater and dance techniques that result in active co-creation of an artwork (e.g., Liz Lerman's "Blind Lead" that involves step-wise group improvisations that result in the creation of "a self-animated human sculpture garden"). Through the iterative use of these and other practices, participants identify a shared vision and then enact that vision in a performance. About this experience, Assaf writes:

> From the moment of forming a circle around a shared vision, to building and enacting that vision on a stage or public platform, artists have the opportunity to create a microcosm in which to rehearse the world we want to live in – the opportunity to create a "show" that embodies and communicates: *This* is what democracy looks like.
>
> *(Chapter 5, p. 95)*

In Heather McLean's "Braiding Comedy in Precarious Times: The Possibilities and Pitfalls of Research Creation in the Settler Colonial University" (Chapter 6), comedic performance is used to advance suppressed Indigenous perspectives on the "absurdities and violence of growing housing and climate crises" in the Canadian city of Kamloops. Through the making and presenting of webinars – led by comedic alter-ego characters (developed by the performers) who engage in a range of absurd, and sometimes distasteful actions (e.g., those evoking slime or feces) – the project *A Buzz in Your Hub* uses satire to to expose "states of contradiction" brought on when Indigenous artists are hired by colonial cultural institutions that do business with developers, whose projects ultimately displace and traumatize communities in which Indigenous artists live and work. Ultimately the project fosters a "relational ethics" as it seeks to "braid" Indigenous and settler perspectives (Jimmy et al., 2019) on a more general housing crisis in Kamloops.

Finally, in "Mediating Provisional Communities: The Production and Management of Collaborative Arts Projects" (Chapter 7), Rui Gonçalves Cepeda produces participatory durational artworks experienced in "ambiguous space" – dislocated from traditional cultural districts to "arteries" in the city where "everyday life happens" – thereby engaging participants as members of the populace rather than as members of an audience. By inviting participants to physically inhabit, walk over, and eventually erase a chalk figure of a bullfighter and bull, The Collaborative Art Project (CAP), *No Veo Nada* encourages citizens to confront and express their (divergent) sentiments on a controversial killing of a live animal in a public spectacle, as well as the government policy that enabled it. In this project the artist functions as mediator, and the aesthetic approach is one of conciliation. Participants are collectively afforded an opportunity to physically express their sentiments by choosing whether and how to transform controversy-cum-artwork. They are thereby given an opportunity to rehearse citizenship and a process for collectively making a world that can support and enable an inclusive culture of democracy.

Conclusion

Entrepreneurship scholar Saras Sarasvathy (2012), best known for her theory of effectuation, has posited worldmaking as an affordance of the entrepreneurial method and an important tool for times of uncertainty, writing:

> The moment we embrace the notion of worldmaking, we cede the notion of inevitability. We are no longer satisfied with the pursuit of understanding *the* world as it is or even arguing about *the* world as it should be. Instead, we also have to grapple with plurality, contingency, and possibility of the *worlds* that *could* be, the worlds we can make as well as the world we find ourselves in. Since we no longer seek to understand what *will* happen, we have to be ready to explore all the different things that *can* happen. And all the things that could have happened but did not.
>
> *(p. 11, emphasis in original)*

Within artistic realms, worldmaking is both method and affordance. The aesthetic strategies chronicled by the authors in these chapters illuminate how creative processes model ways of engaging relational, right-brain, embodied, participatory knowledge systems. At the same time, such processes make possible the realization of community-led worlds, where a diverse set of contributions come to constitute novel, beautifully co-created outcomes.

Democracies, like community-engaged creative practices, are intended as an act of collaborative co-creation (i.e., worldmaking). They invite the agency and diverse contributions of many, sometimes divergent perspectives and actions to contribute to the emergent whole. To do this, leaders, like many artists do through their practices of co-creation, must facilitate processes capable of creating trust, building productive ensembles, welcoming diverse perspectives, and devising forms of collective dramaturgy (ways of making fair decisions together).

When we practice with others in ensemble, we are building relational capabilities needed to create well *together*. Co-founder of the Center for Performance and Civic Practice, Michael Rohd, describes "ensemble" as: "Specific. Alive in context. Multitudinous. Present and Ready" (Rohd, n.d.). He says that ensemble-building begins with community building, that is, making space for relationships, listening, and asking difficult questions, thereby forming a commitment to care, justice, and healing (Rohd, n.d.). It is a commitment to the ensemble-building process that makes civic imagination and co-creation *possible*.

Co-creating in ensemble is a practice of relationality that we can rehearse. It moves from individualism toward collectivism, away from the component parts to the interactive properties that give rise to new, emergent possibilities. When we improvise in conditions of plurality, we create a collective field (a world) that is rehearsing ways of working well together across differences. We are prefiguring functioning democracies.

References

Ayed, N. (Host). (2021, October 22). Neuroscientist Iain McGilchrist on the divided brain [Audio podcast episode]. In *Ideas with Nahlah Ayed*. CBC. https://www.cbc.ca/listen/live-radio/1-23-ideas

Blake, A. (2022). *Embodied awareness, embodied practice: A powerful path to practical wisdom.* (Order No. 30004414). [Doctoral dissertation, Case Western Reserve University]. ProQuest Dissertations & Theses Global.

Connolly, W. E. (2005). *Pluralism*. Duke University Press. https://www.amazon.com/Pluralism-William-Connolly-ebook/dp/B00EHNZ0BA

De Oliveira Andreotti, V. (2021). *Hospicing modernity: Facing humanity's wrongs and implications for social activism*. North Atlantic Books.

Digiovanna, J. (2007). Worldmaking as art form. *The International Journal of the Arts in Society: Annual Review,* 2(1), 115–122. https://doi.org/10.18848/1833-1866/CGP/v02i01/35348

Eno, B. (2022). Forward. In J. Alexander (Ed.), *Citizens: Why the key to fixing everything is all of us* (pp. 3–6). https://www.amazon.com/Citizens-Why-Key-Fixing-Everything/dp/B0BM4J34CB

Escobar, A. (2018). *Designs for the pluriverse: Radical interdependence, autonomy, and the making of worlds*. Duke University Press. https://www.amazon.com/Designs-Pluriverse-Interdependence-Ecologies-Twenty-First-ebook/dp/B07BFXGZWM

Jimmy, E., Andreotti, V., & Stein, S. (2019). *Towards braiding*. Musagetes.

Kimmerer, R. W. (2015). *Braiding sweetgrass*. Milkweed Editions.

McCoy, J., & Somer, M. (2019). Toward a theory of pernicious polarization and how it harms democracies: Comparative evidence and possible remedies. *The ANNALS of the American Academy of Political and Social Science, 681*(1), 234–271. https://doi.org/10.1177/0002716218818782

McMillan, T. (2023). Anishinaabe values and servant leadership: A two-eyed seeing approach. *The Journal of Values-Based Leadership, 16*(1), 148–172. *Gale Academic OneFile*. link.gale.com/apps/doc/A733937539/AONE?u=nysl_me_newsch&sid=bookmark-AONE&xid=0fdc1507

Michie, M., Hogue, M., & Rioux, J. (2018). The application of both-ways and two-eyed seeing pedagogy: Reflections on engaging and teaching science to post-secondary Indigenous students. *Research in Science Education, 48*(6), 1205–1220. https://doi.org/10.1007/s11165-018-9775-y

Rohd, M. (n.d.). *Ensemble, learning cohorts, and the promise & pitfalls of technology*. Center for Performance and Civic Practice. https://www.thecpcp.org/field-notes/ensembles

Rowson, J., & McGilchrist, I. (2013, February 1). *Divided brain, divided world: Why the best of us struggles to be heard.* RSA Report. https://www.thersa.org/reports/divided-brain-divided-world

Sarasvathy, S. (2012). Worldmaking. In A. Corbett & J. A. Katz (Eds.), *Entrepreneurial action* (Advances in Entrepreneurship, Firm Emergence and Growth, Vol. 14, pp. 1–24). Emerald Group Publishing Limited. https://doi.org/10.1108/S1074-7540(2012)0000014013

Vervaeke, J. (2020). *Mindful movement as the confluence of perspectival and participatory cognition* [Video]. The Embodiment Conference. https://portal.theembodimentconference.org/sessions/mindful-movement-as-the-confluence-of-perspectival-and-participatory-cognition-4dee0h

5

CO-CREATING DEMOCRACY

Aesthetics in Action

Andrea Assaf

What Democracy Looks Like

Since I began performing in street protests as a young artist – particularly in the anti-globalization (read, *anti-corporate* globalization) protests of the late 1990s – a recurring refrain from protesters, often accompanied by drums or music, has been: This is what democracy looks like! "*This*" refers to the assembly of protesters themselves: diverse, pluralist, activated, sometimes messy and contradictory, vocal, embodied, defiant, and driven by "the people," the *community* of participants (or multiple communities, as it has often been in the era of decentralization; more on that in this chapter).

My early years in street theater protesting the global march of capitalism left an indelible mark on my consciousness, creative practice, and aesthetics. I protested with the Radical Rockettes and later apprenticed at Liz Lerman Dance Exchange, joined Alternate ROOTS, and became a program associate in the early years of Animating Democracy, a program of Americans for the Arts, initially funded by the Ford Foundation. Through these experiences, I developed my aesthetics as an artistic director. These influences all began to amalgamate into my own ethos, values system, and practices of arts-based activism, cultural organizing, and democratization of artistic process.

The power and responsibility of a theater or performing artist, or a producer of performance, is precisely that we have access to a microphone. Amplification is power. Choosing who and what we amplify is a *response-ability* (Goldbard, as cited in Cohen-Cruz, 2010). *As artists, performers, and cultural producers, we have the power to democratize public discourse by shifting who has voice in the public sphere.*

In this chapter, I reflect on different practices I employ to amplify community voices, and various ways of understanding democracy in creative practice.

DOI: 10.4324/9781003475996-10

Community co-creation offers a structure of democratic inclusion and builds relationships in the service of progressive social change. By telling their own stories on stage and online, and by participating in civic dialogue, community participants increase their voice in the public sphere, their access to democracy, and their capacity to be agents of change.

Centering

The problem of democracy is that majority rule often results in the suppression of the minority. When a vote is taken, and the majority wins, what happens to the minority? The so-called minority might be based on an opinion, belief, or even identity. In a society plagued by systemic racism, classism, sexism, and heterosexism – even white supremacy and Christian supremacy – systems of oppression both shape majority rule and enforce it. The history of colonialism on the land now called the United States of America created a white, or European-descended, majority through the active and intentional genocide of this land's First Peoples. The Doctrine of Discovery, a series of 15th-century decrees by the Catholic Pope, granted moral license to European colonizers by declaring that lands could be considered empty if the inhabitants were not Christian, because non-Christians were not considered human according to the Church. The institution of slavery in the United States specifically ensured that even in places where Euro-Americans were the demographic minority, they held minority-rule power by stripping African Americans of citizenship in the new nation, even of personhood. And they called it "democracy."

I am a student of Ngugi wa Thiong'o, Kenyan playwright, novelist, and theorist, who was detained and exiled from Kenya for his community-based, anti-imperialist theater work. I went to NYU Performance Studies in 1999–2000 because he was there. His work and writings that influenced me include *Decolonizing the Mind*; *Penpoints, Gunpoints, and Dreams*; and *Moving the Centre: The Struggle for Cultural Freedoms*. The latter argues that in all our education, in every land the British colonized (as well as other European powers, but particularly the British in the case of Kenya and the United States), British and European history, philosophy, worldview, and aesthetics were treated as the center and summit of human events, knowledge, and expression. In the United States, the actions, writings, and art of Euro-American men (predominantly) were selectively added to the concept of "greatness," and therefore were also centered in public education. We all internalized this from childhood. As a result, the majority, regardless of race or identity, perpetuates systems of supremacy when reaching positions of access or power. *Moving the Centre* suggests that the process of decolonizing is not only a matter of changing laws and policies, but of shifting who is *centered* in the public sphere, and in our own consciousness – whose communities and voices matter in decision-making, who we see on stage and on screen, whose writings we read and study, whose aesthetics and modes of expression we value. It's a matter of understanding and achieving cultural freedom, as well as political liberation. For artists and producers of culture, a step toward this is moving the center: shifting away from Eurocentrism, to center the values and aesthetic expressions of those who have been colonized, oppressed, or excluded from the public sphere for centuries.

As a queer, third-generation, Arab American artist working in contemporary performance, my work exists on the fringes of culture in my own country, the United States. I live in the margins, and I am committed to the marginalized. In my own work, since 9/11 and the wars that followed in Iraq and Afghanistan, I have endeavored to center Southwest and Central Asian, North, and East African artists and communities – those who have been most targeted by the so-called Global War on Terror, and by the Islamophobic and anti-Arab backlash of the first two decades of the 21st century. Using practices detailed in the "Methodologies" section later in this chapter, I have engaged communities and artists around the country in story-sharing and theater co-creation, in order to shift whose voice is centered in our commemoration and collective understanding of the post-9/11 era.

In 2019, I launched a socially engaged series of new performance works titled *Eleven Reflections on the Nation*, exploring Southwest/Central Asian and North African (SWANA) and Muslim American experiences in the 21st century, with communities across the United States. In its first iteration, in San Antonio, collaborating participants and contributors ranged from nationally acclaimed Palestinian American poet Naomi Shihab Nye and San Antonio's Poet Laureate (2020–2023) Andrea "Vocab" Sanderson; to Gulf War veteran turned professional Flamenco dancer, Tamara Adira, and Mexican American theater-maker and activist Anna De Luna; to an Iraqi musician and songwriter who had a ten-year professional career in Turkey before moving to Texas, where he hadn't been on stage since, Sarmad Mahmood; to Moroccan American emerging theater artist Kauthar Harrak-Sharif and her brother Ahmed; and other community members who had never performed in a theater before, such as Egyptian community organizer Lilly Guindy (who spent three years as a volunteer medic in Tahrir Square during the revolution), Afghani American medical student and poet Najwa Faiz, and more. After, Guindy (2021) expressed what the process achieved:

> This experience is going to change the way I see myself for the rest of my life . . . This is opening the door for a minority group like the Arab Americans of San Antonio. And for those from the community who are not Arab Americans, hearing all these stories is creating a kind of empathy towards peoples' journey in life . . . Because it's so artistic, it's very far from what we hear on the news . . . That's something that San Antonio can move forward from – with more art, more storytelling, and more healing.

Every performance in the series is followed by a public dialogue, with participants, artists, and audience – putting SWANA communities at the center of an art-based civic dialogue on US policy. When centering voices and perspectives that

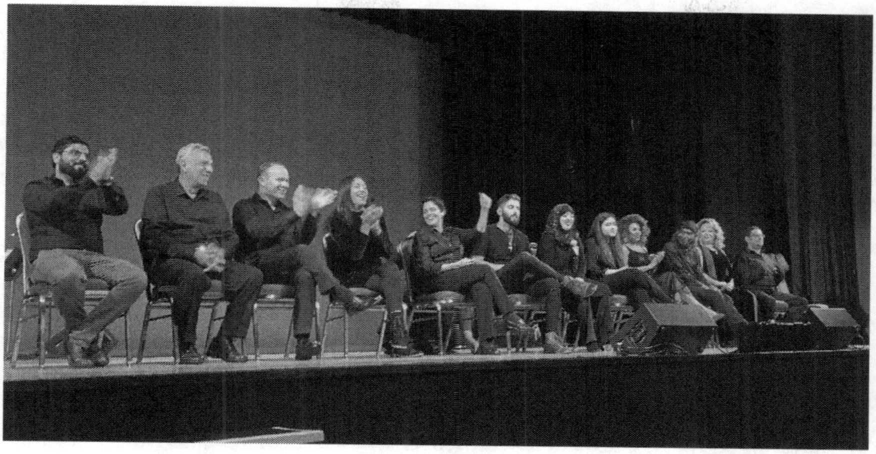

FIGURE 5.1 *Eleven Reflections*: San Antonio cast members in a post-performance dialogue, on the Jo Long stage, at The Carver Community Cultural Center. From left to right: Sarmad Mahmood, Housam Harriri, Ethan Wickman, Anna De Luna, Andrea Assaf, Ahmed Harrak-Sharif, Kauthar Harrak-Sharif, Najwa Faiz, Lilly Guindy, Orlan "T-Bow" Gonzales, Lubana Al Quntar, Akram Shehata. Photo by Gabi Vigueira, San Antonio, 2021.

are usually marginalized, both in the arts field as well as in our democracy at large, aesthetic sophistication and local relevance work together to create the conditions for transformational dialogue – dismantling stereotypes, developing empathy, and building new solidarities.

Decentering

The problem of "centering" is that it still creates margins. Who is pushed to the margins may look different – or not. When groups of historically marginalized people try to work together, vying for center (out of a deep need to finally be seen and heard), it can create divisions – despite the intention of coming together to build solidarity and collective power. We see this in the history of movements: the Civil Rights Movement re-inscribing patriarchy and drawing critique from the Feminist Movement, while the Feminist Movement struggled with internalized racism, and both movements excluded queer and especially trans-identified folks. Centering one area of oppression to combat, at the expense of other forms of liberation, seeds division. Even if there is agreement on decentering white/European, cisgender, land-owning, or upper-class men from their centuries of power and domination, who gets the center when they are removed from it? How do we avoid falling into the painful pit of "Oppression Olympics," arguing over whose identity group is more historically oppressed and therefore most deserving of the center?

For example, in 2022, I was invited to be part of forming a professional network of queer-identified artists and presenters. In the early stages of identifying shared values, a familiar tension arose. A young person proposed "centering" Black Trans Women, from the honest belief that they are the most targeted, at-risk, or disempowered identity group in our complex, intentionally diverse set of intersecting communities, and therefore should be centered in our process as a liberatory practice. But then, a middle-aged lesbian of color spoke up, expressing that all through the Gay Rights Movement, lesbians have been historically marginalized, despite generations of radical leadership; she expressed that she was uncomfortable with centering Black Trans Women, if that would again relegate cisgender woman-identified lesbians to the margins. Though the group attempted to hold both statements in their values list, it became apparent over the course of several meetings that the tension was not resolved and was causing a fissure in the group. When it came up again, the lesbian-identified co-leader further named the question at the root of her discomfort: What was the group's commitment to Feminism? The absence of Feminism as a shared value and commitment was concerning. Through further, sometimes contentious dialogue, the group surfaced another question: What did we actually mean by "centering"? Did we all have the same understanding of what it means to center an identity group? Is it possible to center one group without marginalizing another? And if we do that, are we ethically okay with who is left in the margins? Is there a way to share the center together? Or, *what if there is no center at all?*

This is where the concept of decentralization, as a practice of direct democracy and pluralism, becomes useful. Early 21st-century movements have sometimes been criticized for not having strong (read, *centralized*) leadership. But as Yale professor David Graeber (2002) wrote, "This is what the direct action movement is ultimately about: reinventing democracy. Far from lacking an ideology, those new forms of radically decentralized direct democracy *are* its ideology" (n.p., emphasis from original).

Effective decentralization is extremely difficult to achieve. For historically privileged "leaders," it is very difficult to honestly let go of power, and genuinely move out of the center, without manipulating it from the perimeter. For those of us with historically marginalized identities, the desire to be centered often comes from a deep well of personal and historical trauma; when our traumas are activated, we don't always lead with our best selves. Effective decentralization requires a rooted analysis and conscious practice of equity – an embodied practice. And in order to embody it, we must actively work to heal our traumas. We must rehearse what a new way of being might look like – what *democracy* might actually feel like. As the globally influential creator of *Theatre of the Oppressed* (and Brazilian elected official), Augusto Boal, posited: theater is a rehearsal for life.

At the National Institute for Directing and Ensemble Creation,[1] Black, Indigenous, and diverse artists of color, women, and LGBTQ2S+ artists from across the United States and internationally gather in an intensive peer-exchange to develop curriculum, cross-train, articulate culturally specific aesthetics, and develop shared

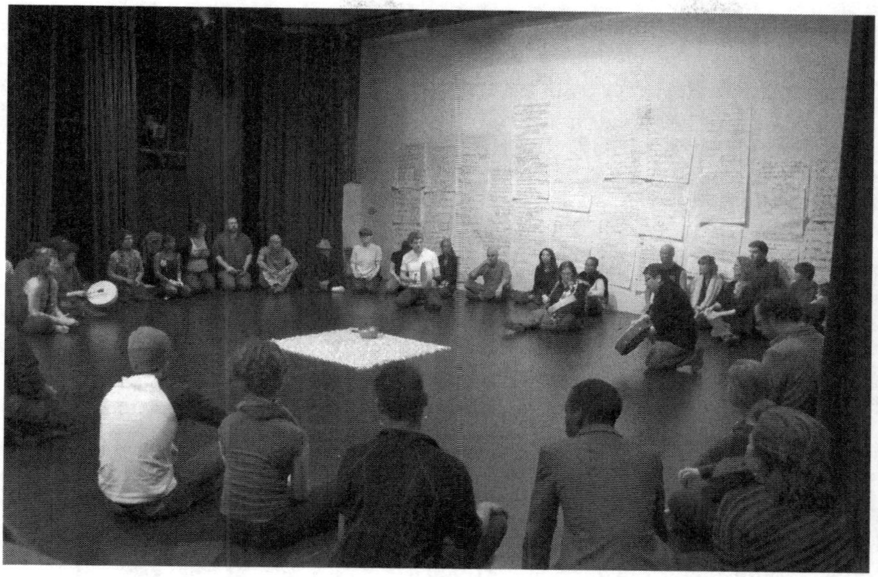

FIGURE 5.2 Participants in the National Institute for Directing & Ensemble Creation pilot, co-organized by Art2Action and Pangea World Theater. The group sits in a circle at Intermedia Arts, while Native American artists offer a song, with Sharon Day, (Ojibwe) Executive Director of Indigenous Peoples Task Force, leading in the center. Photo by Luminous Concepts, 2012.

practices. Tensions often arise in convenings this diverse – around indigeneity and understanding cultural protocols, around gender and appropriate use of pronouns (when some languages don't have gendered pronouns at all), and from not understanding each other's specific histories of oppression and resistance. We address these challenges by establishing community agreements with every new group; by integrating intentional trainings in anti-racism and indigeneity into the exchange-based curriculum; by carefully utilizing diverse co-facilitation when conflicts do arise; and by engaging elders in our field as witnesses to our work, who can reflect back on what they see emerging as the group dynamic evolves.

Margo Kane, an extraordinary Indigenous (Cree-Saulteaux) performing artist, Founder and Artistic Managing Director of Full Circle: First Nations Performance based in Vancouver, Canada, has been a valued participant in the Institute since 2012. In the first pilot Institute, she generously shared this wisdom, which has become a guiding principle:

> There's a teaching that's come to me that talks about the Sacred Tree that stands at the center of the Medicine Wheel. . . . What our intention is – what we've just discussed – is what that metaphor is for me: every point on that circle, every person, has a perspective that's different from the next one. We see the Sacred Tree

> at the center of the circle differently, because we're sitting in a different position around [it]. You can't describe that tree in the middle without having every perspective. So, every point is valid, every perspective is needed, to describe the Sacred Tree that stands at the center of the Medicine Wheel.
>
> *(Kane, 2012)*

For me, this image gets at the heart of what decentralized leadership is. What stands in the center is not an identity, it's a vision. When the group forms a circle around a shared vision – even if there are different perspectives, and understandings of the vision vary – the collective energy is focused on something greater than any one identity. Then the circle becomes a Medicine Wheel, a source of healing. And the tree grows – the seed, the vision, comes to fruition.

I learned this, also, from the great John O'Neal, playwright, theater-maker and civil rights activist, co-founder of the Free Southern Theatre and later Junebug Productions. In 2003, a group of cultural workers and creative instigators met in New York City to plan for a grassroots convening in New Orleans that we were co-organizing, called the National Convergence of Artists, Educators, and Organizers. Caron Atlas, founder of the Art & Democracy Project, suggested we meet at my very tiny studio apartment because it was centrally located. And there I was, a young activist and emerging artist, literally sitting at the feet of John O'Neal (because I didn't have enough chairs). I remember distinctly John sharing this lesson: people don't build community by talking about it, they build community by doing something together – by committing to a shared vision, creating it, and experiencing a sense of accomplishment together. This is precisely what theater does, and what organizing around an issue or action does: we create lasting bonds when we work together toward a shared goal. It's not the outcome – whether the show or action is successful or not, whether we celebrate or grieve at the end – it's the *practice of community co-creation* that enacts lasting change. We hope the show will be applauded, we hope the policy will pass, but whether or not the group experiences setbacks, the quality of community and civic engagement shifts forever through the process of collaboration. It is the leader's job, as facilitator and co-creator, to design the conditions and process for the collaboration experience to be successful. That shared experience of doing and building then becomes the ground on which all future actions are built, in which all future possibilities are planted. Our job as leaders is to nurture fertile ground, and to build strong foundations.

Democracy as Creative Process

> Even though we seldom see it in practice, the possibility of real democracy lingers in collective memory and imagination. Like a muscle that has atrophied from disuse, it can be restored through exercise, even on the smallest scale.
>
> (Goldbard, 2004)

After 9/11, I lost my faith in democracy. In 2001, an African American woman, Representative Barbara Lee, was the *only* member of Congress to vote against war in the immediate aftermath, pleading on the House floor, "Let us not become the evil that we deplore." I was certain that if the US population had been allowed to vote, the majority would have chosen to wage war, not only on Afghanistan and Iraq, but on all Arab and Muslim people. This was also several years before marriage equality for LGBTQ2S+ people became legal in the United States, and I was convinced that if the electorate had been offered a vote on the subject, I would have been stripped of all rights as a queer person. I remember having this conversation with Tufara Waller Muhammad (multidisciplinary artist, political strategist, popular educator, and cultural organizer who was working at the Highlander Center at the time), during a training she was facilitating. I shared my feeling with Tufara, who is African American and Muslim, that if majority rule is the primary tenet of democracy, then I would surely lose, and would forever face oppression as a young, queer, Arab American. But Tufara's answer surprised me. She said to me, "That's because people don't really understand democracy."

What I learned from Tufara is that democracy is not a result, it's a process. It's not the outcome of a vote, but the popular education, dialogic process, and public discourse that leads to the vote – or collective decision, which might actually be better served by consensus-building rather than voting. *Democracy is a way of being in community, a way of organizing and leading collectively. It's a way of centering and decentering at the same time*. Both are necessary to create progressive change, to create a more just society and global geo-politic. To do this, it is critical to move away from Eurocentrism, white/male/Christian/hetero supremacy, to listen to and support the leadership of those who have been most oppressed historically. And here is the challenge, especially for those of us who have been most marginalized: while we do so, we must also collectively, in solidarity with each other, *hold something greater than ourselves in the center* – a shared vision of justice, peace, equity, liberation – and a commitment to making that vision a lived reality for all.

One of my many mentors, choreographer Celeste Miller, says, "Art may not change the world. But it can change how we live in the world." Through our artistic practices, artists can change how people experience belonging, voice, democratic process, and collective action. In the process of co-creating theater with communities, it is possible to generate experiences of self-actualization, empowerment, and democracy in action. We can rehearse that experience, until it becomes a way of life – a way of being in the world.

Methodologies: Ways of Rehearsing Democracy

I use a number of interdisciplinary methodologies in my community-based work. A core practice in my co-creation work is Story Circles, as taught to me by John O'Neal, and those he worked with and influenced, including Linda Parris-Bailey (former Executive Artistic Director of The Carpetbag Theatre, playwright and founder of Parris-Bailey Arts), cultural organizer and song leader Wendi O'Neal, and members of Alternate ROOTS. Story Circles is a very simple but deeply impactful methodology that draws from Black and Indigenous traditions of storytelling, lightly codified by a set of guidelines and agreements introduced by the facilitator. This practice establishes the democratic structure, and importance, of the circle: every voice is equal in a circle. Everyone gets equal time to speak. It is timed, generally three minutes per person, although length is variable as the context demands. Everyone who speaks is asked to tell a story – a true, lived, personal experience. Some facilitators introduce a theme or prompt for the stories, based on the goals of the organizing or creative project; some facilitators use the Story Circle to discover themes or issues that are most resonant and relevant to the group.

Linda Parris-Bailey is a master of story prompts. The art of the prompt is key to determining the direction and depth of the storytelling. Linda crafts prompts that offer participants options in how deep they want to go, but also suggests an empowering or liberatory direction. For example, instead of asking a group to tell a story about a traumatic event in their lives,[2] she might ask them to tell a story about a time they survived or triumphed, and who or what gave them the strength to do so. By prompting a story about *overcoming* adversity, she opens the possibility and gives participants agency in the choice of exploring adversity, without demanding a focus on it; instead, the focus of the story becomes resilience, articulating one's own path to survival or success. After everyone in the circle has shared a story, the facilitator may guide the process into dialogue and creative generation – in the form of theater scenes, creative writing, movement, song creation, digital storytelling, or in whichever discipline the group is working.

Another democratizing creative structure I often use, both in standalone workshops and in devising a full production, is Collective Poetry. Many poets and Spoken Word artists use a variety of methods to create group poems, but I learned this practice first from poet and cultural organizer Alice Lovelace – former Executive Director of Alternate ROOTS, National Lead Organizer of the US Social Forum,[3] publisher of *In Motion* magazine, and much more. First, I prompt participants to write individual poems, which may evolve from Story Circles or other prompts. I invite everyone to share, either their whole poem, or a few lines or a phrase, in small groups or with the full group (depending on time, and the size of the group). I encourage listeners to share back what they heard that resonates with them personally, influenced by the first step of Liz Lerman's Critical Response Process (Lerman & Borstel, 2008), or perhaps what resonates with the themes or issues the group has been exploring. Then I ask permission to edit their poems together. Asking permission is very important: contributing to the collective process must always be an invitation, a consensual process. Every participant has the right to keep their work to themselves, if they prefer, and confidentiality must always be respected. Those who would like to contribute to a collective work turn in their writings, and the next time I see the group, I return with an edited piece that weaves all voices together, and perform it for them, or direct the group in creating an ensemble performance of the poem. From many individual poems, many disparate stories, emerges one Collective Poem – with all its contradictions, interconnections, and shared visions. If there are singers or musicians in the group, some of the poetry may also be turned into songs, or set to music.

Embodiment is very important to me as a performing artist – as important as storytelling, writing, or poetry. For without the body, neither the whole truth nor the whole self is expressed. Healing cannot take place without engaging the body. Muscles and cells store memory, and trauma, that must be released. Countless examples of this are detailed eloquently and powerfully in the book *The Body Keeps the Score: Brain, Mind, and Body in the Healing of Trauma* by Bessel Van der Kolk (2014). Movement-based theater and dance methodologies are key to releasing blocked energy, giving participants nonverbal ways to express themselves (especially when they're not ready to speak or write the most difficult stories), and in building ensemble connection. Leading-following exercises, for example, can develop in the group the experiential knowledge that in a vibrant, thriving, creative democratic community, everyone is a leader, and everyone must sometimes follow for the benefit of the whole; there are times to lead, and times to allow oneself to be led. There are times to speak, and times to listen. Everyone has equal right to speak and lead, and no one must dominate to the detriment of the group dynamic. Everyone's voice is equally important and valuable – and when it's time to act, everyone must take action together.

These are just a few of the methodologies I use to democratize the creative process, and to shift from the "I" of material generation (personal stories, individual writings, movement phrases, etc.), to the "we" of ensemble performance or of community building. In the course of one project, I may use all of these practices and more; or I may decide to focus on a specific practice, based on the ability and interest of the group, and go as deep as possible in that direction. Let me be clear that a democratic, participatory process does not mean that there's no leadership. Just that leading may sometimes mean following, guiding, getting out of the way, or listening more deeply, or asking the group's permission to make the final decision. If the leader has honored the group and the process up to that point, the ensemble will almost always say yes. Trust must be built and earned; and when it is, as in every great movement for democracy, the leader emerges from the will of the people, is endowed and entrusted with the responsibility of leadership, and does so in service to the collective.

Aesthetics: Directing and Democracy in Co-Creation

As directors, or producers of culture, we find something else that happens after all that democratic, creative process: staging an event that an audience attends. This is where aesthetics become important, in the moment of amplification. As a director, I understand that if the community co-created work is not embodied, staged, and

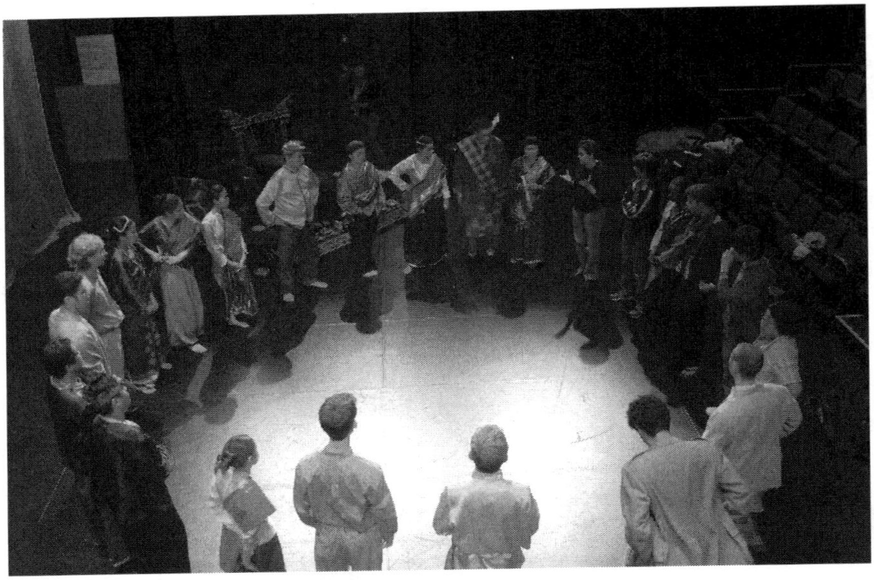

FIGURE 5.3 Andrea Assaf directing Kinding Sindaw in *Parang Sabil: The Ballad of the Kris* at Amherst College, in New WORLD Theater's Summer Play Lab. Photo by Ed Cohen, 2007.

performed with a commitment to aesthetic excellence, the audience might receive a vision of democracy that is disorganized, disheveled, at best uninspiring, or at worst intolerable. As Toni Cade Bombara (1983) writes, "the role of the artist is to make the revolution irresistible." That requires revolutionary aesthetics. If my commitment to the aesthetics of community-based work is not as rigorous or visionary as it is for my professional work, I will inadvertently undermine the intention of the work itself – which is to uplift the value and importance of community voices in the public sphere, and in democracy.

What bears examining, then, is *which* aesthetic values become important in socially engaged, community co-created, or "arts for change" work.[4] *Whose* cultural or aesthetic values are centered or included? How can everyone's strengths be amplified? A values-based practice I learned from Urban Bush Women's Summer Leadership Institute (SLI) is how to apply the community organizer's practice of asset mapping to the creative process. Just as organizers may use asset mapping as a methodology for understanding and building from the strengths of a community, directors or facilitators can use creative/cultural asset mapping as a starting point for a devising process. Sometimes participants do not identify themselves as artists, when in fact they may have a deep well of creative practice to draw from. For example, if a community member has been performing for decades – perhaps as B-Boy or street performer, or a drag performer in queer clubs, or a choral singer in their place of worship, or at pow wows or Indigenous ceremonies – then they may indeed have exceptional technique or embodied knowledge of a creative or cultural form, whether or not they embrace the term "artist." The director or facilitator should recognize and value that expertise, which may become a primary vocabulary to work from, for an individual performer or for the group. When working with Black, Indigenous, or people of color communities, this is a practice of both decentering Euro-American definitions of "professionalism" (which are often tied to capitalism, or money-generation), while recentering Indigenous, traditional, or syncretic forms of cultural knowledge and expertise. Or subcultural, which is equally important: queer culture is a global subculture, for example, that has its own aesthetic systems. Also, military veterans are a very specific (and legally protected) subculture in the United States; they may not be familiar with theater culture or certain dance forms, but they have a tremendously rigorous training in a physical vocabulary, as well as a deep respect for discipline and teamwork, which can provide a strong structure from which to build a collective creative work. The artistic direction, then, becomes a process of identifying where excellence lies, valuing the inherent forms of excellence in the group, and then creating from those values and vocabularies – while also developing new skills, to discover the unique aesthetic specific to that group or project. As adrienne marie brown, author of *Emergent Strategy* (2017), asks: what is the conversation that only this group can have? Or in artistic terms, what is the aesthetic that only this specific group of people, this ensemble, can embody and create?

If the job of the performer is to tell their story well, whether in a verbal or embodied form (or both), then the director's job is to frame the story beautifully and powerfully. What is the visual or sonic world this story is immersed in, or emerges from? How can the final choices of the director elevate the work as a whole? I have been very influenced by Dora Arreola,[5] Artistic Director of Mujeres en Ritual Danza-Teatro, based in Mexico, in the notion of "elevating" a performance through aesthetic choices – an understanding she developed from working with Jerzy Grotowski. Rather than an answer, it's a question that a director must always ask. The director's job, ultimately, is to create the world that the performers live in. The aesthetics of that world impact how the stories are witnessed, heard, and received by the public. In a devised work, the director decides – ideally in collaboration with the co-creating ensemble of artists and community members – what kind of world it will be. Will this world model democracy, by example, or warn us of an antidemocratic dystopia? Will it uncover an ugly truth, and if so, will it offer hope for the future? Will it, ultimately, provide a vision of another world that's possible – a world that the community and artists want to co-create?

From the moment of forming a circle around a shared vision, to building and enacting that vision on a stage or public platform, artists have the opportunity to create a microcosm in which to rehearse the world we want to live in – the opportunity to create a "show" that embodies and communicates: *This* is what democracy looks like.

Notes

1 A joint program of Art2Action and Pangea World Theater, the National Institute for Directing & Ensemble Creation was launched in 2012 and has convened over ten intensive exchanges to date, from 4 to 14 days long, in Minnesota; the program is ongoing, and a book titled *The Fire in the Center: Directors on Directing & Ensemble Creation* is forthcoming from Routledge.

2 In the 2016–2018 pilot study on Art2Action's Veteran Arts Program, the VA research team recommended strongly that prompts should never directly ask participants to share a trauma; further, when working with a community that is known to have high levels of post-traumatic stress – such as veterans, refugees, and survivors of torture or sexual violence – the VA strongly recommends having a therapist, social worker, or trained peer leader present or available to support any participants who may need assistance beyond what the artistic process can provide.

3 The US Social Forum is a series of gatherings in the United States, which grew out of the World Social Forum process, bringing together activists, organizers, working people, and more, toward an intersectional movement for social justice. Alice Lovelace was the National Lead Organizer 2006–10.

4 The "Aesthetic Perspectives" framework developed by Animating Democracy is a tool for examining this for yourself, and how you might apply it to your own work, or work to be evaluated, through a series of guiding questions (https://animatingdemocracy.org/aesthetic-perspectives).

5 Dora Arreola is the founding Artistic Director of Mujeres en Ritual Danza-Teatro, based in Tijuana, Mexico, since 1999. Her background includes training with Jerzy Grotowski, in the Objective Drama and Theatre as a Vehicle phases, 1987–1989, at the Workcenter in Pontedera, Italy. An accomplished international director, she has taught at the University of South Florida (USF) School of Theatre and Dance since 2010.

References

Bombara, T. C. (1983). *This bridge called my back: Writings by radical women of color*. Kitchen Table: Women of Color Press.

Brown, A. M. (2017). *Emergent strategy*. AK Press.

Cohen-Cruz, J. (2010). *Engaging performance: Theatre as call and response*. Routledge.

Goldbard, A. (2004). *Don't do it!* Organizational Suicide for Progressives, archived in Community Arts Network (CAN) Reading Room. http://wayback.archive-it.org/2077/20100906203614/http://www.communityarts.net/readingroom/archivefiles/2004/09/donot_do_it_org.php

Graeber, D. (2002, February 19). Reinventing democracy. For the online publication *In These Times*.

Guindy, L. (2021). *Virtual dialogue presented by Art2Action and The Carver Community Cultural Center*. https://www.art2action.org/reflection-sessions

Kane, M. (2012, December). *From the documentary, "National Institute for Directing & Ensemble Creation – Pilot 2012" from the first full convening (co-organized by Art-2Action and Pangea World Theater)*; filmed at Intermedia Arts in Minneapolis, MN, by Sammy Sarzoza, Stemless Media. https://www.art2action.org/directing-institute

Lerman, L., & Borstel, J. (2008, Winter/Spring). Liz Lerman's critical response process: The core steps and an interview with Liz Lerman. *Contact Quarterly*, 16–20.

Van der Kolk, B. A. (2014). *The body keeps the score: Brain, mind, and body in the healing of trauma*. Penguin Books.

6

BRAIDING COMEDY IN PRECARIOUS TIMES

The Possibilities and Pitfalls of Research Creation in the Settler Colonial University

Heather McLean

I am a cisgendered queer white woman of Scottish, English, and Irish ancestry writing this chapter from Tk'emlúps te Secwépemc, a city colonially named Kamloops, British Columbia. As a feminist urban studies researcher, teacher, and comedic performer, I engage in arts-based and praxis-oriented research to analyze mutual aid, gentrification, and climate crises.

In this chapter I reflect on the possibilities of comedic arts-based research for fostering the principles and practices of a more inclusive democracy. After providing a brief overview of the strengths and limitations of creative research methods, I tell a story about how my alter-ego character Toby Sharp, a self-appointed world leader in creativity and innovation, ended up in a satirical professional development webinar performance titled *A Buzz in Your Hub* with two Indigenous alter ego characters: Donnie Dreamcatcher, performed by Secwepemc and Nlaka'pamux artist and musician Chris Bose (Bose, 2020); and Skus Akwesin, performed by Mi'kmaq artist and musician Nakuset Gould. I describe how this project provided pathways for sharing stories about the contradictions of working for arts institutions and universities that receive funding from resource industries and real estate stakeholders accelerating the displacement and trauma of the communities we work with. Referring to *Towards Braiding* (2019) by Cree curator Elwood Jimmy, education scholar of Brazilian descent Vanessa Andreotti, and white settler education scholar Sharon Stein, I also reflect on the struggles and successes of this Indigenous and settler arts-based collaboration for responding to and addressing housing and climate crises in Kamloops.

Arts-Based Research in the Settler Colonial Neoliberal University

Increasingly, geographers and urban studies researchers are fostering more inclusive democratic values within universities and the communities they are connected

DOI: 10.4324/9781003475996-11

with by practicing arts-based research. By co-creating walking tours, graphic novels, and plays, researchers are investigating the impacts of climate crises, gentrification, the policing of urban space, more-than-human relations, and more (Vasudevan & Kearney, 2015; McLean, 2016; Johnston & Pratt, 2019). Such relational and collaborative methods can disrupt dominant pedagogical and research practices that separate researchers and researched communities, and theory from practice (Nagar, 2014). With poetic and aesthetic practices, researchers are also mobilizing communities in the co-creation of alternatives to oppressive systems and structures and fostering solidarities across differences. As Audre Lorde wrote,

> poetry is not a luxury. It is a vital necessity of our existence. It forms the quality of the light within which we predicate our hopes and dreams toward survival and change, first made into language, then into idea, then into more tangible action.
>
> *(Lorde, 1977, p. 3)*

Feminist and queer performance theorists and artists also add depth and vitality to our understanding of the possibilities of arts-based methods for practicing democracy across diverse communities. Theorist and performance artist T. L. Cowan (2017) writes of cabaret as a method for starting where you are, working with what is available to you, and "hacking the worlds we want to live and see." In a similar vein, La Pocha Nostra values performance as an anticolonial method and methodology of world building to respond to the absurd violence of capitalism and colonialism (La Pocha Nostra, 2020). With dance, ritual, and improvisational performance, La Pocha offers strategies for creating from the glitches and breakdowns of everyday life within capitalism and practicing radical tenderness.

At the same time, feminist, Indigenous, Black, and people of color, critical disability, and 2SLGBTQI+ scholars have raised critical and reflexive questions about the tensions and contradictions of creative methods within neoliberal and colonialist universities and institutions. Political theorist Wendy Brown describes neoliberalism as a "peculiar form of reason that configures all aspects of existence in economic terms" (Brown, 2015, p. 17). Brown traces how neoliberal practices have undermined public educational and artistic institutions over the past few decades. As universities bear the brunt of public funding cuts, administrators have favored research and arts practices that align with "best practices" mirroring corporate values. Critical researchers working within this context experience cognitive dissonance as universities celebrate community-engaged research and creative practices but also promote knowledge, thought, and training that contributes to capital enhancement (Brown, 2015).

As white cisgendered researchers like me engage in arts-based practices, we find ourselves complicit in all kinds of contradictions. As we engage communities, we can accrue institutional and social currency as benevolent at the expense of racialized underrepresented and precarious artists, activists and community workers, as well as disproportionately racialized and gendered adjunct faculty collaborators. Critics also challenge researchers to consider the imbalances reproduced within the competitive neoliberal university when researchers render collectively produced work into sole-authored articles or chapters (McLean & de Leeuw, 2020).

In *Towards Braiding*, Jimmy et al. (2019) add greater nuance to our understanding of the role of arts-based research for building practices of democracy within neoliberal and settler colonialist environments. Specifically, this book offers strategies for "braiding" arts practice across Indigenous and non-Indigenous settler communities. By braiding, they mean developing and practicing strategies to unsettle colonial research and art practices with "relational ethics, reciprocity, (self) compassion, care, humility, honesty, humor, and hyper reflexivity" (Jimmy et al., 2019). They also discuss how, for non-Indigenous white settlers, there is no escaping our complicity in settler colonial structures designed to benefit us. Therefore, braiding work will always be flawed and will risk reproducing uneven power dynamics. At the same time, because both Indigenous and settler communities are bound together as we face unprecedented climate challenges, we have no choice but to start where we are, fail forward, keep learning from failures, and strive towards creating wiser democratic practices together.

A Buzz in Your Hub: Origin Story

Before I reflect on our attempts to braid comedy in Kamloops, I provide the origin story of *A Buzz in Your Hub*. My alter ego Toby Sharp emerged from my doctoral research on the impacts of neoliberal policies on the arts and urban planning in Toronto. Before I embarked on my PhD, I had worked as an affordable housing planner in Toronto for five years. Around this time, Creative City policies were taking off, and there were endless consultancy and think tank-led workshops on how to make cities more creative, innovative, and competitive (McLean, 2016). As private sector consultants and creativity experts led these workshops, they often overlooked the creative residents and organizations whose aesthetic practices did not fit within this neoliberal policy script that was accelerating gentrification across the city.

At that time, I was also engaged in a range of DIY and feminist arts projects in Toronto, including improv comedy, clown, cabarets, and performance art collectives. As intersectional feminist artists, we grappled with our complicities within colonial and neoliberal policy regimes. On one hand, think tanks, arts funders, developers, and planners valued our practices for cultivating neighborhood-scale cultural capital and attracting investors. At the same time, echoing Winifred Curran's (2018) writing on gender and gentrification, the queer and feminist collective spaces I worked with were also co-creating collective and politicized alternatives to neoliberal approaches to the arts. During this time, I was deeply inspired by queer feminist performance theorist and activist Alex Tigchelaar's work with *Dirty Plotz*, a cabaret collective that explored the historic and ongoing missing women, 2Spirit, trans and nonbinary people in the arts (Buddies in Bad Times, 2013). With the enthusiastic care and support of Alex and the feminist artists working with Dirty Plotz, I gave birth to "Toby Sharp: the Tool for Urban Change," to perform in this cabaret.

When my post-doctoral position in Glasgow ended and I found myself back on the precarious academic job market, I moved back to unceded Tk'emlúps te Secwépemc, a city colonially named Kamloops, where I grew up. Kamloops is a small interior British Columbia city with a population of around 100,000. Like all urban centers across Turtle Island, Kamloops is the site of historic and ongoing colonial violence. Mining, logging, ranching, and a large industrial train yard historically supported the regional economy. In 2021, Tk'emlúps te Secwépemc First Nation uncovered 215 children buried in the grounds surrounding the Kamloops Indian Residential School that was in operation from 1890 to 1969 (Tait, 2022). Across so-called Canada, residential schools were part of church and state genocidal practices to destroy Indigenous lifeworlds and to clear land for privatization and capital accumulation. As a white settler writing these sentences, condensing the story of these horrifying schools into a simplistic context section feels like an act of violence. I recommend Secwepemc poet Garry Gottfriedson's (2023) book *Bent Back Tongue* for greater nuance and more Indigenous perspectives about living with the legacy of residential schools in this territory.

Interconnected with settler colonialism and capitalist expansion, Kamloops is also the site of waves of racialized diasporic workers who faced and continue to face precarious work and unsafe labor conditions (CCPA, 2023). Currently, the city is the site of a strong service industry, university, and a robust local arts scene. Like cities across Turtle Island, the city is also a site of increasing gentrification which is accelerating the houseless population. Over the past few years, people have fled expensive housing costs in the greater Vancouver area four hours away in search of affordable neighborhoods to buy homes as well as develop condominiums, breweries, and restaurants (Landry, 2021).

This growing housing crisis is compounded by an accelerating climate crisis in Kamloops. Situated in a semi-arid desert, the city has been the site of record forest fires, including the summer of 2021 when 81 fires circled the city (Ravindran, 2021). Many of us remember packing up our cars and fleeing at the last minute as enormous flames swept through nearby subdivisions (CFJC Today, 2021). A heat dome enveloped the city in 48 degrees Celsius temperatures, the hottest recorded temperature in the Northern Hemisphere. Then, a few months later, record rainfalls landed on burnt forest floors covered in fire retardant, resulting in massive flooding in nearby towns and villages. As Indigenous poets, scholars, Land Defenders and Water Protectors, including Tuscarora writer Alicia Elliot, write, the climate disasters shaping Kamloops are not new; they signal the ongoing violence of colonial capitalist enclosures, plunder, and violence towards earth that settler regimes have practiced for hundreds of years (Elliott, 2020).

This combination of housing and climate crisis shaped the direction of my research. In 2020, I connected with Chris Bose, a Secwepemc and Nlaka'pamux visual artist, poet, musician, and community worker who has worked with Thompson Rivers University's (TRU's) Fine Arts Department and the Kamloops Art Gallery for years. A vital member of the city's small punk scene in the 1990s, Bose's visceral writing explores his life growing up in a family that survived the brutal residential school system. He also writes of the impact of mining across the territory and his life as an artist and single dad navigating the mountain city's low-density urban sprawl by transit.

Chris introduced me to his alter-ego character Donnie Dreamcatcher. Decked out in an Adidas tracksuit with spray-painted gold dreamcatchers around his neck, Donnie is an Indian leg wrestling coach, energy bar salesman, and property developer excited to build condominiums and strip malls and "pave over everything" (interview with Chris Bose, personal communication, 2022). A keen entrepreneur, Donnie aims to profit from the housing and climate crises into what he describes as a "cris-a-tunity." According to Chris, his surreal alter-ego character is a "Fort Indian" who deals with his trauma by hanging around the fur fort, or the neoliberal economy, hoping to cash in on colonialist systems and structures (interview with Chris Bose, personal communication, 2022).

When the world went into COVID lockdown in 2021, my alter ego Toby joined forces with Donnie Dreamcatcher in an informal performance-led arts research project. Our alter-ego characters wandered Kamloops neighborhoods, including roaming around on the beach that was the site of the Secwépemc Unity Camp where Indigenous Water Protectors fought the drilling of the TMX pipeline to carry Alberta tar sands sludge under Secwépemcetkwe, a river colonially named Thompson River after a Welsh fur trader and cartographer. In defense of the

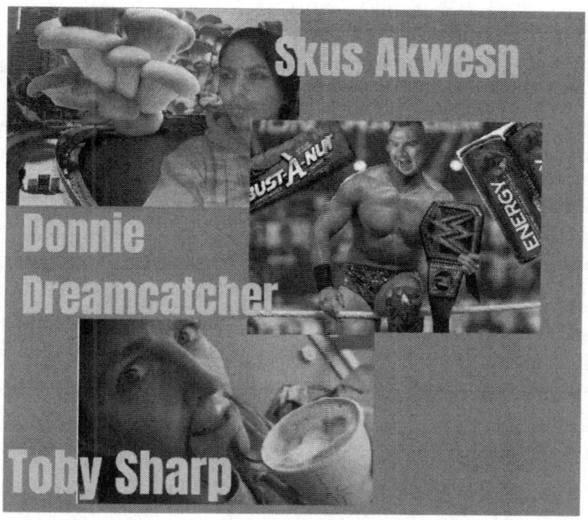

FIGURE 6.1 Three characters from webinar performance A Buzz in Your Hub

Canadian petro-capitalist state, Royal Mounted Police arrested the Water Protectors, some of whom were Kamloops Indian Band residential school survivors (Chandrakate, 2023).

Around this time, an assistant professor friend at the University of Northern British Columbia (UNBC) asked Chris Bose and me if we could prepare a performance for an online conference on the arts and environmental studies (UNBC, 2020). We then asked Nakuset Gould, a Mi'kmaq artist originally from the East Coast, who creates critical and hilarious content about gentrification, sex workers' rights, and the violence of settler colonialism on Indigenous women, to join us (Gould, 2023). Nakuset plays a drag king alter-ego character named Skus. In haphazard and hilarious online improvisation workshops, our alter egos Donnie, Skus, and Toby co-create a bizarre satirical professional development webinar for UNBC that offered tips on how to plan small cities. After positive feedback from planning, geography, and environmental studies students and professors, we decided to then co-create a 30-minute video titled *A Buzz in Your Hub: Entrepreneurial Strategies for the Late Capitalist Death Spiral* for the Vancouver Fringe Festival with the coaching of performance theorist and comedy director Moynan King and video artist and fine arts scholar Dayna McLeod.

Lessons in Braiding

Critically reflecting on how *A Buzz in Your Hub* contributes to broader practices of enriching democracy for this book, I turn to Jimmy et al. (2019) to consider the possibilities and pitfalls of "braiding" art with Indigenous and settler artists. In its unique way, our satirical webinar project braids some hopeful and creative strategies for amplifying underrepresented perspectives in the arts and planning, as well as responding to overlapping precarity, housing, and climate crises. Through this work, we contribute to strengthening inclusive democratic practices and principles.

To show how our satirical webinar enriches democracy in small ways, I start with Donnie Dreamcatcher's contributions to *A Buzz in Your Hub*. In the webinar, Donnie introduces his Powder Keg Project, a micro-housing and food security initiative featuring tiny homes made from porta-pottis – portable blue toilets that we often see on construction sites and in festivals. As Donnie shares his surreal toilet housing slides, he describes how, as an "Indigepreneur," the current housing and climate crisis in Kamloops present "cris-a-tunities." He also explains how his Powder Keg porta-potti homes are the logical next step, the new frontier, in affordable housing. Sharing images of young white men with beards drinking cappuccinos while riding blue toilets down the river as fires engulf the landscape, he describes how these flexible micro-homes can easily turn into little lifesaving boats to escape from climate emergencies. In his punchy used car salesman presentation style, Donnie describes how anyone who purchases a Powder Keg home receives a growler of beer and a $30 charcuterie board.

Donnie's surreal porta-potti project engages viewers in democratic practice because it offers critical and creative Indigenous perspectives on the absurdities and violence of growing housing and climate crises in Kamloops. When Nakuset, Chris, and I discussed his housing initiative, Chris described how the blue mini-toilet homes are a homage to housing insecurity in the city. In the past few years, as housing costs have risen rapidly, and forest fires and floods have disrupted entire neighborhoods, families, precarious young people, seniors, students, and low-income residents across Kamloops and the surrounding region have had to live in modular housing, recreation vehicles, and motels. Forest fires and floods across the territory have particularly impacted Indigenous communities. Indeed, in 2020, the village colonially named Lytton, British Columbia, home to the Nlaka'pamux First Nation that Chris belongs to, was almost completely wiped out by fires.

Chris also described how the porta-potti project satirizes the serious housing crisis that TRU's growing international student population is experiencing. As part of their corporate growth model, TRU currently generates enormous revenue from international students from Africa, India, Vietnam, and China. Often these students seek educational opportunities in Canada to flee the climate crisis in their home countries. However, as this predominantly racialized student cohort arrives in Kamloops, emergency modular housing resembling shipping containers in the university parking lot are some of the few options available (Letterio, 2021).

As we created the webinar, Chris also described how the growlers of beer and charcuterie boards that come with the porta-potti housing are his satirical reference to increasingly exclusionary urban development and university research across Kamloops. We discussed how, as TRU promotes creative community-engaged research, social innovation, and the arts in disinvested neighborhoods, the university also partners with property developers implementing carceral policing strategies to control the city's growing unhoused population. These community-university stakeholders include an assemblage of trendy restaurant and brewery owners and property developers complicit in reproducing settler colonialist gentrification dynamics. Indeed, a large percentage of the growing houseless population in Kamloops are Indigenous survivors of the local residential school system (Holliday, 2023).

Moreover, in the webinar, Donnie invites participants to invest in the Flush Festival, a jab at colonialist innovation, creativity, and property development scripts that universities and public and private stakeholders reproduce. While images of porta-pottis and charcuterie boards awkwardly float by as he speaks, Donnie excitedly describes how this two-day festival of innovation brings together pipeline and mining companies, property developers, and artists to share ideas on micro-housing, property development, and art. As we created the slides for the Flush Festival, Chris discussed how a festival celebrating pipelines transporting highly toxic Alberta tar sand sludge and collaborations promoting innovation, private sector partnerships, art, and tiny toilets seems like a fitting response. For Chris, humor is a rational response to the absurdities of corporate partnerships, real estate development, and petro-capitalism in Kamloops as fires, floods, and heat waves become the new norm.

Meanwhile, Nakuset's character Skus's presentation also strengthens democratic practice in her own unique way as she braids a hilarious critique of the everyday politics of neoliberal partnerships and settler colonial notions of success and mastery. With bizarre PowerPoint slides and a short video, Skus shares Sploosh, a green-pond-scum-smoothie health elixir he created to boost the competitiveness of white settler professionals. In the video, Toby (myself) excitedly drinks a smoothie, goes into a trance and, with green slime all over his face, thinks he has transformed into a world leader in research on Indigenous entrepreneurs. When we filmed the Sploosh promotional video on a lake not far from Kamloops, I literally got stuck in sand and muck as we harvested smoothie sludge, more excellent content for Skus's advertising. In Skus's Sploosh video, as Toby flails in the muck, he mansplains how he is an expert on Indigenous entrepreneurs and Skus slurps his coffee over his voice. Ignoring Skus, Toby keeps babbling on about innovation and his research leadership. When I asked Nakuset why her alter ego would put up with Toby, she said that, as an Indigenous artist, she is stuck working with seemingly benevolent white "Toby-types" who manage projects and institutions. Within these confining roles, she is always coming up with little ways to push back and hold power.

Moreover, *A Buzz in Your Hub* also builds a culture of democracy in small ways because it braids collective alternatives to uneven labor relations often reproduced in community-engaged research projects. As we co-created the webinar, Chris and Nakuset discussed how they continually experience precarity working with settler colonialist universities, arts institutions, and nonprofits. As artists and community workers, they both rely on piecemeal grants from government institutions. They also work for universities and galleries that value Indigenous artists and Knowledge Holders to provide land acknowledgements and Indigenize course content and exhibitions but that do little to make deep structural changes. In my small attempt to address these power imbalances, I used my Research Incentive Grant from Athabasca University to pay Chris and Nakuset Canadian Artist Representation (CARFAC, 2023) fees to create and perform their characters. Our long-term goal is to keep building projects together to access further grants and capacity-building opportunities.

At the same time, as a white, cisgendered assistant professor with the privilege of job security, I can never escape my complicities within colonial research systems and structures. Even with the consent of Chris and Nakuset, by writing this sole-authored book chapter, I accrue currency for practicing benevolent, community-engaged research and arts activism. I also risk coming across as a virtuous researcher who has figured out how to be good at decolonizing research. Because I am never exempt from these complicities, I too need to keep working with reflexivity and care and to hold these tensions. As Indigenous, Black, and queer scholars and activists of color point out (see maree brown, 2017), making space for these complexities and messiness is all part of the work of learning and cultivating democracy.

Conclusion

Overall, I realize that our performances are small acts of chipping away at huge structures and building more inclusive democratic institutions. However, in this chapter, I show how comedy offers one way for Indigenous and settler communities to "hack together" (Cowan, 2017) the worlds we want to live in and to practice creative world building. As we keep co-creating our projects, checking in with each other, and practicing relationship-building and consciousness-raising, we are envisioning and enacting the society we want to live in. Inspired by *Towards Braiding*, we move forward with our alter-ego projects imperfectly, practicing hyper-reflexivity, and learning with these contradictions and tensions. I do this because Chris, Nakuset, and I see our futures entwined in Kamloops and across so-called Canada as we face climate catastrophes and housing crises.

Onwards we go co-creating more buzz. In June 2023, the rEvolver performance festival in East Vancouver screened our video as part of a day of Indigenous performance sponsored by the Savage Society Indigenous theater company. As part of this performance, our alter egos facilitated a porta-potti art collage making planning workshop where people created collages to describe the current housing crisis here in so-called British Columbia, as well as build the kinds of cities they want to live in. To facilitate collage making, we provided cutout images of porta-potties and police, referencing the City of Vancouver's increasingly carceral policies to control and remove unhoused people living here from public space. We also offered cutouts of more-than-human plants and critters for people who are envisioning abundant and caring cities instead. Nakuset plans to share the images in zines for Skus's growing fictitious consultancy company. We are also discussing using these collage images in porta-potti planning workshops with the young artists that Chris works with in Kamloops. As we engage in these creative conversations, we keep co-creating possibilities for more radical and caring democracies.

References

Bose, C. (2020). *Chris Bose website*. https://www.chrisboseland.com/

Brown, W. (2015). *Undoing the demos: Neoliberalism's stealth revolution*. Zone Books.

Buddies in Bad Times Theater. (2013). *Buddies in Bad Times website*. https://buddiesinbadtimes.com/about/history/past-productions/

Canadian Centre for Policy Alternatives (CCPA) (2023). *Half of BC workers lack access to "standard jobs" and 37% are in precarious employment, groundbreaking survey finds*. https://policyalternatives.ca/newsroom/news-releases/half-bc-workers-lack-access-%E2%80%9Cstandard-jobs%E2%80%9D-and-37-are-precarious-employment

CARFAC. (2023). *Canadian artists representation*. https://www.carfac.ca/news/2023/04/14/artist-fee-survey-and-consultation/

CFJC Today. (2021). Large fire breaks out in Juniper-Valleyview area of Kamloops. *CFJC Today*. https://cfjctoday.com/2021/07/01/large-fire-breaks-out-in-juniper-valley view-area-of-kamloops/

Chandrakate, K. (2023). Kamloops Residential School survivor sentenced to 28 days in jail for resisting TMX pipeline. *Spring Magazine*. https://springmag.ca/kamloops-residential-school-survivor-sentenced-to-28-days-in-jail-for-resisting-tmx-pipeline

Cowan, T. L. (2017). Insubordinate, indiscrete, interdisciplinary: Risking perpetual precarity in all the wrong places, or, just being fabulous, a manifesto. *Hook and Eye.*

Curran, W. (2018). *Gender and gentrification*. Routledge.

Elliott, A. (2020, March 26). After the crisis, what kind of world do we want? Post-apocalyptic novels hold lessons – And warnings | CBC arts. *CBC*. https://www.cbc.ca/arts/after-the-crisis-what-kind-of-world-do-we-want-post-apocalyptic-novels-hold-lessons-and-warnings-1.5509721.

Gottfriedson, G. (2023). *Bent back tongue*. Caitlin Press.

Gould, N. (2023). *Nakuset Gould Instagram*. https://www.instagram.com/p/B_BOaQ7hUVd/

Holliday, K. (2023). Kamloops homeless count shows 51 per cent increase in street population. *Castenet On-Line News*. https://www.castanetkamloops.net/news/Kamloops/454248/Kamloops-homeless-count-shows-51-per-cent-increase-in-street-population

Jimmy, E., Andreotti, V., & Stein, S. (2019). *Towards braiding*. Musagetes. https://musagetes.ca/wp-content/uploads/2019/07/Braiding_ReaderWeb.pdfKern

Johnston, C. & Pratt, G. (2019). *Migration in performance: Crossing the colonial present*. Routledge.

Landry, L. (2021). The Loop plans to fight "nuisance" status in Kamloops. *Kamloops Daily News*. https://infotel.ca/newsitem/kamloops-the-loop-plans-to-fight-nuisance-status/it83466

La Pocha Nostra. (2020). *La Pocha Nostra: A handbook for the rebel artist in a post-democratic society*. Routledge.

Letterio, A. (2021). TRU finds short-term solution to student housing crisis. *CFJC Today*. https://cfjctoday.com/2021/09/29/tru-finds-short-term-solution-to-student-housing-crisis/

Lorde, A. (1977). *Poetry is not a luxury*. Chrysalis.

maree brown, a. (2017). *Emergent strategy: Shaping change, changing worlds*. AK Press.

McLean, H. (2016). Hos in the garden: Staging and resisting neoliberal creativity. *Environment and Planning D: Society and Space, 35*, 1.

McLean, H., & de Leeuw, S. (2020). En/acting radical change: Theories, practices, places and politics of creativity as intervention. In A. de Dios & L. Kong (Eds.), *Handbook on the geographies of creativity*. Edward Elgar.

Nagar, R. (2014). *Muddying the waters: Coauthoring feminisms through scholarship and activism*. University of Illinois Press.

Ravindran, J. (2021). A wildfire has destroyed 90% of this town. Indigenous communities have been hit the hardest. *CNN*. https://www.cnn.com/2021/07/08/americas/canada-lytton-wildfire-climate-change-indigenous-intl-cmd/index.html

Tait, M. (2022). Healing through drums: Norman Retasket on how in the wake of unmarked grave discoveries he found meaning in making drums – and his own story of surviving the Kamloops Indian Residential School. *Globe and Mail*. https://www.theglobeandmail.com/canada/article-kamloops-residential-school-survivor-drums/

UNBC. (2020). *Inspiring women among us 2020: Sharing power now! Diversifying leadership*. https://www2.unbc.ca/events/55297/inspiring-women-among-us-2020-sharing-power-now-diversifying-leadership

Vasudevan, P., & Kearney, W. (2015). Remembering Kearneytown: Race, place and collective memory in collaborative filmmaking. *Area, 48*(4), 455–462.

7

MEDIATING PROVISIONAL COMMUNITIES

The Production and Management of Collaborative Arts Projects

Rui Gonçalves Cepeda

In this chapter, I argue that collaborative art practices provide platforms for the existence of a culture of democracy in a community. I draw from my practice as founder and director of the Trienal, a transcultural festival held in Portugal, in 2010 and between 2013 and 2015, that presented traditional art formats, such as sculpture, photography and installations, but, as well, commissioned and presented collaborative art projects (CAPs). My argument develops around the conflict existing in the implementation of governmental political agendas concerning the legislation and execution of cultural guidelines. More specifically, using Santiago Morilla's artistic commission *No Veo Nada* (2013) as a case study, this chapter reviews how the application of conciliatory strategies and of narrative mediation (in behavioral relationships) have occurred in the dispute amongst different parties, i.e., a local community – the Reguengos de Monsaraz community – and an administrative governmental institution – the Inspecção-Geral das Actividades Culturais [ICAG].

The festival, named Trienal, produced durational artworks working with and in regional communities and appealing to specific communities and cultures creatively and improvisationally. In particular, within the Trienal framework collaborative art practices (CAPs) and the artworks produced supported the existence of democratic discourses and practices in communities. Following Grant H. Kester's (2004) description, CAPs work with what is endemic to the region where they are to happen, or what we, the Trienal directors, have denominated as its *terroir*. *Terroir* is a French term borrowed from the winemaking industry and offers something embedded culturally in a socially or historical context, particularly at an emotional level. Together with a subjective dimension, which is related to image and senses, the term *terroir* "refers to a specific place and includes the social and technical features common to that place," in addition to "[g]eological and geographical features, such as climate, soil and geology, [which] all influence perceptions of

DOI: 10.4324/9781003475996-12

terroir" (Spielmann et al., 2014, pp. 225–226). The *terroir* here can be defined as an ambiguous space in which artistic projects with a collaborative participatory nature will happen. This ambiguous space is seen as a temporary space – external to the sociopolitical paradigm defining the discourse in conflict – that provides for the arts producer or manager in collaboration with artists, local communities, and regional and national institutions conditions supporting the realization of participatory aesthetic interventions supporting democratic discourses. Those parties are just two of the multiple constituents that define the whole that is Portugal as a representative democratic state based on the rule of law. I finish this chapter by concluding how the specific conditions for the production of an act of collaborative participation in artistic interventions can be, first, considered to be a social desire to renew democratic standards, and, second, to drive society's cultural life towards the realization of an inclusive culture of democracy.

Production of *No Veo Nada*

No Veo Nada (2014) was born from a commission given by the Trienal to the Spanish artist Santiago Morilla (b. 1973, Madrid). Morilla's project consisted, first, of a drawing made on the floor of the old *Praça de Armas*. The drawing was erased during a bullfighting spectacle with *touros bravos,* a particular breed of bulls used in bullfighting. Specifically, that act of aesthetic expurgation took effect while the interaction between man and animal occurred. Second, the aesthetic experience functioned as a metaphor for the drawing up and erasure of institutional narratives, legal determinations and political impositions, and the transience of life's values. These are all themes that accompany Morilla's artistic work and are at the heart of the dispute between two parties – a local community and a governmental body. Morilla integrates and interacts with the surrounding environments as if they are a global territory that needs to be mapped. By "territory," or the *terroir*, it is meant what is offered by the location (the historical village of Monsaraz), its natural environment (the Alentejo region), and the local historical and cultural heritage (the population's traditions, habits, and customs). *No Veo Nada*, like many of Morilla's other artworks, "lives during its production, in the way of relating to the context in which it is found and produced" (Morilla, personal communication, March 2020). Finally, the collaborative participatory art project *No Veo Nada* was framed and contextualized by a relationship of conflict that was created by an act included in Monsaraz's religious festivities – the killing of a live animal in a public spectacle.

The religious festival held in honor of the *Nosso Senhor Jesus dos Passos* [*Our Lord of the Passion*] has been happening every year since 1877, in September.

After several Kafkaesque months mediating the different narratives regarding the same disputed story – the legal or illegal act of killing an animal in a spectacle of live entertainment – what was expected was for the local population to appear in the old *Praça de Armas* during the killing. The *Praça de Armas* is used as a prime location to host a variety of events by the responsible local authority,[1] situated in the medieval village of Monsaraz, Portugal. The spectacle involves locals participating in the act of erasing the face of the Spanish matador, Manolete, while a bull charges and dies before their eyes. The aim was for all those people attending the aesthetic intervention to be accomplices in the bull's death in the arena; to witness the first legal *touros de morte* spectacle to be held in the historical village of Monsaraz, to actively question an institutional form of cultural censorship, and to experience a redistribution of civic authority and leadership. My role as an art and cultural manager is to engage in the demanding and complex task of accessing the *terroir* influencing specific communities, and, as a producer of CAPs, to objectively formulate, propose, and create a temporary relational space that would allow for active participation in an aesthetic experience. My expectation is that by occupying and existing in the relational space, to that "provisional community" was given the sovereignty to present its own cultural values and attributes as materials that then become part of the process of production. This supports agency and participation by a CAP, and encourages a civic culture of democracy in society that will endure beyond the short-lived aesthetic experience.

In *No Veo Nada,* Morilla transferred with white chalk to the floor of the *Praça de Armas* the face of the famous Spanish bullfighter Manolete. Manuel Laureano Rodríguez Sánchez (1917–1947, Spain), known as Manolete, was a famous Spanish *matador* (bullfighter), who bled to death after being hit by a bull in a *corrida* held in the bullfighting arena of Linares (in Andalusia) in 1947. The whole of Manolete's face could only be distinguished from the castle keep. During the bullfighting spectacle, the bull, aficionados, and other dilettantes jumped, stumbled, and drank in the face of Manolete (Photo 1). Morilla argues that "it is the bull and the bullfighters, the people who step on the drawing and the other uncertainties that will make the work" (personal communication, March 2020). According to him, the different participants distort the impassive face of the *matador*, changing the shape and limits of the drawing: "people interact and comment on the work, are interested in it, step on it, destroy it and inhabit it" (personal communication, March 2020). Morilla adds that in this way, people and bull create a monstrous and infinite portrait; both metaphorically disfigure the image until it is completely erased from the real world. Conceptually, with this erasure of the drawing under people and animals' feet, they all interacted as if they were in a painting representing a symbolic double death – that of the *matador* and that of the bull – but also, that of a convention conveyed in legal conventions and institutional determinations, popular certitudes, and religious dogmas.

Popular Festivities of a Religious Nature: The Bullfighting Spectacle

Usually in Portugal, in popular outdoor celebrations or festivities of a religious nature, local community members actively participate in setting up the festival as visitors, traders, performers, etc.; but, more importantly, they are involved in the

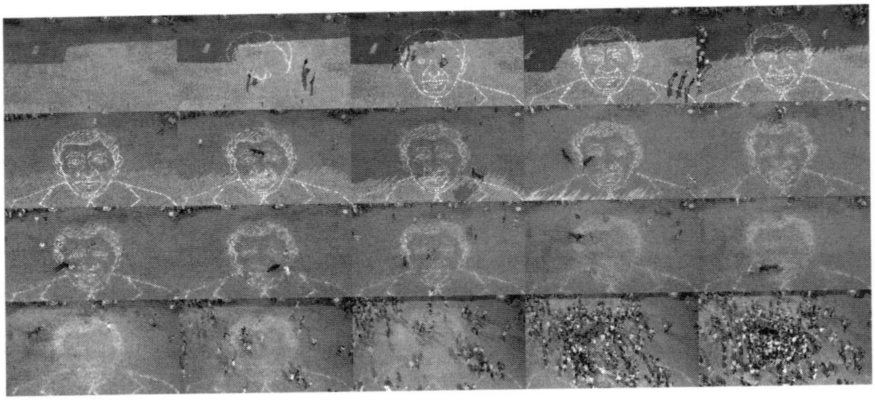

FIGURE 7.1 Santiago Morilla *No Veo Nada* [*Can't See Nothing*], 2014. Courtesy: © the artist. Video stills of the video recording of Morilla's collaborative project *No Veo Nada*. Starting with the drawing of Manolete's face in white chalk on the floor of the old Praça de Armas (top-left), through the subsequent interaction between man and bull, and finishing with the erasure of Morilla's drawing and the killing of the bull (bottom right).

commission that plans, organizes, and delivers the event (*comissão de festas*). It can be argued that those popular festivities of a religious nature are the result of an inclusive community planning process to celebrate particular cultural traditions and the ways of life of local communities. This type of popular festivities can also be perceived as being what Helguera (2011) defines as a "collaborative participation" within his multi-layered participatory structure. Furthermore, the level of participation and engagement bolsters the ability to develop relationships among different stakeholders, experience in dealing with decision-making processes, and understanding of the benefits (impact) that would derive from these decisions. One consequence is that the level of participation and engagement changes and fosters local communities' levels of confidence in their own cultural traditions and ways of life (Kidd, 2018).

The regulation concerning the practice and realization of bullfighting spectacles in Portugal is written and legally defined in the Portuguese Constitution. According to Decreto-Lei N.° 89/2014, de 11 de Junho, bullfighting is an integral part of Portugal's popular culture heritage and is under the supervision of the Ministry of Culture. According to the *Regulamento do Espectáculo Tauromáquico* [Regulation of the Bullfighting Spectacle], "bullfighting spectacles are considered those that consist of dealing with wild animals, in fixed or mobile venues that are specially designated for them" (Diário da República, 2014, n.p.). However, in Portugal, it has been prohibited to kill bulls in entertainment spectacles since 1928. *Decreto-Lei N.° 15.355 de 14* de Abril de 1928, by the then Ministry of the Interior, established an absolute ban on bullfighting with *touros de morte* [killing of the bulls] throughout the Portuguese territory. However, for almost a century, the prohibition on bullfighting spectacles with *touros de morte* was only understood to be applied on the premises licensed for the purpose, commonly known as "praças de touros" or "arenas."

A national referendum carried out in 2002 called for the approval of a regime of exception to that law to allow the killing of bulls. Subsequently, in 2002, an exception was introduced in the law in which the condition of exceptionality to the killing of bulls would be due to cultural and social specificities. If framed by particular historical and traditional circumstances, such as a popular religious traditions, this would not justify the general prohibition in force in the rest of the country. According to the 2002 *Decreto-Lei*,

> any spectacle with *touros de morte* is exceptionally authorised in the case that they are to observe local traditions that have been maintained uninterruptedly, at least in the 50 years prior to the entry into force of this decree, as an expression of popular culture, on the days when the historic event takes place.
>
> *(Diário da República, 2002, n.p.)*

As is argued by a local public official, "the death of the bull is a symbol of the culture of the population of Monsaraz . . . [it is a] tradition that has remained uninterrupted for over a century" (Lusa, 2011, n.p.). For 12 years (from 2002 to 2013), nonetheless, the population of Monsaraz continued to contentiously exercise their legal or illegal manifestation of popular culture as they always have done, even if it had to be exercised, literally, under a blanket.

Morilla's artistic project was intentionally included in the Trienal's program of activities as a conciliatory strategy between two contending parties (local community vs. public institution). This conciliatory strategy changed the institutional narrative surrounding the event, as being an aesthetic experience rather than being a popular festivity of a religious nature held in honor of a religious character. The transformation to *be* an aesthetic participatory experience occurred when those people who contemplate from the comfort of their seats the spectacle led by the *torero* in the *arena* (nominal participation), move from their seats into the *arena*, and, rather than contributing with a single task – running in front of the bull (direct participation) – they not only provided content (creative participation) but also shared responsibilities with the *torero* for the developing of the spectacle structure (collaborative participation) – the killing of an animal in a spectacle of live entertainment. On an operational level (artistic practice), the artist operated as a mediator by strategically providing an interactive, relational space where different parties could meet – the artistic project *No Veo Nada* – conceptually engages and develops alternative conciliatory narratives between the parties in dispute. Symbolically, the legal or illegal drawings derived from conventions conveyed in a legal book were erased by the participants in the collaborative art project during their interaction, thus moving from an institutional imposition to a moment supported by freedom of choice.

Citizen Discourses on a Culture of Democracy

Constitutionally, Portugal is a sovereign republic with plural democratic expressions and political organizations that exist through the separation and interdependence of powers, a Western democratic state based on the rule of law, with a view to achieving and growing a culture of democracy through democratic participation. By strategically incorporating the sociopolitical narrative in dispute in the aesthetic intervention, *No Veo Nada*, as an artistic project with a conferred autonomy from the controlling politics, disrupted the prevailing politics. In 2014, due to the pluralizing effects of arts, in contrast to the monopolization, the political institutionalizing of sociocultural tendencies, under the current political and legal regime it was the first time that, in the village of Monsaraz, a bull was legally killed during the popular religious festival.

In cooperation with distinctive educational and cultural agents, Portugal governmental cultural policies promote a *democratization of culture* by encouraging and ensuring access, by all citizens, to cultural enjoyment and (collective or individual) creation. Democratization of culture guarantees "citizens access to artistic enjoyment and cultural production, correcting inequalities (social, economic or territorial) in the access" (National Plan for the Arts, 2021, p. 22). This policy encourages citizen participation in the arts and enables a continuous provision of a wide range of aesthetic and artistic experiences, while promoting and implementing cultural offerings for the education of communities and all its citizens. Although democratization of culture is a democratic governmental policy, it is a practical initiative by cultural organizations or national bodies to promote access to culture. As such, it is a policy that fails to engage civic society, since cultural democratization is fundamentally implemented *downwards* (Matarasso, 2019). This governmental policy aims for the participation of the people in the building of a nation-state by raising the educational and cultural standards of the people, and once that happens, the people, as citizens within the nation, could become more equal in the access to opportunities for political governance.

A second governmental cultural policy agenda, *cultural democracy*, favors the pluralization, the territorialization of decisions, and the sharing of power (Carta do Porto Santo, 2021). Democratization of culture and cultural democracy are often set in opposition. What divides and unites those two concepts is "their divergent approaches to pursuing the same overarching social democratic ambition: to address, via state action, the damaging effects of capitalism," particularly values related with inequality, freedom, and identity (Gross & Wilson, 2020, p. 329). First, in contrast to democratization of culture, cultural democracy is fundamentally democratic, with an egalitarian nature, since the cultural is "not fixed and universal but the result of a continuing process of . . . democratic negotiation between people" (Matarasso, 2019, p. 77). In the Portuguese case, the government – the state – contributes to the achievements of cultural democracy "through a regulatory policy applied for the distribution of information and the structures of supply"

(Evrard, 1997, p. 168). Second, with this policy, the role of the government "is not to interfere with the preferences expressed by citizens-consumers but to support the choices made by individuals or social groups" (Evrard, 1997, p. 168). According to what is expressed in the Portuguese Constitution, the effective implementation of these choices has the objective to achieve economic, social, and cultural democracy and deepen a participatory democracy. By shifting from an interfering paradigm, in democratization of culture, to one based on choice, cultural democracy may be defined as one founded on the freedom of individual choice.

The reason I am identifying those two policy discourses has to do with the conceptual and spatial shift in the inherent value of the sociopolitical narrative in a democratic society and its importance to the understanding and experience of cultures of democracy in the wider sense. This distinction allows us to unveil and address the institutional validation of the cultural value implied by what is considered to be the democracy of the masses, and to confront it by means of questioning through an aesthetic intervention, with the cultural validity conveyed by the concept of freedom of the minority. In a Western democratic society,

> citizens have the right not just to vote, but also to take in every aspect of democratic life, to express and defend their values, and to try to persuade others of their ideas. That process is not only political. It happens in daily life.
>
> *(Matarasso, 2019, p. 74)*

In democracy, individual citizens have the right to learn within their own cultural contexts, to be able to have the capacity to define oneself as active participants in society. In this light, democracy is sustained when citizens have a voice, instead of being regarded as the silenced *other*; "[d]emocracy is expressed in and sustained by a culture that enables people to affirm, express and question their own and other people's values and the relationship between them" (Matarasso, 2019, p. 74). Having a culture of democracy in a society's agenda would promote diversity of views and active participation; it enables people to participate in policy disputes and decision-making, and it provides fair and equitable access to resources while aiming for win-win outcomes, rather then win-lose situations. This enables inclusive societies to contribute to citizens' involvement in the democratic process and in decision-making.

Although participation in artistic practices is not a substitute for the deficit of a culture of democracy in society, the act of participation in artistic projects can be perceived to be a social desire to renew democratic standards, especially in social-liberal democracies. Within this framework, "[c]ulture and the arts can 'create a space of expression' beyond institutions, at the level of the person and can act as mediators, thus paving the way for the 'shared public space(s)' necessary for intercultural dialogue" (Anheier, 2017, p. 13). In social-liberal democracies, the idea is that culture is no longer produced and imposed from above. Individuals are not only users, a potential audience for a cultural product or experience; rather, they are citizens likely to be involved in local life in all its dimensions, including in the collaborative formulation of public cultural policies.

In CAPs, participants have been dislocated from artistic or cultural spaces to the arteries of a city, to spaces where everyday life happens. Here they are seen and accepted by the different stakeholders (participants, public powers, and those at whom they are aimed) as being members of the population rather than being members of an audience. In CAPs, participation exists when the visitor, who now has become an active participant, "shares responsibilities for developing the structure and content of the work in collaboration and direct dialogue with the artist" (Helguera, 2011, p. 17). Active participation in CAPs gives the community the ability to express itself publicly and the confidence to have an active voice as citizens in decision-making in matters that are of concern in the public sphere, i.e., public policies.

Conclusion

From the point of view of the *No Veo Nada* producer, what mattered was how to inscribe an aesthetic discourse as a conciliatory strategy in the narrative regarding the realization of a bullfighting spectacle with *touros de morte*, rather than looking for aesthetic situations that could validate a cultural policy.

The second strategic component in the *terroir* is, strategically, to reflect, at an operational level, on existing theories on participatory art and, more widely, on a civic culture of democracy. Locality is one component in the *terroir*. In the Trienal's case, the knowledge of how to evaluate the region's internal and external environments allows producers to discover (symbolic) spaces that can be provisionally occupied jointly by different parties, while opening up possibilities for engagement and liberatory participation in artistic activities within a collaborative framework.

The communication in *No Veo Nada*, with the local community and its representative bodies, such as the local borough or religious institutions, was essentially *upstream*, which is a cultural democracy strategy. The proposed strategy was to negotiate, with the community and the other stakeholders, what is of value (sociocultural, political, symbolic, or spiritual) for the formation of the community's identity. In this case, what was important for the community is the organization, realization, and promotion of the annual festivities where the killing of the bull is legally included.

Additionally, by relating and including himself in the community, Morilla "hacks" the landscape and the sociopolitical representative use of space by the community, its external and internal environments – the *terroir. No Veo Nada* is "a project that revolved around a site-specific performance and intervention, designed specifically to be produced in the 'arena' of the bullring of the castle in the village of Monsaraz" (Morilla, personal communication, March 2020). For the artist, while conceptually reflecting upon those theories, his art works are collaborative, rather than solely participatory, because, first, local "contingencies [are] . . . invited to act and produce the work," and, second, those works are, "in some way, voluntarily and also involuntarily co-production" (personal communication, March 2020). While Morilla's first reflection can be considered to be based on a social desire to renew democratic standards, the second consideration can be based on what drives society's cultural life towards the realization of an inclusive culture of democracy.

Actual participation in aesthetic collaborations gives to the participants a two-fold voluntary and involuntary social empowerment. This invites participants to make a choice whether to participate or not. When one chooses to participate, one may also choose to alter the work, its object, its subject, and its meaning. To a certain extent, artistic collaborative participation also enters the fields of action under participatory democracy.

Note

1 The Município de Reguengos de Monsaraz is the entity which is responsible for the safeguarding of the historical village of Monsaraz, including the castle.

References

Anheier, H. (2017). *Cultural participation and inclusive societies: A thematic report based on the indicator framework on culture and democracy* (p. 13). December 2016. Council of Europe Publishing.

Carta do Porto Santo. (2021). *A cultura e a promoção da democracia: para uma cidadania cultural europeia. Report*. 2021PORTUGAL.EU. https://www.2021portugal.eu.

Diário da República. (2002). *Lei n.º 19/2002 de 31 de Julho*. Retrieved May 2020, from https://dre.pt – my translation and italics.

Diário da República. (2014). *Decreto-Lei n.º 89/2014, de 11 de Junho* (p. 3080). Retrieved May 2020, from https://dre.pt – my translation.

Evrard, Y. (1997). Democratizing culture or cultural democracy? *The Journal of Arts Management, Law, and Society*, *27*(3), 167–175 (168).

Gross, J., & Wilson, N. (2020). Cultural democracy: An ecological and capabilities approach. *International Journal of Cultural Policy*, *26*(3), 328–342 (329).

Helguera, P. (2011). *Education for socially engaged art: A materials and techniques handbook*. Jorge Pinto Books.

Kester, G. H. (2004). *Conversation pieces. Community + communication in modern art*. University of California Press

Kester, G. H. (2011). *The one and the many: Contemporary collaborative art in a global context*. Duke University Press.

Kidd, S. L. (2018). *Art as infrastructure: An evaluation of civic art and public engagement in four communities in south Los Angeles County*. Evaluation. Los Angeles County Arts Commission. https://www.issuelab.org/resource/art-as-infrastructure-an-evaluation-of-civic-art-and-public-engagement-in-four-communities-in-south-los-angeles-county-2.html

Lusa. (2011). Monsaraz promete voltar a cumprir tradição proibida. *Diário de Notícias*, 9 de Setembro de 2011. Retrieved May 16, 2020, from https://www.dn.pt/portugal/sul/monsaraz-promete-voltar-a-cumprir-tradicao-proibida-1985866.html – my translation.

National Plan for the Arts Executive Committee. (2021). *National plan for the arts: A strategy a manifest. 2019–2024* (p. 22). Report. Ministry of Culture and Ministry of Education.

Spielmann, N., Jolly, S., & Parisot, F. (2014). *Terroir* in the media: The poetry of people, place and palate. *International Journal of Wine Business Research*, *26*(3), 224–240, 225, 226.

PART THREE
Learning Environments

INTRODUCTION TO LEARNING ENVIRONMENTS

Learning and Practice – Democracy in Action

Susan Badger Booth

Participation in civic life is essential to a healthy democracy, so naturally a strong education in civics is the bedrock of participation. Outcomes of a civics curriculum will often include students being able to name the branches of government or their local and federal representatives, but the authors in Part Three suggest there are skills and practices that are much more fundamental than how governments work. This part of the book offers four case studies on why democracies work, and in turn why they may be at risk.

All the cases in Part Three ask students to both learn about and participate in democracy. As a professor of arts management and administration, I taught my students democratic principles through applied participatory field work. For over a decade I took students to the Americans for the Arts (AFA) National Arts Action Summit. This pilgrimage to the US capital always began pre-conference with students analyzing the current AFA *Congressional Arts Handbook*. Once current issues were reviewed, students prepared mock congressional interviews in the safety of their classroom. By the time we were talking with legislators, students could paint a picture of how "Boosting the Creative Economy" or "Funding the National Endowment for the Arts" (AFA issues, 2022) would advance their own careers. It was at this magic moment where I saw students transform into advocates. *Culturally Responsive Teaching* was employed in three of the four case studies in Part Three, and in my arts advocacy class, this technique allowed my students to see themselves in the issues they were presenting to their legislators.

In 2021, I took my last class to the National Arts Action Summit. The number of Michigan participants for that year's summit was at an all-time high. In fact, over 90% of our state delegates were either from my current class or alumni from previous years, including our state captain. As in Sims's "The Power of Storytelling" (Chapter 11), I challenged my students to identify the roots of social issues in

DOI: 10.4324/9781003475996-14

stories and work through them, in my situation advocating for advancing national arts policy by speaking with elected officials. As I developed an alternate curriculum for my course, I considered how creative practice might become a form of civil action as was suggested in "Reflections on Doing Visual Politics" (Chapter 8). How can I use my students' creative practices to leverage and inform the need for government support for the arts at the local and national levels?

Part Three on learning environments includes a diverse collection of international case studies describing how teaching artists work with students from Minnesota to Kathmandu. Ten authors, including both educators and artists, describe how creative practices are used to develop skills such as questioning power, giving voice, thinking about relationships to other beings, and seeing multiple viewpoints simultaneously. Teaching artists are working artists from any discipline who take on parallel roles as educators. In the cases documented here, three describe teaching artists in K-8 schools working predominantly with elementary school students, and in one case the audience is college students from Australia, Bangladesh, and Nepal.

Rebecca Winthrop, author of *The Need for Civic Education in 21st-Century Schools* (2020), suggests, "schools can and should play an important role in catalyzing increased civic engagement. They can do this by helping young people develop and practice the knowledge, beliefs, and behaviors needed to participate in civic life" (p. 2). The following chapters exemplify the "practice" Winthrop notes in the "creative practices" employed by all the teaching artists.

Educational philosophies used in "All the Relatives" (Chapter 9), "The Ray of Hope Project" (Chapter 10), and "The Power of Storytelling" (Chapter 11) all employ Culturally Responsive Teaching, which "combines curriculum with a narrative that contains various entrances and exits, and allows all students to engage with and see themselves in the content" (Acuff et al., 2012). This represents a significant change in how art appreciation has been taught historically, and now works as a catalyst to move students into a world where creative practices are used for social change. Students in all of these case studies are not just observers but creators and co-creators, experiencing democracy in action, reframing place and transforming space, visualizing the complexity of decision-making processes. Both "All the Relatives" and "The Power of Storytelling" use the theories of Jack Zipes to ground much of their pedagogical framing with a methodology that helps participants navigate and transform social scripts while becoming more confident narrators of their own lives.

In Chapter 8, "Reflections on Doing Visual Politics," the authors describe a framework of creative practice as civil action using photography as the creative medium. This is more age appropriate for the college student audience whom these teaching artists are working with. Educators in three different locations/countries (Naarm/Melbourne, Australia; Kathmandu, Nepal; and Dhaka, Bangladesh) use scholar/artist Ariella Aisha Azoulay's theory of reframing photography as a relational practice. Azoulay dismisses art history, aesthetics, and ethics and instead uses photography as the medium for building relationships around shared civic concerns. Two concerns of note are: (1) overcoming the unnecessary dichotomy between the aesthetic and the political, and (2) establishing civil discourse and how this might be realized through forms of collaboration which seek to address matters of shared concern with local communities.

Chapter 8, "Reflections on Doing Visual Politics" by Alan Hill, Kelly Hussey-Smith, Marnie Badham, Shehab Uddin, and Sagar Chhetri, was a multinational project connecting 60 students in three different countries at the Pathshala South Asian Media Institute in Dhaka, visual activism platform photo.circle in Kathmandu, and RMIT University's School of Art in Naarm/Melbourne (Naarm is the traditional Indigenous name for Melbourne). Although participants were encouraged to engage globally, they were asked to act locally focused on creative practice as civil action. Through reflection on a trans-local pedagogy of creative practice, they explore how photography and creative practice can function as a form of democratic participation when framed through the lens of relationality and the civil. Thus, photography takes on a political ontology through the way it brings people into relation, and the "civil" potential to do so over matters of shared concern.

In Chapter 9, "All the Relatives," Maria Asp and Sonja Kuftinec offer a 25-year-old storytelling methodology to animate cultures of democracy rooted in self-expression and collaboration across differences. "All the Relatives" builds cultures of democracy through three primary means: (1) transforming space and place, (2) questioning power, and (3) telling new stories. One student reflects, "it showed me I could act with my peers." "We saw so much growth in the students emotionally and academically. Kids became more vocal, literally speaking out for themselves and they participated more in other classes," notes one classroom teacher. This program shows an intentional pedagogy to prepare students for their role in democracy.

Student learning outcomes and research findings in these four chapters offer a diverse array of lessons learned and content to emulate in our own communities. In Chapter 10, "The Ray of Hope Project," author/teaching artist Alika Hope uses music and storytelling to teach about the US abolitionist movement of the 19th century. As Alika brings the unheard voices of abolitionists of color to the forefront in her historic reenactments, African American audiences made connections between their ancestors' slavery or enslavement practices and modern-day slavery such as child sex trafficking. Engaging with students' learning outcomes change, redirecting the future of Ray of Hope. Student responses to Alika's workshops allowed them to focus more deeply and invite participants to not only learn about, but practice democracy.

As noted earlier, an education in civics cannot just include how democracies operate. These four chapters help students consider civic values, civil discourse, and free speech and engage with those whose perspectives differ from their own. In Alika's project, this work prepares students for their roles in our democracies, as they must have the chance to practice civic behaviors. This should include giving students agency to vote, volunteer, attend public meetings, and engage with their communities.

In Chapter 11, "The Power of Storytelling," we see a shared educational philosophy with Chapter 9, although author Kiyoko Motoyama Sims adds to this philosophy by leveraging her experience growing up in Tokyo, Japan, and reflects deeply in the area of cultural intelligence or CQ. She describes CQ consisting of four factors: metacognition, cognition, motivation, and behavior. By living inside of characters' viewpoints through creative activities, the participants (students) deepen their intercultural capabilities by expanding their cultural knowledge and awareness of complex thought processes. This exercise visualizes the complexity of the decision-making process. It encourages the students to see multiple viewpoints simultaneously and allows them to change their minds by hearing other's perspectives. Stories provide bonds with unexpected protagonists, new communities of belonging, and models of empowerment (Stewart, 2019) that develop competencies critical to civic engagement and democratic practices, which are particularly important to newly immigrated populations such as the Somali American students Sims finds in her workshops.

These four chapters build a pedagogy of employing creative practices in education that develop skills in civic engagement. During the past few decades, youth civic engagement in the United States has been declining, but is the pendulum shifting? In fact, data shows that Gen Z and Millennial generations are becoming more engaged. "It's estimated that more than a quarter of registered voters . . . between 18 and 29 years of age cast a ballot in" the November primaries of 2022. "The turnout was an illustration that this is the most politically engaged cohort of youth voters in recent history" (Townley, 2022, p. 1) Additional follow-up is needed on all four of these case studies to measure the impact of how these programs build competencies of civic engagement.

References

Acuff, J. B., Hirak, B., & Nangah, M. (2012). Dismantling a master narrative: Using culturally responsive pedagogy to teach the history of art education. *Art Education, 65*(5), 6–10. https://doi.org/10.1080/00043125.2012.11519186

Americans for the arts, congressional arts handbook. (2022). National Arts Action Summit. https://www.americansforthearts.org/sites/default/files/2022_NAAS_Handbook_FINAL.pdf.

Stewart, C. (2019). The dangerous power of art education. *Art Education, 72*(6), 25–29. https://doi.org/10.1080/00043125.2019.1648144

Townley, D. (2022). US midterms: Why gen Z and millennials came out to vote and why it marks a generational shift. *The Conversation*. https://theconversation.com/us-midterms-why-gen-z-and-millennials-came-out-to-vote-and-why-it-marks-a-generational-shift-194947

Winthrop, R. (2020). *The need for civic engagement in 21stcentury schools*. Brookings Institution. https://brookings.edu/policy2020

8

REFLECTIONS ON DOING VISUAL POLITICS

Photography, Collaboration, and Creative Practice as Civil Action

Alan Hill, Kelly Hussey-Smith, Marnie Badham, Shehab Uddin, and Sagar Chhetri

In her seminal book, *Civil Imagination: A Political Ontology of Photography* (2015) curator and theorist Ariella Aisha Azoulay reframes photography as a relational practice. Rejecting art historical readings of aesthetics and ethics, Azoulay proposes an understanding of photography as having a political ontology through the way it brings people into relation, and the "civil" potential to do so over matters of shared concern. She brings together photography and political theory to conceptualize the "citizenry" of photography that she defines as "a special laboratory for the study and analysis of political relations" (2015, p. 70). Through reflection on a trans-local pedagogy of creative practice, we explore how photography and creative practice can function as a form of democratic participation when framed through the lens of relationality and the civil. We propose that the cultures produced through these practices offer opportunity at the intersection of democracy, creative practice, and education to motivate political action, intercultural understanding, and collaboration (Badham, 2019; Hussey-Smith, 2023). The chapter examines Doing Visual Politics: Creative Practice as Civil Action – a collective learning space which sought to contribute to cultures of democracy in Naarm/Melbourne, Australia; Kathmandu, Nepal; and Dhaka, Bangladesh.

We identify two specific concerns found in Azoulay's work that offer potential in developing innovative forms of praxis capable of overcoming the unnecessary dichotomy between the aesthetic and the political – and, in so doing, promoting cultures of democracy. The first is civil intent, and specifically what its identification and promotion as a teaching framework can offer in terms of developing forms of creative practice expressly aimed at actively participating in visual culture. The second is the ambition to establish civil discourse and how this might be realized through forms of collaboration that seek to address matters of shared concern, with local communities and situated in context. Through dialogic methods and critical

DOI: 10.4324/9781003475996-15

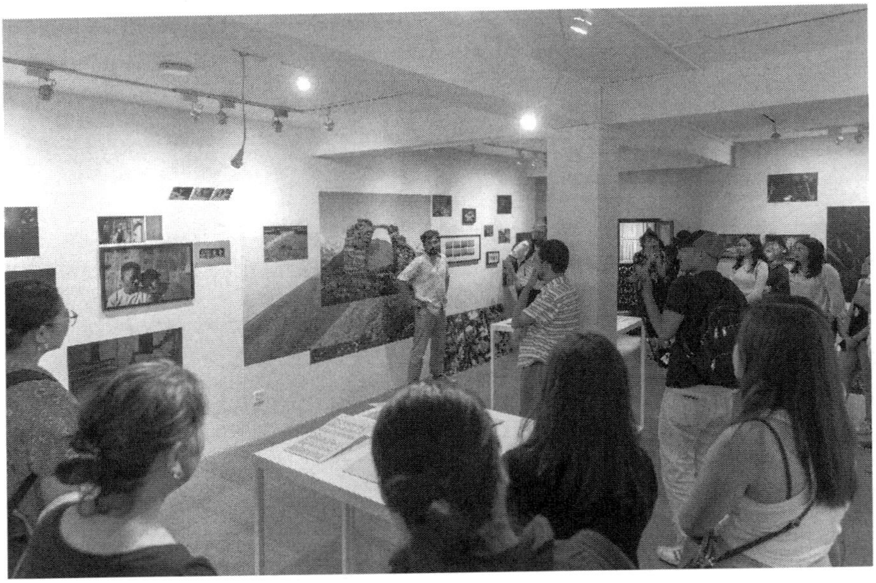

FIGURE 8.1 Sagar Chhetri speaking at the opening of the *All This Weight* exhibition at Patan House, Kathmandu, June 27, 2023. Photograph by Shikhar Bhattarai/photo.circle

reflection on the teaching and learning experience of Creative Practice as Civil Action, this chapter examines the motivations and practices that enable engagement in cultures of democracy through creative practice. We reflect on how these pedagogic approaches play out in different cultural and educational contexts but are primarily interested in if and how using this framework shifts participants' creative practices.

A Civil Framework: The Theories

Azoulay defines the civil as "the interest that citizens display in themselves, in others, in their shared forms of coexistence, as well as in the world that they create and nurture" (2015, p. 8). In *The Civil Contract of Photography*, she uses this lens of political theory to articulate the way in which photography creates communities "of people between whom political relations were not mediated by a sovereign ruling power" (2008, pp. 17, 23). This application of the concept of citizenship is not about a package of rights bestowed upon individuals – such as being a citizen of a nation-state – but, rather, "a hypothetical partnership between individuals that enables them to relate to one another as having equal access to this partnership" (2015, p. 73). Azoulay argues that the plural space created by photography is "an interface that enables people who inhabit different spheres of existence to share a common world," thereby establishing the "citizenry of photography" (p. 105). This leads to the conception of the civil contract of photography, which aims to recognize and reconstruct the political space where "photographed persons are participant citizens" who can call on spectators to "recognise and restore their citizenship through my viewing" (2008, p. 17).

The framework employed in Creative Practice as Civil Action extended Alan Hill's research reframing documentary photography as a civil practice by incorporating Azoulay's theories into practitioner knowledge to contribute to an emerging paradigm that integrates photography with political theory and visual culture (Hill, 2022). This research sought to clarify the laudable but often vague social agenda of documentary photography and to answer underlying questions and presumptions about the civil potential of creative practice more fully. Therefore, through our trans-local teaching of this articulation between creative practice and political theory, our pedagogic framework is comprised of two key elements: the adoption of civil intent, and the aim to establish civil discourse.

Civil intent allows us to recognize that "every citizen bears responsibility toward a common world and proceeds on the understanding that if citizens neglect their responsibilities, or incite others to do so, damage will ensue" (Azoulay, 2015, p. 105). As such, civil intent is simply a gaze, speech, or action that expresses this interest – a straightforward proposition that becomes a very useful tool for photographers and creatives to question their intentions and reflect on them through the lens of political theory. However, Azoulay argues further that civil intention/gaze also needs to be adopted by audiences, because it "enables the spectator to exceed the limits of professional discourse and to regard the image, not as source and end in itself, but first and foremost as a platform that bears the traces of others," and that this form of looking "departs from the form routinely sanctioned by the professional discourse of art and participates in a shared civil space" (p. 118). In this way, Azoulay argues that if we can regard photographs with civil intention and recognize the civil intention of the photographer (and/or photographed person/s), then we can see that photography can establish social relations.

Considering intent in these terms is important for creative practitioners – as is considering how to encourage viewers to adopt civil intent – because this intention will enable the recognition of the civil space potentially established. This begins with the challenging task of encouraging viewers to withhold the judgment of taste – which the regime of art encourages them to do – and instead regard photographs and artworks with civil intention, because this "enables me to treat the full spectrum of shared human life as political and to formulate a new discourse concerning civil intention as a special form of agency within it" (Azoulay, 2015, p. 10). Adopting civil intent and developing strategies to encourage audiences to suspend judgments of taste open the potential for civil discourse, which might then "suspend the point of view of governmental power and the nationalist characteristics that enable it to divide the governed from one another and to set its factions against one another" (p. 2).

> Civil discourse is not a fiction. It strives to make way for a domain of relations between citizens on the one hand, and subjects denied citizenship by a given

> regime on the other, on the basis of their partnership in a world that they share as women and men who are ruled. It seeks to isolate potential factors in the real world that might facilitate the coming into being of such relations of partnership, instead of the power of the sovereign that threatens to destroy them.
>
> (2015, pp. 2, 3)

This description arises in the specific context of Azoulay's discussion of regime-made disaster, wherein the relationships might literally be between citizens and noncitizens. But if read through the lens of the citizenry of photography, where the regime may not necessarily be a nation-state but some other "governing" force, then this understanding is useful in thinking about how photography can establish relations – and civil discourse – with our co-citizens.

Doing Visual Politics: A Trans-Local Network

The Doing Visual Politics network sits across three institutions with shared social justice values: Pathshala South Asian Media Institute in Dhaka, visual activism platform photo.circle in Kathmandu, and the RMIT University's School of Art in Naarm/Melbourne. For almost a decade, this network has been interrogating and expanding disciplinary understandings of what we refer to as *visual politics* – the practices and discourses at the intersection of photography, visual activism, art and social practice, and public pedagogy. The network and its projects have emerged from long-term relationships and collaboration between Australian-based photographers and educators Alan Hill, Kelly Hussey-Smith, and Shehab Uddin; Shahidul Alam and others from Pathshala; and NayanTara Gurung Kakshapti and colleagues at photo.circle.

Doing Visual Politics brought together more than 60 students from Australia, Bangladesh, and Nepal with a group of leading visual politics thinkers, practitioners, and researchers in Kathmandu in 2016 and 2018. Our first collaborative workshop sought to develop a transdisciplinary approach spanning art, photography, media, design, and social science methods. Based in Kathmandu, the workshop comprised a three-day symposium and a week of workshops with international guest mentors, with an evening program of talks and panel discussions. Over two subsequent weeks, students worked collaboratively to break down cultural, institutional, and disciplinary boundaries and engage with the local community to produce photographic, multimedia, written, and installation works, culminating in publications and exhibitions. In 2018, transdisciplinary groups of students and mentors developed visual research projects in response to issues relevant to the local context, such as the politics of aid, (con)testing national visual archives, media-driven narratives, and familial visual practices. The project acknowledges the complexity of cross-cultural practice and places ethical considerations at its core. In these workshops, participants engage directly with their local communities in a supported, collaborative, and critically reflexive context, as they are immersed

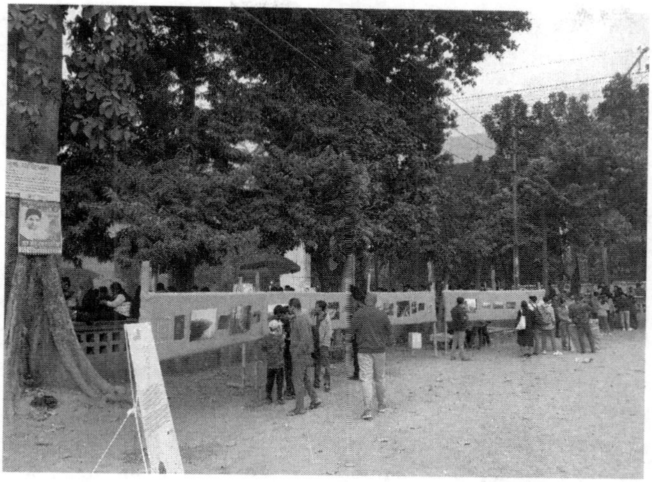

FIGURE 8.2 Eti Mohanagar (This Metropolis) exhibition at Dhaka University Teacher-Student Centre, December 2022 – the first of three exhibitions organized by Pathshala participants. Photo: Taslima Akhter.

in a learning community comprised of peers, experienced professionals, and academics from a wide variety of cultural backgrounds. Throughout this transformative process there is a rich exchange of ideas, politics, and philosophies, with new understandings developed and embedded in the work produced.

Creative Practice as Civil Action: The Teaching Collaboration

In late 2022, these three partner organizations activated our third collaborative workshop. Taking the form of a trans-local and transdisciplinary community of practice across sites in Naarm/Melbourne, Kathmandu, and Dhaka, the workshop set out to explore a practice-based rethinking of the aims and discourses of art, photography, and conventional education by reconsidering if, how, and when creative practice could constitute a form of civil action. While Creative Practice as Civil Action built on the success of two previous in-person workshops, this iteration was distinct in two ways. First, this workshop adopted a trans-local mode, where instead of traveling to one location, we ran simultaneous workshops at home, enabling participants to engage in creative thinking and practice relevant to their local communities and contexts while learning from and exchanging with their international peers. The second distinctive feature was the specificity of the framework and the explicit attempt to reimagine creative practice as civil action through the integration of political theory into the pedagogy. This approach – now explicit – grew out of our earlier iterations in which this focus on the civil functioned in more tacit and intuitive ways.

Each organization hosted a group of eight to ten student participants, along with a lecturer and a mentor bringing contemporary practice perspectives. At Pathshala and photo.circle, nearly all participants were students of photography, while RMIT students came from a range of practices: painting, sculpture, printmaking, sound design fashion, and photography. Like previous iterations, the workshop began with a symposium comprised of a series of online panel discussions introducing related photography and art practices and discourses. These presentations – held over three weeks – prompted students to think about creative practice as civil action and made clear the expectation that the work produced in their course would be contextually relevant and publicly exhibited.

At RMIT and Pathshala, the practical workshop then ran for two intensive weeks. The direction of the projects undertaken were left up to the groups in each location to determine, but a collective approach was encouraged. At Pathshala, the group focused on the student responses to the (mega) city itself, including issues like traffic congestion and road safety, resulting in three public exhibitions of their project *Eti Mohanagar/The Metropolis*. The Naarm/Melbourne group was located at a new urban research lab in the suburb of Brunswick, where the local government had recently changed its name from Moreland to Merri-bek ("rocky country" in the local Woi wurrung language) following revelations that the former namesake was a Jamaican slave plantation. As a result, the group produced a zine and exhibition called *Learning Merri-bek: Fragments of Connection*, featuring responses to what they learned about the Indigenous and non-Indigenous history of the place they were working. At photo.circle, the workshop was embedded within a larger five-month educational project where students were already developing individual projects, so for these students, Creative Practice as Civil Action provided an opportunity to look at an ongoing project in a new way. Their work culminated in the publication of a collective book, exhibition, and public program, *All This Weight*.

The reflective dialogue we undertook with teachers in each of the three sites pointed to critical expansion in pedagogy for each person in the team. Working trans-locally was reported as a strength for students to reflect more deeply on their own positionalities in relation to engaging in creative practice in their own social, political, and cultural contexts. In Dhaka, mentors Saydia Gulrukh and Taslima Akhter explained how Bangladeshi students come from a particular political context where individualism is typically favored over collectivism; therefore, in this workshop they began shifting their work to be about activism and collaboration. Difference within the group, and in the international intercultural context, was described as key for the students "seeing self." Sagar Chhetri in Kathmandu was also committed to this international collaboration. He spoke about the pedagogic framework as a focus on process over outcomes – holding space for students to engage in resistance, questioning, conflict, growth, collaboration, and transformation. In Naarm/Melbourne, Shehab Uddin and Jody Haines described the experimental pedagogical strategies as an extension of their politically motivated photographic practices. They discussed the potential of interdisciplinarity in creative practice through non-hierarchical teaching and learning and the need to center "care" in these creative practices as civic action. The collaborative experience of the symposium and engagement with the theoretical texts by Azoulay offered a valuable (and shared) framework for civil intent and action, yet each local project was substantially different, not only because of local context but also what each teacher and student brought to the particular learning collaboration.

Creative Practice as Civil Action: Student Reflections

Students involved in the program were interviewed in four focus groups and were asked questions about creative practice and civil action, the ethical complexities arising from the workshops, and how collaborative processes and projects might relate to ideas of participatory democracy in different contexts. The following three sections focus on the students' reported learnings and understandings from the workshop in relation to creative practice as civil action.

Identifying Civil Intent

"What is my goal? What is my aim here?" (RMIT student D)

A distinguishing factor of this workshop was the explicit pedagogic intention to blend creative practice with contemporary political theory. The workshops began with a provocation from Azoulay observing that "where there is no civil intention, there is civil malfunction" (2015, p. 107). Students were asked to consider what Azoulay's concept of civil intention meant in their specific contexts. Students described civil intent as something beyond disciplinary and professional boundaries. One student commented that it is a practice that "kind of reaches outside of itself" (RMIT student B). Unlike the "civic" which is related to governance, the "civil" is an open processual and dynamic space of possibility and action (Hussey-Smith & Clarke, 2023) unmediated by governing power (Azoulay, 2015). For this student, their civil intention was about "creating something that also has a political agenda" and attempting to "affect things more broadly outside of just the creative practice, and [the] insular kind of ecosystem that a lot of creative projects tend to exist in."

Despite its connections to political theory, many students spoke about the importance of articulating their own positionality in understanding their civil intent. Students in photo.circle described civil intent as a process of learning to connect the personal with the political. One student commented that "instead of being too self-indulgent, how can we take it beyond that and make [a broader] statement?" (photo.circle student B). Another student shared that they were prompted to think about "political feelings" (photo.circle student C) as a bridge between themselves and the world. Pathshala students spoke about civil action as a process of moving beyond binaries of self and other. One student commented that "we learned something different about working with each other . . . we learned that it's not that easy working collaboratively or being involved in [social] issues" (Pathshala student A). Another commented that "we are taught to work individually but when we work as a team, we have to learn to cooperate through our thinking process" (Pathshala student B).

Another student explained that civil action produced "an expansion of the field [of art]" that focused on an "ability to articulate my own positionality and context" while being in "dialogue with different positionalities" (RMIT student D). This relates to Azoulay's analysis of civil intention as requiring "a different kind of work than that required by human beings within their regular form of action" (2015, p. 107). This acknowledgement that the space of the civil is created through multiple perspectives, vantages, and experiences shows how the introduction of political theory shifted the boundaries of what a creative practice can do in the world. According to one student, identifying their civil intention "almost eliminated the possibility of any apolitical way of perceiving what I was doing . . . that was part of what I wanted to get out of it [to] be more in the world" (RMIT student A).

Beyond Aesthetics: Ethics and Civil Action

Students were supported to expand their creative practice beyond the "judgement of taste" (Azoulay, 2015, p. 10), and consider how their creative practice might become a form of civil action. Just as Azoulay uses political theory to show how photography creates political communities whose relations are constituted through shared concerns (the civil) rather than mediated through forms of governance (the civic), students used the framing of creative practice as civil action to guide their work. This departure from more familiar aesthetic practices, discourses, and evaluation caused some discomfort. RMIT student A shared that "coming from [fine art], I had no prior knowledge really of things like Azoulay or like a political end to my work." Another Pathshala student commented that "before this workshop, we were thinking about the technical aspects of the photograph: the beauty, how we compose these photographs but after this workshop, we were thinking about how to connect with people" (Pathshala student E).

The emphasis on process was impactful, with one student commenting that "the creative outcome to me was less important than the knowledge that had leached into me. . . . It was like . . . merely the beginning of a different way of thinking" (RMIT student A). A photo.circle student commented that their hierarchies of aesthetic interpretation were challenged through sharing their work with individuals directly connected to their project (photo.circle Student A). This fusion of political theory, civil action, and creative practice brought the students into relation with multiple viewpoints and experiences which raised ethical concerns about taking "action."

One RMIT student commented that most of the workshop was spent talking through the ethics of working on stolen Wurundjeri lands (the local First Peoples). Instead of finding a more comfortable topic, they used this discomfort as a "starting point" for group discussions and asked themselves, "Why are we doing this? Who are we doing this for?" (RMIT student C). They said while lengthy conversations in front of the whiteboard generated critical discourse, they came to realize the limits of critique as only one part of civil action. In comparison, Pathshala students explained their understanding of civil action through their experiences working with communities outside the classroom during their public exhibitions. They commented that the relational experiences with different communities and with each other profoundly impacted their thinking about civil action beyond professional cultures and aesthetic traditions in photography.

Pathshala students commented that working with publics was a significant transition that highlighted for them that creative practice as civil action was not only representational but also relational. In response to this, one student stated that prior to the workshop, "we never felt the need to make a connection with people" but "now we are thinking that . . . the connection with people [is] the primary thing for this work" (Pathshala student F). Another student commented:

> The placement of our exhibition was interesting because we went to the people, rather than a gallery. So, we were in a public place and tried to relate with people viewing the exhibition. And we also put up some [paper where they could write] their thoughts about our mission.
>
> (Pathshala student A)

As Azoulay suggests, civil discourse is possible when (creative) work is treated as a platform for relations (2015, p. 18).

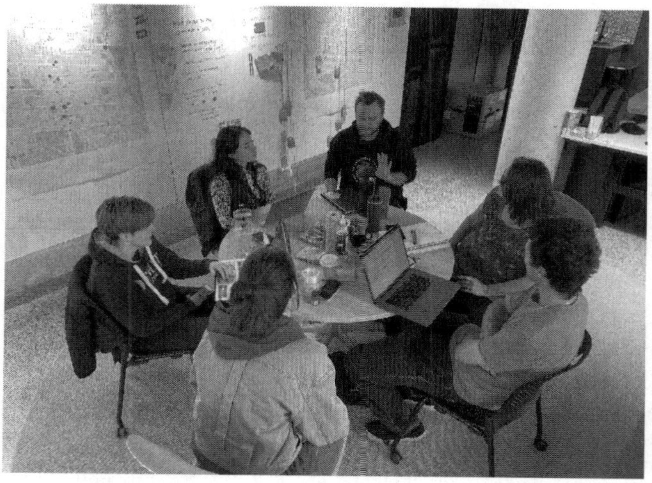

FIGURE 8.3 Student discussion as part of the Creative Practice as Civil Action workshop, RMIT Placelab Brunswick, unceded Wurundjeri Country, Naarm/Melbourne, December 2022. Photograph by Alan Hill.

Pathshala students also highlighted the importance of designing collaboration into the foundations of their chosen project on local road safety:

> When we finally did the exhibition . . . we started to make connections with people. Then somehow our curation also changed through [these connections]. Maybe if we started to think about the connection with people from the very beginning, then perhaps our exhibition would be more effective.
>
> (Pathshala student F)

These new relational challenges – such as receiving direct criticism from community stakeholders and inviting feedback at public exhibitions – assisted the students to understand that multiple perspectives and interdisciplinary contexts were key to understanding practice as civil action and how creative practice can help establish relations by opening space for dialogue about issues of shared concern.

Creating the Conditions for Civil Action

Pathshala and RMIT students spoke at length about how the collaborative emphasis across relational, educational, and disciplinary boundaries shaped their conversations, process, and outcomes. Pathshala students spoke about how the workshop helped them identify and question their reliance on binary understandings of practice: "we had to think beyond the binary . . . to work as a team, we had to cooperate in our thinking process. So that was the first challenge for us, like, we had to make one decision and make a team." They went on to explain that prior to the workshop, they were always late for class, but the collective atmosphere and responsibility of the project meant that they tried to arrive on time (Pathshala student B).

RMIT student C commented that while the lecturers were responsive and provided leadership there were "no weird power dynamics or hierarchies . . . Just a really level way of doing things meant that we were all a lot more open." RMIT student A explained that "there was some conflict within the group because of our interdisciplinary backgrounds. And I think we were able to, for lack of a better term, democratically make compromises." Disagreement and dissent generated critical questions for the group. RMIT student B commented on the "sense of urgency" that developed in relation to creating an environment where everyone felt comfortable to speak. They recounted scenarios where students who had been quiet initially started to share their discomfort with the direction of the project. This became valuable to their learning because these quieter voices raised important ethical questions that guided discussions and creative outcomes. Here we see students realize that different perspectives and experiences are not barriers, but pathways to co-create forms of action based on the specifics and contexts of these complex problems. RMIT student B continued:

> If there were people that were quiet and not participating, there was a real sort of urgency to get them to participate and . . . to give their own . . . perspectives in

a way that maybe they wouldn't have if they just were in a normal [classroom] environment where it wasn't asked of them.

In the Pathshala focus group, students commented that being forced to work together and navigate tensions in the group resulted in a greater intimacy in the group. A student reflected on how classes had previously been competitive, but this focus on civil action became about shared and distributed responsibility. Pathshala students highlighted the tensions that emerged in the group when different positionalities and experiences were brought into focus and that in some cases, these issues had caused deep self-reflection.

While photo.circle students did not work together on projects, they did encounter challenges around collaborating with the community – often on sensitive social and political topics. One student commented on how collaborating with community gave them confidence. "I showed my work to a lot of non-practitioners . . . and it was liberating and interesting how they could get into the work without any sort of explanation" (photo.circle student A). The same student spoke about working on a project about a significant political movement in Nepal but realizing after consultation with individuals associated with the movement that "some conversations should be left for the people to talk about in their own time." Here, processes of listening, valuing different knowledges, and self-determination became part of their expression of civil action – a reflection consistent across all three locations and contexts.

Conclusions

Creative Practice as Civil Action attempted to explore connections between photography, political theory, and visual culture as a framework for practice, using scholarship to make explicit the democratic potential of creative practice. What we found from working with students and educators in three distinct educational contexts is that these perspectives have not generally been part of their education to date, but that they do offer potential for examining intent, approaches to authorship, and methodologies addressing matters of shared concern. Positionality emerged as a key theme for both students and educators, which accords with the emphasis placed on relationality, reflecting the contrast of locating the practitioner within a political community, where their positionality becomes both apparent and significant. This appears to extend through the methods and priorities in the production of creative projects, where participants regularly commented on the heightened significance of "process" rather than on aesthetic "products" or outcomes. These findings can be understood as participants finding meaning and value in the civil framework introduced through its explicit surfacing of understanding of the civil and enabling participants to go beyond superficial understandings of their social motivations. In addition, the collaboration, negotiation, and collective decision-making within these learning communities seems to outline an additional dimension of democratic practice where we see evidence of the development and rehearsal of civil skills.

This form of creative education seems, then, to offer potential as a lived culture of democracy. For RMIT student C, it was refreshing to just "create an outcome that worked for the project and not be filling the criteria."

References

Azoulay, A. A. (2008). *The civil contract of photography* (R. Mazali & R. Danieli, Trans.; First paperback ed.). Zone Books.

Azoulay, A. A. (2015). *Civil imagination: A political ontology of photography*. Verso UK.

Badham, M. (2019). Spectres of evaluation indeterminacy and the negotiation of value(s) in socially engaged art. In *Co creation* (No. 5, pp. 205–216). CAC Brétigny.

Hill, A. (2022). *Beyond good intentions: Reframing documentary photography as a civil practice* [Doctoral dissertation, Griffith University]. Griffith Research Repository. http://hdl.handle.net/10072/416288

Hussey-Smith, K. (2023). Towards community praxis in community-oriented art education. In G. McQuilten & D. Palmer (Eds.), *The world we want*. Intellect Books.

Hussey-Smith, K., & Clarke, A. (2024). The future of photography and collaboration in education: Co-creating with civil intent. In M. Bertrand & K. Chambefort-Kay (Eds.), *Contemporary photography as collaboration*. Palgrave Macmillan.

9

ALL THE RELATIVES

Animating Stories of Democratic Participation Through Speaking Out

Maria Asp and Sonja Kuftinec

An elderly man in a plaid shirt and purple-shaded sunglasses sits amongst wildflowers. Behind him a sturdy branch wrapped with red, white, and black material leans against a tree trunk. He greets viewers with a Dakota phrase which he then translates to English. "In the language of the first Minnesotans, this is a greeting which means 'hello, my relatives, with a good heart I greet all of you with a handshake.'" Viewers are positioned in relationship with the speaker, as a "relative," but centering Dakota language and people: "the first Minnesotans." The speaker continues, inviting the audience to consider an upcoming lesson and story through a Dakota worldview:

> We have a phrase *Mitakuye Owasin*, all my relatives. It serves as a greeting, but more importantly, it's a teaching from our people. An ancient teaching which means we're talking about all living creation – the four-legged, the two-legged, the winged, the fish of the sea. They're all of our relatives.
>
> *(Speaking Out Collective, 2008)*[1]

This video greeting from Dakota elder and educator Dr. Chris Mato Nunpa (Wahpetunwan Dakota) orients elementary school students to a tale featuring cottonwood trees. But more importantly, he orients viewers to Speaking Out Collective's work with Indigenous artists and educators, building curriculum for Minnesota school teachers mandated to teach about Tribal Nations and through Indigenous ways of knowing.[2] A Dakota history and its worldview of interconnected being, and of place as relationship, complicates a US settler colonial narrative while also complementing core democratic values. In this chapter, we detail how Indigenous narratives and their teachings work alongside a 25-year-old storytelling

DOI: 10.4324/9781003475996-16

methodology to animate cultures of democracy rooted in self-expression and collaboration across differences.

This kind of collaboration requires skills in empathy, respectful critique, and co-creation. For over two decades, the co-authors have worked with an arts-based critical literacy practice – Speaking Out Collective (Speaking Out) – that animates cultures of democracy in schools and community centers through story. Developed by Dr. Jack Zipes in 2004, the Speaking Out methodology helps participants navigate and transform social scripts while becoming more confident narrators of their own lives (Zipes, 2004).[3] By learning to question, remake, and act out stories, children and adults practice making more equitable worlds together. Our primary case studies focus on students in Twin Cities public elementary schools. We argue that Speaking Out builds cultures of democracy through three primary means: (1) transforming space and place, (2) questioning power, and (3) telling new stories.

Reframing Place and Transforming Space Through Story

The greeting featuring Dr. Nunpa does more than center Dakota worldviews narratively. By taking place outdoors, the greeting activates the idea of interconnectedness with all beings, including trees, flowers, rocks, and soil. For Dakota people, land is a relative rather than a space of demarcation or ownership. Learning is also relational and can take place beyond classroom settings. Yet, when introduced to a lesson on the cottonwood trees growing a few miles away from classrooms on the banks of *Haha Wakpá* (the Mississippi River), many students report never having seen such trees up close. Classroom teachers work with Speaking Out teaching artists to prime the tale of "The Cottonwood Trees" with images and simple questions that invite attention to other beings. For example, "What are the trees near you that keep their leaves the longest?" A class at Anishinabe Academy took a field trip to the river, enlivening all the students' senses. "We can smell the river!" they announced while skipping rocks and writing poems to the trees. "The Cottonwood Trees" thus gently introduces students to new ways of thinking about their relations to other beings, about where learning can happen, and about how to learn *from* rather than simply *about* Dakota people. Such relational practices also animate cultures of democracy beyond ownership and property.

"The Cottonwood Trees," composed with Speaking Out by Indigenous storyteller and puppeteer Jennings Mergenthal (2023a), relates the story of Joey and *Deksi* (his Uncle Earl) who takes Joey on weekly walks along *Haha Wakpá*.[4]

> Every time they went on a walk, *Deksi* would teach Joey something new about the plants and animals that lived by the river, where the best fishing spots are, or one memorable time, how to make the best fart noises.

On this day, *Deksi* teaches about cottonwood trees. He notes that the trees require a lot of water, and "that's why they're by the river banks." Then he cuts open a branch to show Joey the star inside, relating a Dakota tale of how the star dropped from the sky to be closer to the people. *Deksi* teaches Joey about the buds that produce oil that can heal pain, and about the cambium layer of bark that can be ground to flour, but also about how to ensure sustainability by only taking what's needed. "Remember, it's not just you that the tree needs to feed." He points to eagles nesting above and then explains phytoremediation – "There's a good spelling quiz word for you!" – detailing how trees process heavy metals that can poison the soil and water. "The cottonwood trees are a vital part of this river ecosystem and important relatives to us all."

Students not only listen to a story featuring relationships to place, but they also transform the classroom and their relationships within it. They work together to move the desks, allowing space for them to sit together in a circle. The storyteller and teacher are now also on the same level with all the kids. Within the circle, students also learn to moderate their own expressive physicality. When spaces and bodies are regimented for much of the day, students can get easily over-activated. "I want to fly into the circle like this!" a student might cry out as their foot swipes close to a classmate's cheek. They learn to recognize that their personal freedom is limited at the point where it infringes on others: a core element of democratic culture-building.

Students build skills that foster relationships through games. They make shapes together without talking: an eagle's nest, a branch with buds, flying cotton fluff, the river, Uncle Earl's pickup truck. They learn not only how to communicate and work together nonverbally (which reduces arguments), but also that there are multiple "right" answers to creative prompts. "Look around and see how many ways there are to form a nest!" Circle games can also be places where students practice self-expression, collaboration, and how to share space and time by taking turns. Prompted to physically express an emotion like "This is unfair!" one student will freeze in place. Then a second and third add onto the first, learning to complement each other's ideas. They build rhythm orchestras together. They find ways to jump at the same time without a pre-ordained leader. They practice attunement and collaborative success learning that the classroom can be a space that is "leader-full."

Questioning Power and Making Rules Together

In addition to learning how to attend to each other and share space, the Speaking Out curriculum invites children to consider dynamics of power and authority. Students learn how to make rules for how to be together, which are core principles in activating cultures of democracy and respectful classrooms. Students *feel* what it is like to be successful together, building on the Dakota teaching of relational being. When a student struggles, we ask, "How can we be good relatives and help them through this moment so they get to retain their dignity?" Students learn that community is a shared responsibility. One classroom teacher noted: "Speaking Out was the only time during the week that all the kids could come together no matter what

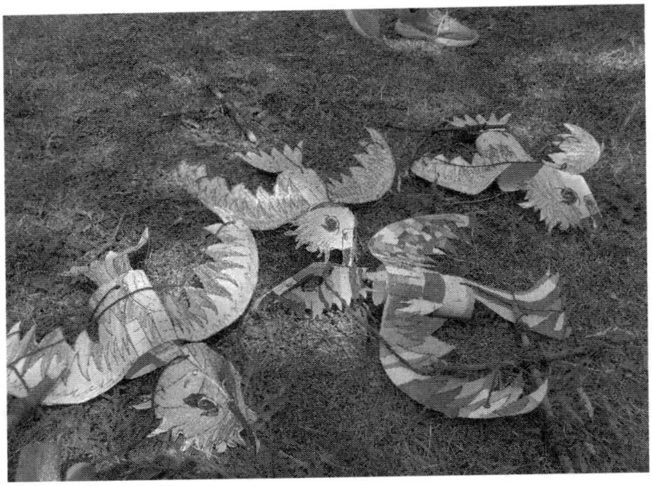

FIGURE 9.1 Minneapolis Public Schools third-grade students eagle marionettes. Photo by Maria Asp.

issues they were having with each other." As one student reflected, "It showed me I could act with my peers."

Other Indigenous stories reinforce these principles. In "Walleye Wars," composed by Ojibwe storyteller Madeline Miigwan Johnson (2023), friends in the story work through biases handed down from their families. They expand their thinking, and attitudes change. The story also complicates settler narratives around property rights and cohesive nation-state borders, introducing the idea of Native sovereignty and what it means to "follow the rules" when they are negotiated between nations. Makwa, an Ojibwe server in a cafe, overhears a conversation in which young people disparage Native fishing rights. "They don't have to follow the rules like the rest of us do." In response to this narrative, which Makwa discovers is shared by her friends Susie and Abdullahi, Makwa relates a counter story. "A long time ago there was no United States. There was no Minnesota and Wisconsin." She talks about the other nations – Ojibwe, Dakota, Potawatomi – and the ways that they resolved conflict through conversation, and how these nations later negotiated fishing rights with the United States in exchange for land use by settlers. Youth within the story learn to process emotions together and ask questions. "I guess learning can be uncomfortable at times and it's better when we help each other."

Students listening to the story, then animate its principles of thinking through complex narratives and relational compromise using some of the interactive tools of Theatre of the Oppressed.[5] "Zoom into the moment in the story where Makwa brings the customers their coffee. Is there anything she can say that might open up their thinking?" Students then take on the role of the customers and Makwa with the goal of expanding thinking rather than escalating conflict. The teaching artist acts as a "Joker," asking the class reflective questions: "Is learning happening? Did that choice raise or lower the tension? Can tension sometimes be productive?"

Students also make more personal connections to the story, practicing moving through conflict with grace. In small groups they create images of what concerns them with varying focus on the world, the neighborhood, and their school. They practice conflict resolution scenarios. "You are a group of friends. One of the friends is upset and overwhelmed. How do the other friends respond?"

Kids who are already under-resourced tend to struggle most with written literacy, and this disparity was amplified by COVID school closings. Speaking Out motivates them to access the written word as a technology of democratic participation through bringing joy into classroom learning. One student who lives in a foster home had been particularly struggling. However, after playing with a story of Anansi the spider, he wrote two full pages and triumphantly read his story to the class. As one fourth-grade teacher in the student's school noted, Speaking Out gets kids excited about their writing. "We saw so much growth in the students emotionally and academically. Our kids became more vocal, literally speaking out for themselves and they participated more in other classes."

In addition to learning how and where to speak out and how to access written literacy through play, students in Speaking Out also learn how to name and question power and authority. They do so through canonical stories as well as Indigenous tales. Kids ask why parents would abandon children (as they do in "Hansel and Gretel"), whether stepmothers are always "evil," and whether true riches can be measured in things. In remaking "Hansel and Gretel," one Somali boy assumed the role of the oldest child with multiple siblings and offered himself to be locked away so that his siblings wouldn't suffer. In responding to "The Pied Piper," students probed assumptions from the perspective of the rats in the tale, asking, "why should they have to move from their homes?" In stories relating Greek myths, students offered the thought that gods could be fickle, linking Greek gods to Marvel superheroes who destroy whole cities to save a single person. They wonder why Zeus would treat Prometheus so badly for sharing fire with humans. In taking on the role of Zeus, one student characterized the dangers of authoritarian power: "I'm going to make more humans so I can zap them with my lightning!" At the same time, when staging the story with their own spins, students in character might refuse to submit to Zeus's harsh leadership.

Teaching artists also work with classroom teachers to animate perspectives on power through creative means. In a 2021 class conducted via video due to COVID restrictions, graduate student teachers leading a Pied Piper lesson took on the persona of an antagonistic three-headed mayor at a Town Hall. Positioned as parents, the younger fourth-grade students (many of them first-generation Somali Americans) demonstrated their understanding of electoral politics by shouting that they were going to take the mayor to court and replace them with their teacher Ms. Amanda. "All in favor of kicking them out?" "Now it's time to vote for new people!"

Speaking Out invites students to question power relations ("Who makes the rules? Who has other kinds of power?") and perspectives ("Who don't we hear from?") in canonical tales. While telling "Robin Hood," for example, children might be assigned to listen to the tale from distinct perspectives: Robin Hood, the Sheriff, the poor people. Students consider how the story positions their character group, listening for what they say and do, and for what is said about them. Afterwards, students dialogue within their groups: How were they represented in the story? Did they make rules? Was anything missing? Did they have a voice? One student in the "poor people" group shared,

> I will tell you what was missing; like everything about us! We don't have names, and we are just an excuse for Robin Hood and the Merry Men to steal. How does he know what we need? When does he actually talk to us?

Their questions demonstrate that they understand core principles of creating cultures of democracy questioning modes of power that dictate to rather than being in relation with "the people." And after a lively discussion, students add missing scenes and change the story to make it their own.

Children also learn to question normalized hierarchies such as gender roles. In acting out their version of Little Red Riding Hood, the grandma might talk tough and carry a baseball bat. They craft dialogue questioning the speed of marriage in many fairy tales: "I need a background check before I'm marrying you!" They question tropes of desire: "Why that man want to kiss a dead woman??"

Through these techniques of storytelling, discussion, and enactment with more canonical tales, students practice questioning power and creating new narratives together. The Dakota curriculum adds historical complexity and multiple points of view. This curriculum can also teach students how to make effective change.

Making Change and Telling New Stories Together

A set of stories about a fourth-grade class field trip in Minneapolis illuminates how the Dakota curriculum might teach about and prompt social change within and outside of classrooms. "Field Trip," written by Jennings Mergenthal (2023b) for Speaking Out, unfolds in three parts. Each part centers on fourth-grade Dakota student Rachel, who lives in Minneapolis. In the first part, Rachel's teacher, Ms. Larsen, introduces the idea of a field trip to Historic Fort Snelling, a nearby settler landmark. Rachel tries to share a counternarrative from a Dakota perspective and instead gets sent home with a note about being a "disruptive influence on the classroom learning environment." Rachel's grandmother, *Uŋci* (Dakota for grandmother), rips the Fort Snelling permission slip into pieces, leans down to her granddaughter, and tells her:

> Your teacher may not understand, but we will help her see that when it comes to the story of our people; our land, and our representation in history, there is

always more than one side to every story. And the story you'll hear at Fort Snelling will not be one that includes Dakota history and Dakota experiences.

In the second part of "Field Trip," *Uŋci* relates a story of place to Rachel from the Dakota perspective, upending assumptions about geographic boundaries and positionalities. She sketches out a section of *Haha Wakpá* (the Mississippi River) where it meets *Mnísota Wakpá* (the Minnesota River). In order for Rachel to understand where she is on the map, she asks her grandmother to draw Minnesota in. "Surely, if that would help you, little one. But just remember, 'Minnesota' didn't exist at this time. And these state lines are just imaginary." Rachel watches her sketch with absorption, then interrupts, "Wait, hang on, *Uŋci*! You drew Minnesota the wrong way up! . . . the little bump on top is supposed to point North! We learned this in Geography in school." "Ah," replies *Uŋci*, "but who said that 'up' has to be North? . . . You've got to decolonize your thinking, little one." Rachel's grandmother then relates that the Dakota spatial perspective orients towards downstream and towards an origin story rooted in the Bdote–the sacred origin site of the Dakota people, where the two rivers meet. This terrain was later "traded" by a few Dakota leaders in 1805 to unauthorized US treaty signer Zebulon Pike. *Uŋci* walks Rachel and the listening audience through the complexities of that unsanctioned treaty signing, the resultant wars and decimation of the Dakota people, and their survival as present-day communities living alongside the rivers. She then encourages Rachel to share this story with her classroom to help them learn.

The story has cleverly shifted between two sites of learning, the classroom and the home, with two different models of teaching and worldviews: settler and Dakota. The third part of the story shifts back to the school, where the two perspectives come together (and occasionally clash). Self-exiled from the field trip, Rachel conceives of a plan with her classmates to introduce Dakota history through questions rather than counter-statements. She initially allies with her friend, Ahmed, and they compose questions on the back of the ripped-up pieces of her permission slip. Her classmates commit to asking these questions to the Fort Snelling guides: "Can we see where the Dakota prisoners were held at the fort?" "How do you honor the Dakota people who died here?" Rachel stays back at school and uses her time with the principal to teach him about the Dakota history she learned from her grandmother. When her classroom teacher Ms. Larsen returns, at first angered by the student revolt, she reconsiders her perspective and asks Rachel to help her understand, apologizing for not listening originally. "Saying sorry is like a land acknowledgement, Ms. Larsen," Rachel responds. "You have to back it up with action." Ms. Larsen then activates her new understanding, prompting the fourth-grade students to write letters to the Minnesota Historical Society (who run Fort Snelling) questioning the erasure of Dakota people and perspectives. Rachel then asks if the class could go on another field trip, to the Bdote next to Fort Snelling, but this time chaperoned by her grandmother. She and her grandmother both receive permission slips, and Rachel gets praised for being a "positive influence on the class."

The third part of "Field Trip" leans into building relationships, engaging with multiple perspectives by posing questions to authority, and to the ways that the power hierarchies of learning can shift. Importantly, the teachers and principal are positioned not as enemies, but as potential allies who can learn alongside their students and use their power to organize collective action. The second set of permission slips also counters how written words and policies, like treaties, have been used to disempower Dakota people. Here they represent the honoring of new relationships.

To animate the story, students again work with Theatre of the Oppressed techniques, taking on the roles of Rachel, Ms. Larsen, and a fellow bystanding student. The teaching artist reminds the class that we ALL often have multiple thoughts and emotions going through our minds at once, and it's not always obvious or understood through our actions. The fourth graders consider the moment when Rachel is blurting and Ms. Larsen tries to calm her down. They freeze into three images: Rachel raising her hand; the teacher trying to redirect Rachel; the fellow student watching. Other students then embody the range of emotions that each character might be experiencing, first standing in frozen images behind each character, then sharing the thoughts of that emotion. Through building this scenario, students recognize and work through the situation's complexities and what might prompt different actions.

In these stories and in their embodied responses, elementary school students are positioned as problem-solvers and change-makers. After listening to, discussing, and activating these stories, these students might even extend learning outside of the classroom. Teachers have taken students on field trips to the Bdote. In one fifth-grade class, a student shared the story with family members, who were then inspired to visit the Bdote and experience place-based learning together.

While the field trip stories offer fictionalized accounts of complicating historical narratives and modes of learning, another Speaking Out tale relates a personal narrative of social change. "*Maká Pahá*" (Dakota for Burial Mounds) details how St. Paul "Eastsider" and Dakota native Crystal Norcross (2023) educated herself. The story gestures to trauma and cultural loss, noting how Crystal's grandmother's federally mandated boarding school education in the mid-20th century violently cut her off from Dakota culture. But Crystal also shares about her own education through the Red Schoolhouse, created by the American Indian Movement, which was founded in Minnesota. Learning about her culture prompted Crystal to ask questions about the Burial Mounds in St. Paul, where Dakota history had been erased through problematic anthropological dating. As a teenager in 2008, Crystal cleans up the Mounds from the litter of the Fourth of July celebrations, which inspires others. "Some neighbors saw me and they came out and helped me." She continues to educate herself about the Mounds and eventually is elected to a Community Council. Through this political involvement, Crystal learns that the St. Paul Parks and Recreation Commission plans to build a splash pad on the Mounds. Crystal keeps asking questions and educating the Council, who, after learning about the sacredness of the site to Dakota people, change their plans. Crystal then gets the Parks Commission to shift the funds dedicated to the splash pad to correct the mislabeled signs at the park. "And we did. It's the summer of 2021 and you can see the change."

Conclusions

Crystal's story works on registers that both complement and complicate democratic practices in the United States. The story points to the federally mandated erasures of Indigenous people and cultures. But the story also highlights how individuals can become change agents through popular organizing and education. In not only listening to, but also taking on the perspectives of others through theater, students actively *practice* democratic culture-building. They do so not only as individuals but as part of a collaborative group. They learn to become change-makers together.

As John Bell details in his article on the Sioux War Panorama (1996), theatrical storytelling has been used to disseminate narratives of cultural dominance. The Panorama of the Indian Massacre of 1862 featured imagery rolled on a "cranky," or moving panorama of narrated images, presenting white supremacy rationalized by the master narrative of manifest destiny to settle the continent. When students hear the more complex narrative of the Dakota Wars, they "speak back" to that history with their own handmade crankies built from paper cups and construction paper. They animate what it means to relate history from multiple perspectives and ways of knowing.

The development of participatory democracy in the United States has a complex and contradictory history. The radical freedoms that philosophers like John Locke envisioned and that underlie founding documents of US democracy were premised, in part, on a sense of superiority over Native Americans and on an understanding of land as property rather than relation. When programs like Speaking Out take up the complexity of Indigenous stories and worldviews, they do so in ways that complicate historical narratives while also activating cultures of democracy. In order to promote and encourage this culture, it's best to start early.

Through Speaking Out, students can learn to question power in canonical tales. They collaborate on new ways of thinking through and restaging those tales. They extend empathy to embrace multiple perspectives and solve conflict through compromise. They learn that they are writers, creators, collaborators, and change agents. They learn to embrace all the relatives. And they do so wholeheartedly through play.

Notes

1 The video was created for Speaking Out Collective's "Truth Telling Residency Series," made possible in part by the National Writing Project with funding from the National Endowment for the Humanities and the Minnesota Humanities Center, with additional funds from the Arts and Cultural Heritage Fund created with the vote of the people of Minnesota on November 4, 2008.

2 The Minnesota Department of Education details these policies within a document outlining K-12 academic standards in Social Studies, available for download at https://education.mn.gov/MDE/dse/stds/. A study conducted by Odia Wood-Krueger (Métis) through the Shakopee Mdewakanton Sioux Community found that even those educators most eager to engage with the Education initiative felt under-resourced (2022).
3 For detailed accounting of the Speaking Out program's theories and origins see Zipes (1995, 2004). Also see https://www.speakingoutcollective.com/.
4 To develop stories, Speaking Out consulted with Indigenous educators and artists including Dr. Chris Mato Nunpa (Wahpetunwan Dakota), Odia Wood-Krueger (Métis), Ramona Kitto Stately (Dakota), and Graci Horne (Dakota/Lakota). They shared key points from these consultations with Indigenous story writers. Tales were subsequently tested with kids and revised for clarity. This process additionally indexes the back-and-forth embraiding of oral and written modes of storytelling.
5 Theatre of the Oppressed is a set of theatrical practices designed to create more equitable communities. In Forum Theatre, for example, participants ("spect-actors") try out different solutions to engage problematic scenarios. Rainbow of Desire techniques explore the complexity of human emotions and ideologies. For more on Theatre of the Oppressed, see Boal (1985, 1992, 1995).

References

Bell, J. (1996). The Sioux War panorama and American mythic history. *Theatre Journal, 48*(3), 279–299.

Boal, A. (1985). *Theatre of the oppressed* (C. A. McBride & M-O. L. McBride, Trans). Theatre Communications Group.

Boal, A. (1992). *Games for actors and non-actors* (A. Jackson, Trans.). Routledge.

Boal, A. (1995). *Rainbow of desire: The Boal method of theatre and therapy* (A. Jackson, Trans.). Routledge.

Johnson, M. M. (2023). *The walleye wars*. Unpublished manuscript.

Mergenthal, J. (2023a). *The cottonwood trees*. Unpublished manuscript.

Mergenthal, J. (2023b). *The field trips*. Unpublished manuscript.

Minnesota Department of Education. Retrieved May 11, 2023, from https://education.mn.gov/MDE/dse/stds/.

Norcross, C. (2023). *Eháŋna Wičháhapi* or *Maká Pahá*. Unpublished manuscript.

Wood-Krueger, O. (2022). *Restoring our place: An analysis of Native American resources used in Minnesota's classrooms*. Shakopee Mdewakanton Sioux Community.

Zipes, J. (1995). *Creative storytelling: Building community/changing lives*. Routledge.

Zipes, J. (2004). *Speaking out: Storytelling and creative drama for children*. Routledge.

10

THE RAY OF HOPE PROJECT AND WOMEN COMPOSERS FESTIVAL

Reframing Narratives

Alika Hope and Penny Brandt

The Ray of Hope Project began as a musical program to teach about the abolitionist movement of the 19th century that then grew into an organization centered on creating democratic artistic learning environments addressing 21st-century social justice issues. In this chapter we describe how the Ray of Hope Project was formed and discuss the democratic cultures and ways of working it both requires and fosters. We also address how the voices of composers, writers, and activists have been removed from or diminished in dominant historical narratives. Through this work, we realized that it is one thing to present and perform about those who fought for democracy, and quite another to actively role-model democracy as a creative practice by including youth and giving them voice to guide and enhance the focus of our work while addressing contemporary issues of human rights in the United States. We describe how the project has evolved over time and how it has become an integral part of the teaching of creative practices and the modeling of democratic culture through our work.

Alika Hope founded the Ray of Hope Project (ROHP) in 2013 with the goal of using African American spirituals to shed light on the combined antislavery efforts of Blacks and whites in 19th-century New England. The project included musicians and actors who incorporate African American spirituals with live music in participatory programs. We use historical records of successful African Americans to teach about slavery and 19th-century abolition movements. Collaborations with schools, libraries, and museums throughout the United States enabled ROHP artists to create poems and performance material. The project also uses the music and lyrics of 20th-century social justice songs to create conversations around current issues of global social justice issues. ROHP won a Gold Global Music Award and partners with other organizations using the arts to advance democracy and social change. In 2018, the Ray of Hope Project and the Women Composers Festival

DOI: 10.4324/9781003475996-17

of Hartford, then led by Penny Brandt, worked together to present a community engagement project and create a documentary to highlight historically underrepresented voices in classical music.

The Ray of Hope Project was founded as a direct response to the lack of inclusion of the voices of African American abolitionists in hegemonic antislavery narratives. Initially, ROHP presented performances and workshops around important African American abolitionists in New England whose voices and roles were excluded or diminished in history. They often worked in tandem with white abolitionists but did not receive the same "air play." As we began working with middle and high school students, the students expressed interest in creating reflective artistic work around current struggles that either they or their contemporaries experienced. When we started workshopping themes of enslavement, the students responded with discussions around child trafficking, loss of liberty, and other current issues in their BIPOC neighborhoods, which they felt directly connected to their ancestors' enslavement.

The work of ROHP takes on greater urgency now in maintaining a healthy democracy in the United States. Democracies require fair and complete histories taught in schools as well as open dialogue. Denial, distortions, and discouraging civil discourse are antidemocratic. As ROHP grew, opening the content and the learning process in the classroom to student voices became part of our practice.

Ray of Hope: The Backstory (Alika Speaking)

In 2006, the Children's Aid Society, a well-established nonprofit in New York City that began over 100 years ago, became a regular client. The relationship began when I was at Borough of Manhattan Community College, which is a CUNY college. I was a full-time professor in the teacher education department, teaching early childhood education courses, when one of the Children's Aid Society's sites invited me to participate in a federal assessment. They eventually had me coaching several of their sites. This relationship provided the springboard for me to branch out as a consultant and trainer. By 2013, I had several private clients in New York City, mostly early childhood programs like Head Start, and began coaching teachers and supervisors around social emotional learning, diversity, and music in the classroom.

Over the next several years, a particular Head Start program director, Esther, became a close friend. She had a staff of mostly Dominican and African American teachers and students in the Washington Heights/Inwood area. Esther kept asking me to do various training workshops, and I started making them up from scratch, programs such as "Young Children, Diversity, and You" and "Colorism within the African-American and Latine communities." I had a lot of fun over the years developing these workshops. Esther knew I was a professional musician and actor, and in 2013 she said, "I'd like you to come in and do a large workshop with a bunch of teachers from different sites around music and early childhood." I asked if they had the budget for me to bring in a musician or two, and Esther said "Sure, no problem." So, I brought in a musician I'd been playing with and performing with professionally for about a year, Ray Morant. Thinking back, I now see how Esther's encouraging me to develop workshops that met the needs of her staff was a great example of a democratic practice in action.

Ray and I led a workshop on music and early childhood in Washington Heights. Ray did some guitar-playing and drumming, I sang and talked academically about all the research on music and brain growth, and it was a great time. They were very impressed, the teachers learned a lot, and we made new friends. As Ray and I were driving back to Connecticut, I said to him, "I really want to do more of this work – using music and movement and acting to help teachers help children." And he said, "Yeah, I think that's a great idea." I remember this so distinctly: I was exhausted, because I also had young children at home who I was returning to after this performance about young children. And I said, "I need . . . we need a name for this thing, this project that we're going to do." I said, "What about something with our names," and Ray just blurted out "Ray of Hope!" And that day in the car, in 2013, ROHP was born.

Presenting and Performing Those Who Fought for Democracy (Alika Speaking)

At that time, my kids and I loved a historical reenactment museum open to the public with acres and acres of houses, actors, and animals. We'd often take my little kids up there so they could run around and learn about colonial history. And I noticed there wasn't much about the African American experience in New England. It was bothering me. I wanted to know what was going on in African American families during this colonial period! There were some exhibits on Indigenous people/Native Americans (in addition to the mostly European American exhibits). I kept thinking to myself, "There had to be some Black people around; why doesn't this historical place in New England have anything on African American history?"

When I got home, I emailed them, saying, "I noticed you really don't have much about African-American history . . ." and – on a whim – I added,

> I have a performance project, the Ray of Hope Project, and I would love to come and do a performance for you, for all ages, about African-American history in that time period. I think it would be a nice thing to add to your location.

I heard back the next day. Their coordinator of special events said, "Oh my goodness, Alika. Thank you for reaching out to us. We've been looking to add some of that to our programming."

Several months later, ROHP had their very first official performance. Ray and I were dressed in historic clothing that my mother helped us to sew and create. We brought a bunch of props. I ended up choosing to sing African American Spirituals, because I'd been singing them my whole life and knew the history of them. We ended up doing a workshop about Spirituals during an arts weekend they have every year. I was sure to tell people that many of the African American Spirituals come from a time after a lot of the colonial things that happened at this place. But it was a start. I talked about what was happening for African Americans, and I had some portraits of successful African Americans in Boston during the 1800s, and it went over really well. They asked us to come back the following year. I realized something new was being born.

In our second year performing there, a shooting in a Black church had taken place around the same time (Charleston, South Carolina, June 2015). The audience was almost all Caucasian people for our performance, and they were so moved. And even though we were doing "historical reenacting," people came up to me asking what they could do, how they could make a positive change in society to stop hate, and I entered into some powerful one-on-one conversations. The seed started to grow – the seed of creating a more hopeful, more compassionate, more empathetic, more democratic society through ROHP.

First Voice: Hearing from the Unseen (Penny Speaking)

I met Alika around 2010, when she messaged me through my website. She was looking for a pianist to rehearse some music at her house so she could also keep an eye on her young children. I learned she was a wonderful singer and actress with remarkable flexibility across styles; she sang opera and show tunes and also covered R&B hits with bar bands. She hired me to play for a benefit for Connectikids and for some of the Ray of Hope Project gigs. I also learned that she was connected to many communities of musicians from Hartford.

In 2014, I was asked to be the first president of the newly incorporated Women Composers Festival of Hartford, an organization that had existed informally since 2001, presenting music by women composers. I got involved because I was writing a dissertation on Italian composer Elsa Olivieri Sangiacomo Respighi (1894–1996), wife of the more famous Ottorino Respighi (1879–1936). I was excited to find other people who were interested in my research, and I enjoyed learning about music by other women composers. But I also felt there was something wrong with the way we were going about choosing music and presentations.

As someone who grew up in a home with less access, I taught myself to play piano by reading books. I struggled in graduate school with a mixture of implicit sexism and classism and often felt I didn't belong. By the time I was planning for the 2015 festival, I knew I wanted it to be a place where anyone could belong – especially anyone from Hartford, where the festival was located. Our concerts were held at Charter Oak Cultural Center, a vibrant multi-cultural arts center committed to social justice through the arts. In Hartford, nearly 30% of families live beneath the poverty line. More than two-thirds of the city's population is BIPOC. And yet, our festival performers and presenters were predominantly white, college-educated, and from middle- to upper-middle-class homes. Our programs showcased new music by living composers from these demographics with a smaller amount of historic music by women composers from 19th-century Europe or the early 20th-century United States. How could we possibly justify the "of Hartford" part of our name?

Because the festival was focused on classical music, and because I knew Alika was a well-trained soprano, I asked her to sing at the festival. I wanted to include songs by African American composers Florence Price or Margaret Bonds to increase the diversity of our offerings, and I offered to work with her to learn them. She said she would like to perform, and we talked about some possibilities. Then she got this thoughtful look on her face. "I wish there were a way to get the Ray of Hope Project involved. I know it's a women composers festival," she said, "but do Spirituals count? I mean . . . we don't really know who wrote them, and some of them could have been composed by women."

Oh.

Talk about a lightbulb moment. Here, we have an entire genre of music, where we don't know the gender of the composers, because enslaved people don't get author's rights. We know that women like Harriet Tubman used Spirituals to help guide enslaved people to freedom through the underground railroad (Bradford, 2018, p. 17). But we don't know anything about the individuals who composed them.

For the 2015 festival, I arranged for our first concert to be free and open to the public. It was a lecture recital at Capital Community College for an audience of around 200 – our largest audience to date. We presented "The Invisible Woman," with research on how and why women composers have "disappeared" from history books. We had music by Barbara Strozzi (1619–1677) and a newly composed piece by WCFH founder Heather Rupy Seaton (b. 1975). But up first was Alika Hope, singing "Sometimes I Feel Like a Motherless Child," creating a space for us all to mourn generations of women creators whose work was prevented, destroyed, or rendered invisible by enslavement.

By audience reaction, this was the right choice. We forged a connection between a new music festival and the community in which it was located. Because the Spiritual was in English and sounded familiar, many people in the audience were more interested in connecting to the music and understanding the cause. The experience allowed them to listen curiously to the unfamiliar Strozzi duet in Italian and to Rupy's postmodern dissonance. The experience was transformative for me as President and later Artistic Director of the organization. I realized that there were people like Alika already doing good work in Hartford, and that our organization could benefit only if we found ways to invite them to help plan the festival. We could democratize our process and incorporate many more voices from the community in our programs, resulting in deeper connections and increased audiences.

That same year, I decided to add a 12-hour marathon of music by women/non-binary composers, to stand in opposition to the many organizations who said, "There just isn't any music by women out there for us to play." We didn't have the resources to pay for or curate 12 hours of music by women/nonbinary composers, so we just invited people to sign up and play what they wanted to play. My only role was to schedule the performers in a way that would make it reasonably easy to change the stage around between acts. The response was incredible, and the first marathon was almost indescribable as a beautiful, stained-glass, eclectic collage. Because we advertised the opportunity for any type of music created by women, we received applications across genres from a more diverse group of composers and performers than we had ever received. There was a harp duet, an electric violist, a couple of singer-songwriters, and a pianist playing a Florence Price sonata. A local college student presented show tunes by women. Alika sang another set of Spirituals. I played a cradle song by Teresa Carreño. A composer twisted synthesizer knobs to create electronic music while drawing a self-portrait. We ended with a brass quintet playing a new piece that we had won a grant to commission. Overall, the folks in charge of the Women Composers Festival of Hartford had stopped trying to curate and instead simply opened our doors and said, "What do you want to do?" The day was so much richer and fuller than anything the organization had been able to plan on its own.

Listening and Growing (Alika Speaking)

As people continued to ask us to do performances, I didn't think I could handle all of the requests; I was homeschooling my children, working, trying to change the world. I didn't have the time or energy to negotiate contracts! I found a talent agent in Boston who I thought might be a great fit, and she took us on. That changed everything, because suddenly I had someone who was able to find and book programs for us and ask for the kind of money that my soft heart was not very good at asking for.

Our first gigs were about how Blacks and whites worked together in the East to free slaves in the South. Initially our work was around talking about, performing about, singing the songs of, and reading the readings of white abolitionists like William Lloyd Garrison, Prudence Crandall, and also Black abolitionists, intermixed with singing and conducting dialogues with the audience or participants.

From there, we started doing after-school productions, a kind of "Black history through music." I ended up hiring an additional eight musicians and actors, and we did some performances for community libraries and for a couple of well-known museums. We received a grant to work with the Oregon Jewish Museum to create and lead a residency that brought together students from a Jewish high school and a predominantly Black high school in Portland that centered on breaking down barriers and bias. I also gave a lecture about Jewish abolitionists. I remember this rabbi sitting in the front row listening with rapt attention as I discussed the Jewish antislavery abolitionists I'd researched. In that moment I felt so connected to him, to how our mutual ancestors had fought for access to freedom and democracy for all.

The Ray of Hope Project was actively doing performances and all-school assemblies. I'd also meet with individual classes and have them create their own responses to music or have them write Spirituals with their own words, and various things that were aligning with the Common Core curriculum at the time.

Soon, ROHP started to shift based on what people in the community wanted. We were at a middle school, in the Hartford area, and a student asked, "Do you do anything around child sex trafficking?" And I was . . . kind of in shock, but I said, "Tell me more about that." These were middle schoolers, and they knew all about it. Because of the questions these students asked, I met with this class of seventh graders a couple of times, and we looked into the history of child and sex trafficking in the Hartford area. I asked them to create PSAs, and they did some skits on trafficking, how they felt about it, and how it was affecting community and awareness. That was our foray into greater social justice work.

We ended up performing at the inaugural International Human Rights Arts Festival in New York City in 2017. That was wonderful, because it was a festival that still happens every year and has grown a lot. I brought five men and Penny with me, and we not only performed the Spirituals, but we started talking about larger social justice issues – particularly in the Black community. But it was because of those middle schoolers that I felt at peace expanding beyond just talking about slavery and abolition.

By the time the International Human Rights Arts Festival came along, our performances and workshops had morphed into a larger focus on social justice in the African diaspora and/or Black Americans. And that just shows the power of democracy in our performances, because after events with the kids, we would just ask them what they were interested in. And because we were able to work with kids from age three up to seniors in high school, no performance of ROHP was ever the same.

Some Lessons We Learned

1. *Think **outside** the box*. Sounds so simple, right? Of course we think outside the box – we're artists! But sometimes, when someone asks us to create something for schools or children or a community center, we feel like, "Oh, we better do this right, or we may endanger the lives of future generations." You can always think outside the box and brainstorm, have ideas that are grandiose and wild and things that you could never do without a spare $5,000 for extra instruments. And then you can bring those ideas back down to the constraints you have. But if you don't start by first thinking outside the box, you'll never know what your limits really are.
2. *Think **inside** the box*. When we are creating programs, we need to align them with educational, organizational, and community standards. We often refer to Common Core or state standards for educational institutions, which can easily be found on websites for state education departments, but this can also refer to understanding the common culture of a neighborhood or the mission of a particular organization. The better we were able to align with those guidelines and expectations for groups we were performing for, ironically, the more freedom

we had to create great programs. We knew we were making teachers, principals, and other stakeholders happy. We could take those existing standards ("inside the box") and get really creative with them. This also applies to aligning with granting organizations in order to secure funding.

3. *First Voice: Involve the opinions of different generations.* When you're doing historical programming, if you are able, ask people who may have been alive during that time period. For example, when we were doing a musical piece about segregation, my father – who was born in Mississippi in 1946 – as a child lived in a segregated state. I did a video interview with him because he was a firsthand source. He talked about what it was like being a Black boy in Mississippi during segregation. His firsthand account and information, words, and video all really helped to bring life and reality to something that is kind of foreign or feels "way-back-when" to kids. That also democratized our creative practice, because I didn't just go to a history book to get information – I actually talked to someone who was there, and somebody whose voice during that time period of segregation definitely would not have been heard or acknowledged. Similarly, when we would go to schools, particularly middle schools, I always tried to ask middle schoolers how we could make a workshop better and asked what they would like to talk about. That was very helpful. When the students wanted to talk about child sex trafficking, this was a touchy subject, and I had to clear some things by the teachers and principals of the schools. When we were able to weave that subject into slavery that took place in this country a couple of centuries ago, it created a strong connection for those teens and preteens.

   (**Penny Speaking**) When I took over the Women Composers Festival of Hartford, most of our score calls were directed to "emerging composers" with an age limit of 35. I happened to meet Elizabeth Austin (b. 1938), who had studied with Nadia Boulanger in the 1950s in Paris, but gave in to societal pressures, married, had kids, and gave up composing for several decades. She lamented to me, "What about me? I'm 80 and I never emerged. Where is the score call for me?" After that, I removed all age limits from WCFH. We started having multigenerational events. Women who had lived through several feminist movements began sharing their stories and offering mentorship and friendship to younger composers. It became a richer experience for everyone!

4. *Inclusivity matters.* Democracy in action means making sure that everyone's voice is heard. Democracy in action means *inclusivity* in action. I remember one fifth-grade class that as I walked in, the teacher made sure I knew who the "bad" kid was. Well. I, of course, reinterpreted that as "Oh, this is the 'BAD' kid? I'm going to make sure he's a star of what we do." I watched that young man, a fifth grader, and got to know him by asking questions. What I understood was that he needed more attention. He had learned that the way to get attention was to engage in difficult behaviors. But he also had a very loud speaking voice, and he didn't quite have control over some of his bodily actions. He would sometimes flail his arms or jump up and sit down in class. Even though I have a MA

in special education, I wasn't going to diagnose him there. What mattered to me was trying to find his strengths and bring him into the process. I realized he liked jumping around and had a loud voice, and I wanted him to be a leader in the class. So, I asked that young man to stand next to me during our workshop days, and when I needed something to be done in a call-and-response manner, I would often ask him to lead the call and response. He loved doing it, and the class started responding to him. We were able to get some democratization in the classroom and help him realize that he's not a failure – he's a leader.

Reference

Bradford, S. H. (2018). *Scenes in the life of Harriet Tubman*. W. J. Moses.

11

THE POWER OF STORYTELLING

Practicing a Culture of Democracy With Young Students

Kiyoko Motoyama Sims

Introduction

Over the last 25 years I have been involved in the learning space as an educator, teaching artist, and arts administrator. My experiences include practical classroom teaching, training educators, developing curriculum, working with students of diverse ethnicities, socioeconomic backgrounds, abilities, and life experiences ranging from age five to adulthood; and collaborating with an army of talented teaching artists. I have seen how arts strategies activate young people's imaginations and empower them to become critical thinkers and inspired citizens with intercultural competency. I refer to intercultural competence as the capability to function effectively across cultures defined in one of the leading cultural competency models, Cultural Intelligence (CQ) (Leung et al., 2014). CQ consists of four factors – metacognition, cognition, motivation, and behavior (p. 494). Citizens with intercultural competence appreciate multiple points of view, are aware of their biases, adjust their behaviors, and take actions towards a more equitable society. These skills are essential to the culture of democracy, where multiple viewpoints continue to intersect and evolve. In this chapter, I explore my own growth as a practitioner and how storytelling and theater strategies create an educational environment where students critically examine and transform narratives, participate in problem-solving through collaboration, develop their intercultural competency skills, and practice activating their power as change agents.

Background

I was born and raised in Tokyo, Japan. I went to girl's schools from PreK to 12th grade, which were feeder schools to the Japan Women's University (JWU), the

DOI: 10.4324/9781003475996-18

oldest women's university in Japan. I attended JWU and graduated with a major in English, earning a teaching license for middle and high schools. The educational philosophy at JWU and their feeder schools were fairly liberal in the context of a male-dominated Japanese society. They nurtured our leadership skills and taught us that young women have the power to accomplish anything if they put their minds to it. However, JWU's pedagogy was predominantly based on the banking model, where teachers downloaded their knowledge and the students were assessed based on how much they remembered from the lectures. Arts strategies beyond the fine arts and performing arts classes were not commonly employed. Teachers did not encourage students to actively question materials presented to them. Discussion-based or project-based work was rare. As a result, learning opportunities to develop your own idea, debate, and collaborate with others were limited. This is not surprising, as Japanese culture cherishes the importance of being part of the group over individualism.

After graduating from JWU, I moved to the United States to pursue graduate studies in theater arts. As I built my career as a teaching artist/administrator, my philosophy towards education pedagogy began to shift. I was fortunate to experience two significant events which changed my perspective on the power of storytelling and arts strategies. My first opportunity came when I met Rhodessa Jones, Co-Artistic Director of Cultural Odyssey and Founder and Director of the Medea Project based in the San Francisco Bay Area. She invited me to join the Medea Project as an associate performing artist in the late 1990s. The Medea Project: Theatre for Incarcerated Women is "an award winning performance workshop committed to the personal and social transformation of women" ("Rhodessa Jones & the Medea Project," n.d., para. 1).

The Medea Project brought a team of artists and a social worker to the San Francisco County Jail to work with women inmates. Through storytelling, theater, dance, and creative writing workshops, we used "The Ugly Duckling" by Hans Christian Andersen as a framework for the inmates to examine the cause of their incarceration and reimagine their lives. These workshops led us to create a performance piece presented at the Lorraine Hansberry Theater and performed by both artists and inmates under the direction of Jones. As an assistant to the director and an associate performing artist, I witnessed how a fairy tale became a springboard to delve into social justice issues and transformed the narrative to reflect the lives of inmates. I learned that the story even in the fairy tales was not fixed, and arts strategies could be used to reshape the story.

The second significant opportunity came when I became a teaching artist with the Neighborhood Bridges Program (Bridges) at the Children's Theatre Company (CTC) in Minneapolis in 2005 and later joined the administrative team. Eventually, as Director of Community Engagement, I supervised Bridges in collaboration with Maria Asp, Bridges Program Director at that time. Founded by Jack Zipes, Bridges is a critical literacy program with the goal of empowering young people to "become the storyteller of their own lives" (Zipes, 2004, p. 52). The Bridges philosophy was grounded in pedagogical framing by Zipes, Gianni Rodari, and Paulo Freire. It "challenges students to identify the roots of social issues in a story and work through them collectively" (Sims, 2014, p. 5). Meeting Zipes was a transformational moment. His pedagogy embraces a student-centered approach, employs the tales as a framework to deep dive into cultural contexts, and encourages learners to transform the narrative. During my 15 years at CTC, I saw how storytelling could nurture young students to open up their minds, develop their social and emotional learning skills, and become critical and creative thinkers.

My experiences in the Medea Project and the Bridges program helped me realize the power of storytelling, which fosters participants to activate their imaginations, cultivate their intercultural competency skills, and practice exercising citizenship as change-makers. Since then, arts strategies have become the bedrock of my teaching philosophy.

"The Wolf and the Sheep"

I am going to share examples from three genres – fables, stories based on real lives, and tales from historical events to unpack how students learn from stories and creative activities.

Fables offer effective framing where students can analyze power structures and bias embedded in the story. As tales are written as metaphors, young people identify and challenge social and cultural values in the context of the story. During my time with the CTC's Bridges Program we often used strategies to uncover multiple points of view through the text.

Let's look into how key strategies were applied in the short fable "The Wolf and the Sheep" by Aesop. First, students were divided into small groups and asked to listen to the story from an assigned character's perspective. In "The Wolf and the Sheep," each group can be assigned to the wolves, the sheep, the dogs, or the farmers. It is intentional to use at least one character group which is marginalized in the story. The participants listened to the tale:

> Once, the wolves sent an embassy to the sheep to make a peace treaty between them for the future. "Why should we continue such deadly strife?" the wolves asked. "The dogs are the cause of it all. They're constantly barking at us and provoking us. Send them away, and there will no longer be any obstacle to our eternal friendship and peace." The silly sheep listened, and the dogs were dismissed. As a result, the flock was deprived of their best protectors, and the sheep became an easy prey for their treacherous enemies.
>
> *(Zipes, 1992, p. 109)*

Following the storytelling, each character group held a small group discussion and shared what they discussed with the whole class. A teaching artist provided prompts such as "What bothered you about this story?" "Is there anything missing from your character's point of view?" "Did you have power in the story?" These prompts are designed to uncover hierarchies and biases through critical literacy. I refer to critical literacy as "an orientation to reading (listeners/viewers), how readers position texts, and how texts are positioned within social, cultural, historical, and political contexts" (Lewis et al., 2010, p. 1). These questions led to rich discussions. The group of the wolves found themselves to have the most power in the story, but they often were not comfortable that their characters were portrayed as villains. The sheep were bothered by how the story described them as "silly," and they ended up being victims of injustice. As for the question about power, the sheep group often said they actually had the power to say "no" to the wolves but did not exercise their agency. The groups of dogs and farmers did not enjoy being silenced in the story. I remember students assigned as dogs sharing that they didn't even get to say ANYTHING. While the farmers who owned dogs and sheep recognized their potential power to avoid this tragedy, they did not like the absence. This discussion revealed multiple perspectives embedded in the text and offered the springboard for the following creative activities.

After participating in theater games, each character group was asked to create a short scene reflecting their viewpoint and power. We encouraged students to change the narrative if they did not agree with the original tale. They could create alternative endings or the scene which was missing from Aesop's tale but was important for their characters. They had about 10–15 minutes to rehearse and perform. During this process, as a teaching artist, I did not direct the students. I facilitated the process so that the students could work autonomously. Young people had to negotiate and agree on what scene they wanted to create. If there were disagreements, they had to work through as a group and resolve on their own.

I witnessed a variety of creative scenes from my students. The wolves' group performed a scene preceding this story. The wolves were starved as they had not eaten for days, and as a result, they planned to attack the sheep out of necessity. They wanted to show the reason why the wolves had to eat the sheep and justify their action. The sheep created a scene when they were debating the wolves' proposal and ended up saying "no" to the wolves. The dogs decided to get involved and convinced the sheep that wolves were trying to trick them. The other group of dogs performed the scene where they discussed how to break the news to the farmers that the sheep were eaten by the wolves. They were afraid of losing their job as a protector of the farm. The farmers intervened when the wolves came to eat the sheep. The students enjoyed watching how each group reimagined the Aesop narrative as the performance afforded a fresh look to the original tale. According to Lewis et al., creating a new scene by transforming a narrative that "challenge[s] assumptions of the story or the way the listener is positioned by the story" indicates one of the patterns of critical literacy skills (2010, p. 4). I often noticed that the groups who were marginalized showed pride after changing the narrative and regaining their power. They were given opportunities to practice how to advocate for themselves, deconstruct hierarchies, and address injustice as a change agent.

At times, students could not come to an agreement, and there was no scene to perform. In these instances, I used a student-centered approach. I asked the group to reflect on their rehearsal process and let them identify what they would change for their future collaboration. As young citizens, they need to learn how to negotiate and compromise. It is important to provide productive spaces where the students can experiment, learn from their mistakes, and discover their own collaborative strategy.

Fables such as "The Wolf and the Sheep" offer a safe way to introduce the lens of social justice. Creative tools based on viewpoints allow students to experience the narrative from the character's point of view while recognizing the multiple layers of perspectives in the text. I believe that valuing the other viewpoints, which are marginalized, and developing empathy is the first step to nurture young citizens' intercultural competencies. These skills deepen their knowledge and awareness of others. Performing alternative scenes afford opportunities for the students to exercise critical literacy skills, practice activating their citizenship as a change-maker, and address social inequity through collaborative problem-solving.

The Paper Bag

I'll also share my experience of teaching *The Paper Bag*, a story written by Emily Dahdah, and look into how the story, based on real-life experiences, fosters the students to develop all four factors of their intercultural competency referred to in the CQ model; motivation, cognition, metacognition, and behavior. In the Twin Cities area, we work with many Somali American students. In some classrooms, they are the largest cultural group. Minnesota has the largest Somali American population in the United States (CBS Minnesota, 2019, para. 1), and Somalis are almost exclusively Muslims (International Institute of Minnesota, 2017, para. 4). According to Minnesota Compass data between 2015 and 2019, 77.8% of the Somali population live in the Twin Cities, and 56.9% of them are under 18 (2022).

While the Bridges curriculum included Somali stories, they lacked the contemporary tales from the Somali American community. We as Bridges staff wanted to address this gap as the students needed to see themselves reflected in the curriculum. Culturally relevant curriculum (CRE) with which students identify is one of the key components to create an educational space that "validat[es] students' experiences and values" (Bryan-Gooden et al., 2019, p. 4). With a three-year grant from the Doris Duke Foundation for Islamic Arts' Building Bridges Program, we had an opportunity during 2017–2020 to work with the Somali community, collaborating with the local writers who wrote tales based on community interviews. One of the stories was "The Paper Bag," in which Dahdah reflected experiences of a Somali American educator in the Twin Cities.

The Paper Bag centered around fictional characters, 13-year-old Fatima, who traveled to New York City with her 8-year-old brother, Abdul, to visit her mom. Although Fatima had traveled multiple times on her own, this was the first air travel experience for Abdul. As they were waiting to board the plane to New York, both were subjected to an additional search as another traveler reported that a paper bag held by Abdul could be a security threat. The paper bag contained his favorite candies, which his father had given him.

After being cleared by security, Fatima and Abdul boarded the plane only to find out that they would be sitting next to the lady who reported the paper bag as a security threat. She demanded the flight attendant find her another seat, but was told that the plane was full. Although Abdul wanted to go home, Fatima told him, "I want you on this plane, Abdul" (Dahdah, 2018, p. 2). The story ends as follows:

> Fatima and Abdul took their seats, and the woman moved herself as far to the window as she could and as away from them as possible. Abdul started eating his candy bars, and Fatima started thinking, "This can't keep happening." She wanted things to change, not so much for herself, but for her brother. She knew she had to do something.
>
> *(Dahdah, 2018, p. 2)*

The story illustrates how everyday lives of young Somali Americans are affected by Islamophobia. Based on teaching in various classrooms and hearing reflections from other teaching artists, I discovered that *The Paper Bag* fosters multiple layers of learning. First, for Somali students, the tale offers the opportunity to provide leadership in the classroom by sharing their culture and experiences. I remember observing how Somali students' engagement deepened when I told this story.

I also saw the profound impact on the students who were not Somali Americans or Muslims. For these students, this story often landed emotionally and gained cultural knowledge which was different from theirs. Participants were able to develop CQ cognition, also known as CQ knowledge which is referred as "one's level of cultural knowledge or knowledge of the cultural environment" (Goh, 2012, p. 401).

Following the discussion, I asked the students to develop alternative endings and reminded them that they could change the narrative if it bothered them. I was always amazed by their creativity. In one scene, two passengers volunteered to switch their seats with Fatima and Abdul so that they did not have to sit next to the woman. In another scene, several passengers took out their cell phones and started filming as the woman began complaining. As a result, she became quiet. I also saw the scene where the flight attendant asked the woman to leave the plane. All the scenes had a common thread; the students wanted to help Fatima and Abdul and find a way to practice their agency. It was heartwarming to observe how participants wanted to empower two young characters and find possible strategies to intervene. By creating alternative scenes, the young people recognized the power of bystanders and reshaped the narrative by using their critical thinking and collectively problem-solving as young citizens.

This theater activity fosters students to develop metacognitive, motivational, and behavioral facets of CQ. By analyzing the original ending, which was unsettling to many of the students, they became aware of the complex cultural interactions among characters on the airplane and worked together to create an alternative ending. This process reflects metacognition, also referred to as CQ strategy, which "can be described as one's level of awareness and ability to plan in light of the cultural understanding" (Goh, 2012, p. 401). It also shows the sign of a motivational factor: they all wanted to reconstruct the narrative to support Fatima and Abdul. Performing a newly constructed ending reflects behavioral intercultural competency, which is considered as CQ action/behavior, "the level of adaptation when relating . . . in culturally diverse situations" (Goh, 2012, p. 402).

The 1963 Children's Crusade

The 1963 *Children's Crusade,* a story based on the Children's March, creates an opportunity to examine the historically important, but often overlooked, moments from the young characters' point of view. By living inside of characters' viewpoints through creative activities, participants deepen their intercultural capabilities by expanding their cultural knowledge and awareness of complex thought processes.

The Children's March took place in Birmingham, Alabama, in May 1963. Thousands of African American children successfully carried out the march under the leadership of Rev. James Bevel, Rev. Ralph Abernathy, and Dr. Martin Luther King (Clark, 2021, para. 15). These leaders originally wanted to organize African American adults to march against segregation. However, it was too risky for adults, as they could lose their jobs or house. As a result, children were recruited. During the span of several days, thousands of children marched, got arrested, and overwhelmed the system. The Children's March "moved President John F. Kennedy to express support for federal civil rights legislation and the eventual passage of the Civil Rights Act of 1964" (National Museum of African American History and Culture, n.d., para. 3).

I worked with a writer, Greer Lichtenberg, who developed *the 1963 Children's Crusade* based on available research materials. The story is written through the viewpoint of three African American high school students who participated in the march. The narrative reveals how they had to weigh the risks of joining the Civil Rights Movement and work through challenges by participating in the march.

I taught this story to elementary to high school students and saw a powerful impact. The tale made a strong connection to the students, as the narrative was told from the young students' viewpoints, relevant to their age group. One of the theater strategies I often utilize is to show the spectrum of students' thoughts in the classroom space. This activity is particularly effective to develop their intercultural capabilities in the area of cognition/knowledge and metacognition/strategy. For instance, following the storytelling, I asked the high school students to imagine themselves as teenagers recruited to participate in the Children's Crusade. If they were going to the march, they could stand towards the left side of the classroom. If they were not, they could move towards the right side of the classroom. If they were not sure, they could stand in the middle. The students are encouraged to stand on any part of the spectrum, as often these thoughts are not easily divided into yes or no. In this classroom, most of them stood towards "yes," and some stayed in the middle. I asked volunteers to share the reasons for their decisions. Most of them wanted to participate as they believed in the cause. Students who were supportive of the march but expressed concerns about their safety decided to stay in the middle.

Next, I told the students that they were a parent of an African American child recruited to participate in the march. If they allowed their child to go, they could move towards the left. If they did not allow their child to march, they could stand towards the right. This time, selecting where to stand was not easy. The high school students took time to think through their options and picked their place carefully. I noticed most of them stood towards "no," a few students stood in the middle, and a couple of them stood in the "yes" area. I invited students to share their reasoning. One student, standing on the right side of the room, said that there was a possibility of their child getting hurt and they would like their child to stay home. Another student who stood in the "yes" area mentioned that they believed in the cause of the Civil Rights Movement and wanted to honor their child's decision. After the comments, some participants recognized their bias, changed their mind, and moved from the "no" to the "yes" area. Stepping inside of the character's mind led students to deepen their respect towards march participants and their parents as they found making decisions in pivotal moment of history difficult.

This exercise visualizes the complexity of the decision-making process. It encourages the students to see multiple viewpoints simultaneously, and allows them to change their minds by hearing other's perspectives. This strategy nurtures the fluidity of the storyline; the narrative is never fixed. This activity offers students to gain cultural knowledge by embodying the character's minds in the historically charged moment and practice their strategy – how to be aware of others' decision-making process, check their biases, and make a plan to change their opinion (Goh, 2012, p. 401). All these factors are essential capabilities for intercultural competency.

I often ended my teaching by asking the students about the issues they feel strongly about and letting them explore actionable steps towards their cause through writing. I heard a variety of topics, including racial justice, gender equity, environmental issues, LGBTQIA+ rights, and immigration. I wanted my students to apply their learning to their lives and start activating their power and agency as future leaders.

Conclusion

Implementation of stories with creative activities has generated multiple levels of learning and a culture of democracy in educational spaces. First, storytelling offers a framework where students develop critical literacy skills, including questioning the text, uncovering the roots of social and cultural contexts embedded in the narrative, and reimagining the story.

Second, introducing culturally relevant stories fosters deep engagement among all learners. The students who find close connection to the story cherish their opportunity to take a leadership role, while others challenge their assumptions and expand their viewpoints. As a result, young people value their own voices and learn how multiple viewpoints can coexist and be appreciated.

Third, as most arts strategies require group activities, students develop their collaboration skills, another essential tool for young citizens. Whether the learners are discussing the story or performing a new scene, they need to work together and solve problems collectively. Because of the student-centered approach, students are positioned to lead, advocate, negotiate, compromise, and achieve consensus as a group. I have seen that navigating through challenges and finding their own solutions only strengthens the development of their interpersonal and leadership skills.

Finally, the storytelling and theater activities allow students to develop all four factors of intercultural competency – CQ motivation, cognition/knowledge, metacognition/strategy, and behavior/action. Listening to and analyzing a story from a character's point of view and playing theater games allows the students to be in someone else's skin and empathize with the character's emotion. When learners are exposed to the characters that differ from their background, they expand their cultural knowledge and deepen their awareness in cross-cultural understanding. As the participants validate the character's perspective and identify injustice, they explore strategies to change the text, reflecting their social justice values, and take action by devising an alternative scene, empowering marginalized characters. These activities lead students to realize their power as change-makers.

It is my hope that storytelling and arts strategies can be actively integrated in a variety of learning spaces where learners develop their creativity, deepen their global perspectives, and, as a result, become critical thinkers and citizens with intercultural competency. I encourage both educators and students to collaborate and create a culture of democracy where young citizens continue shaping their narrative with confidence, practicing their agency as future leaders and actively contributing to a global society with ever-shifting paradigms.

References

Bryan-Gooden, J., Hester, M., & Peoples, L. Q. (2019). *Culturally responsive curriculum scorecard*. Metropolitan Center for Research on Equity and the Transformation of Schools, New York University.

CBS Minnesota. (2019). *What is the history behind Minnesota's Somali-American community*? Retrieved August 20, 2022, from https://www.cbsnews.com/minnesota/news/minnesota-somali-american-population-good-question/

Clark, A. (2021, January 28). *The Children's Crusade: when the youth of Birmingham marched for justice*. History. Retrieved August 20,2022, from https://www.history.com/news/childrens-crusade-birmingham-civil-rights

Dahdah, E. (2018). *The paper bag*. Unpublished manuscript.

Goh, M. (2012). Teaching with cultural intelligence: Developing multiculturally educated and globally engaged citizens. *Asia Pacific Journal of Education, 32*(4), 395–415.

International Institute of Minnesota. (2017). *Somalis*. Retrieved August 20, 2022, from https://iimn.org/publication/finding-common-ground/minnesotas-refugees/africa/somalis/

Leung, K., Ang, S., & Tan, M. L. (2014). Intercultural competence. *Annual Review of Organizational Psychology and Organizational Behavior,* 1, 489–519.

Lewis, C., Janowiec, A., Erasmus, Y., Flynn, J , & Ingram, D. (2010). *Critical literacy in neighborhood bridges: An exploratory study*. Center for Applied Research and Educational Improvement, College of Education and Human Development, University of Minnesota.

Minnesota Compass. (2022). *All Minnesotans: Somali population*. Retrieved August 20, 2022, from https://www.mncompass.org/topics/demographics/cultural-communities/somali

National Museum of African American History & Culture. (n.d.). *The children's crusade*. Retrieved August 20, 2022, from https://nmaahc.si.edu/explore/stories/childrens-crusade

Rhodessa Jones & the Medea Project: Theatre for incarcerated women/HIV circle. (n.d.). Retrieved August 20, 2022, from https://themedeaproject.weebly.com/rhodessa-jones.html

Sims, K. (2014). *Children's theatre company* (pp. 5, 6). Theatre Communication Group Special Report on Education 2013.

Zipes, J. (Ed.). (1992). *Aesop's fables*. Signet Classics.

Zipes, J. (2004). *Speaking out: Storytelling and creative drama for children*. Routledge.

PART FOUR

Civic Processes

INTRODUCTION TO CIVIC PROCESSES

Get With It: A Play of Civic Processes

Roberto Bedoya

The chapters in Part Four, Civic Processes tell the story of "get with it," as my mom would say when her children complained about an injustice, a challenge, a problem that asked for a creative response. "Get with it!" lingers in me as a drive that figures the ethics and aesthetics in civic life, in our nation's democracy. It lingers in me via the dramaturgy of cultural and public policy mindful of the setting, the script, the stage, the blocking, the settings, and the performance that brings democracy into being. I came to reflect on the dramaturgy of policymaking through the writings of the scholar Maarten Hajer, a Dutch political scientist and regional planner associated with the argumentative turn in policy analysis in the field of public policy.

Another writer of influence is the Canadian poet Robin Blaser, who said:

> Cultural condition always approaches what we mean by the word "world" or the process of composing one. . . . The world is never separately – by simplicity's trick – social, political, artistic, or sacred, but, rather, it is made up of an entanglement of discourses having to do with men, women, earth and heaven.
>
> *(Blaser, 1993, p. 18)*

Democracy is a slippery and complex entanglement as experienced by this cultural practitioner, policymaker, and haunted poet-paladin. My love of entanglements comes with the work of prompting engagements via arts and culture in civic life and the composing it ensues. My love of policy is linked to the arguments made that employ political, public, and poetic will that is manifest in societal support systems. My love of the poet-paladin is for the ways of making meaning employed in producing democracy that involves the muses, the knights, the interlopers, the explorers, the social visions, the doubts in the complexity of it all.

DOI: 10.4324/9781003475996-20

This reflection on the essays is also a reflection of entanglements, governance, and imagination that shapes our troubled democracy and demands that we keep open democracy as a process that can imagine and support our civic imagination, our lives together as a "We the People." How? To that end, these chapters offer some thoughts on proceedings and the cultures of democracy and stories about pathways.

SETTING Wiring #1

Mom story: At the end of her life (she lived to 95), she was bed-ridden, not in pain but fragile with a wandering mind. I was visiting her; she was living with my sister, and when it was time to leave, I said my goodbye, left, and was walking down the hallway from her room and she announced "Mijito," beckoning me back. I returned and she said, "I know why you are so social." I smiled and said "Okay – why?" . . . "Well I was pregnant with you in '51 and was going door to door in our neighborhood and registering all the Mexican-Americans in the neighborhood to vote. So you've been to a hundred doors before you were even born!" I laughed, thinking "yup."

SETTING Wiring #2

Irene Story: In 1989, I participated in Maria Irene Fornes's INTAR Hispanic Playwrights Lab in New York City, which was profound, life-enriching, and a gift. Irene was a genius. From her workshop I am still unpacking what I learned about imagination and poetic will – art as order, disorder; beauty as plural; mystery as god; paradoxes as royalty.

Sitting at the workshop table, discovering how I love characters, love drama, and have little appetite for the "play" with "acts" and predictable actions (e.g., the gun appears on the stage and the inevitable shot). I am mindful of the conditions of learning, whether it is through art, dialogue, or argumentation, how one also needs to be aware of its performative dimensions. Irene's workshop experience shaped my career as a cultural worker and how I understand cultural policy as a form of administration and a form of critical inquiry, and to that end the labors of being a deliberative practitioner – a poet-paladin. The poetic will, the world of composing meaning coupled with public will and political will that shapes civic life.

The collected chapters in this section speak to the actions of democracy in making. Let's imagine them as a play that looks at how policy and imagination condition each other. Let's call it:

Get With It: Civic Process

Form:

A comedy of errors
A melodrama
A tragedy
A musical
A farce

A opera
All of the above plus, plus

Characters:

Government
Governance
Artist
Bureaucrat
Policy
Imagination

The Setting:

Your Locale

The Set:

Across America, the utopian ideal of "We the People" that brings into being the porous and promiscuous dynamic of the culture of civic life.

Blocking/Stage Actions:

Lisa Jo Epstein

Epstein offers up the ethical and aesthetic ways that community engagement practices are relational. She illuminates in her essay that being in relation to one's own social positionality, the politics of resource and position, time, is not the transactional frame of relationships but being in relation, which is to lean into transformation – the democratic actions of civic life.

Script:

Karen Mack with Elizabeth Cho

The narrative of story circles as a tool to organize people that prompts democracy via visions and development of an inclusive and just society. The story circle as form of movement organizing that builds social capital.

Vincent Russell

Civic health – its condition and animation through civic engagement events that foreground "fun" generates agency among the players and enlivens our civic imagination as a keystone of participatory democracy and well-being of civic life.

Actors:

Johanna K. Taylor, Amanda Lovelee, and Mallory Ruksana Nezam

Reimagining democracy through the work of building trust in the ways of government. They map the impact of various cultural practices from deep listening to collaborative performance, where the creative work of artists trouble and push government systems into the sphere of governance processes that enliven our civic imagination.

Bronwyn Mauldin and Artists 4 Democracy

The developments of Radical Democracy and Radical Imagination in our democratic processes via networking and organizing for a just society. Defending democracy through civic engagement.

The essays referred to in Part Four address art, culture, and democracy through multiple acts of imagination. "Get With It" as theater, where the conditions of civic life: violence and love shape how we fit together our Civic Imagination – the intersection of the Civic Body – policy, governance and the public realm – and Creative Practice. How we imagine our lives together via design, movement, sound, and visual culture. The cultures of democracy are embedded in the "We" of processes, in our civic imagination.

Artists and cultural workers who choose as a subject of artistic inquiries the "We" ideals of democracy, the social and political aspiration of groups, or the social contracts and obligation in civil society, understand and engage with the public sphere. In their practices and work these artists often feed the mechanism of persuasion that affect cultural and public policies, and affect the aesthetic and emotional ways of the public, which these chapters illuminate.

Projects described in Part Four speak to the decision-making processes of deliberative democracy at the level of affect, metaphor, and judgment and justification. These practices construct meaning and produce knowledge that brings into being a public. This form of artist claim-making also enters into the social action of policymaking through transformative learning, which allows for an understanding of experience and narrative as important components of the policy process. This sort of artistic practice calls into question the role of the citizen and expert, or citizens and experts in this process and the relationship between them by unhinging the authoritative cage that the expert(s), e.g., the elected official or the scholar may assert that forecloses possibilities and discovery revealed by the cultural practices of civic processes.

As I am an arts manager, my entanglements with policy are linked to understanding of the dramaturgy of policymaking and its impulses. How the social actions of policymaking and the social actions of imagination generate a never-ending play of scenes, actions, characters that prompt our civic life, our belonging. That the composing of the world of a fully realized democracy asks for an awareness of the sovereignty of context at play in locales, in relation to phenomenological ways of being. That the argument one makes for advancement of the cultures of democracy need to argue for discovery, poetics, engagement, coming into being that is the future. A never-ending story of a commitment to figuring it out – figuring it out as to sculpt how we advance our democratic best selves, understanding how beauty is an articulation of how we imagine our lives together, and understand our relation to the land, other species, and the heavens.

Reference

Blaser, R. (1993). Recovery of the public world. In E. Alderson, R. Blaser, & H. Coward (Eds.), *Reflections on cultural policy: Past, present and future* (p. 18). The Calgary Institute for the Humanities.

12

DEMOCRACY IS IN THE MAKING

Just Act's Model for Rehumanizing Community Engagement

Lisa Jo Epstein

Introduction

The invitation to contribute a chapter about my model for resident-driven, arts- and community-based engagement in planning and development led me to critically reflect on my social practice art and how I've learned through lived experience that democracy is in the making. Imagining democracy, like imagining utopia, can cease to be a product to be procured, but a direction to pursue through purposeful practice that will take "us to another place" (Duncombe & Lambert, 2021) where pernicious patterns of an oppressive democracy built on racial capitalist othering no longer reign. The predominant conception of democracy can never be the end-point or solution to our current social and political morass because systems of domination and racism that we have propagated under the guise of democracy have led us to the trenchantly unjust world we now inhabit. I proffer the idea of democracy as an experiential creative process of awareness and culture-building that we, as a multiracial populace, can choose to practice in order to collectively rebuild *our* community, not *the* community. When we consider democracy as an ever-evolving, embodied practice, then wonder, care, and curiosity about why, what was and is, and what is emerging are welcomed into the room as our teachers and guides for decision-making.

In 2015, I founded Just Act in Philadelphia as an applied theater, arts, and story-based catalyst for healing, change, and activism to build a just world. In an effort to contribute towards building "a world of belonging without othering" (Othering and Belonging Institute, n.d.), I structured Just Act's creative placemaking engagement initiatives between 2015 and 2022, in partnership with residents and community development corporations serving their neighborhoods, to foster awareness of and to catalyze new relational practices – to ourselves and to each other – through

DOI: 10.4324/9781003475996-21

interactions that yielded embodied knowledge and a felt-sense of mutuality, connection, and solidarity. Arts-based, resident-led activities rehumanized the planning and community engagement process, dissipating distrust and skepticism while greatly strengthening each assembled group's abilities to flex the muscles of their personal, collective, and civic imaginations around a multitude of issues as well as honoring their gifts, needs, dreams, and visions.

Leaving behind a fixed paradigm of what resident engagement should be, and replacing it with a flexible, creative process that connects us with each other and grows a sense of belonging to something larger, requiring all to be involved, reminds me of what happens in a devised theater creation process. A collective of diverse people, guided by a felt-sense of possibility, join to make something visible outside themselves from something invisible inside about which they care and desire to publicly share. Participation in new critical, creative exchanges relies on, and respectfully takes into account, each person's lived experiences. Valuing multiple social and cultural perspectives, they are committed to be in service to each other. As co-creators, they share personal stories and ideas through words, images, and improvisation, externalizing hidden emotions, experiences, and perspectives. Bearing witness to, and generously receiving each other's stories while participating in a collective journey towards the unknown, all are changed and newly accountable to one another. Together, they weave a future creation in form and content reflective of a pluralistic perspective.

We Are All Civic Artists

Adopting the definition of democracy as a creative process transforms everyone's role into that of civic artist. Guided by a shared vision for social justice that has not yet manifested, through conscious practice we can develop the capacity to be changed by listening and receiving from others, while learning, like theater artists, to accept that ideas may be preserved, built upon, edited, or edited out. As civic artists, our work becomes a daily, social practice of making, constructively reflecting on that making, then remaking "ways of being in space together that help us see beyond false constructs of superiority and inferiority without asking us to sacrifice what has shaped us" (Brown, 2021). Democracy, therefore, as a social process horizontally activated by civic artists, can be considered the ultimate act of public creativity.

Upon accepting our role as civic artists, the terms defining community engagement change: process, risk, and playful experimentation meaningfully take center stage, where product/overproductivity, defensiveness, and fear traditionally reigned. There is a shift in thought and action from reactive to relational; from perfectionism and problem-solving to inquiry, curiosity, and possibility-making; from outcome-driven to process-based; from fast to flexible; from scarcity to abundance and dignity. As our art is a daily, ever-evolving practice, no proverbial curtain will rise and fall, so we should not expect applause for our actions, as Rev. angel Kyodo williams reminds us (Kyodo williams, 2022). But we might feel unexpected joy.

Unlike typical planning and creative placemaking projects, Just Act's process can be considered our art product. In "recognition that the diversity of cultures nourishes human creativity," meaningful engagement co-designed and led by cross-neighborhood and cross-sector stakeholders-turned-civic artists is key for animating peers to exercise their imagination, intelligence, and collective wisdom in a public way (Polayni Levitt in Kennedy, 1996). I call this work an art-powered practice for bridge-building between the way residents emotionally experience where they live and how developers and city stakeholders reflect on a neighborhood's status.

What's Identity Got to Do With It?

I find the Emergent Strategy Ideation Institute's question "How do we get in right relationship with change?" a productive framework for reflecting on my role as a social practice artist dedicated to embodied social justice (Emergent Strategy Ideation Institute, n.d.). To get in right relationship with change, I must first acknowledge my positionality. As Just Act's principal artist-facilitator who is white-bodied, middle class, a cisgender woman, heterosexual, mostly able-bodied, Jewish, with decades practicing Theatre of the Oppressed and facilitating arts and community-based engagement planning projects primarily with Black and Brown residents, I am constantly learning about experiences of social injustice and oppression as the participants with whom I join are living them. I'm always learning about and unlearning ways I've been conditioned to think and act as a white-bodied person with unearned privilege – such as the ability to enter and leave certain neighborhoods, or assumptions I've been told to have about such neighborhoods – and how to be accountable to my BIPOC collaborators. Positioned as a trusted "arts partner" for community engagement, I purposefully leverage my privilege as creative convener to decenter white-body supremacy by introducing strategic arts-based processes that interrupt habitual power differentials and promote a sense of belonging. Residents are positioned as leaders, co-creators, and decision-makers who shape every layer of a project.

Community Engagement Is a Racist System

The city planner Marie Kennedy defines "real community development as combining material development with the development of people." Kennedy's use of the word "real" points to habitual practices as *not real*, since they ignore the "interrelationship of economic, physical and social development" (Kennedy, 1996). Proactively rebuilding our social, human architecture and economy that is led by, for, and with Black, Brown, and Indigenous people who have been systematically overlooked and excluded from civic processes must be valued as much as changes in physical improvements. However, pairing the trajectories of place *and* people is not the norm because the vertical system of community engagement, like that of urban design, is "built on a system of privilege, the extraction of resources from the colonised and capitalist ways of doing" (Hormazabal et al., 2021, p. 126). Physical improvements are a tangible, quantifiable product, while growing people power is not. It flips the script on the structurally unjust and undemocratic system of power-over by centering residents as authors of a new narrative that supports power with and within. Such "people" outcomes are not measurable with standard forms of evaluation.

In a society riven by systemic inequity and inequality, my experiences of resident participation in neighborhood planning for equitable development have shaped my understanding of the constructive role engagement could play in catalyzing social change and social justice if only thinking shifted "about who is in charge and where power resides" (Block, 2008). Normative community engagement practices are typically focused on achieving inclusivity "wins" (i.e., diversity of public input from numbers of people in "the community"). Without purposeful activation and commitment to social justice, such engagement amounts to "inclusion without belonging."[1] This is not to say that gathering analytical information isn't productive and necessary. However, in the widely practiced engagement scenario that perpetuates "in-and-out groups, often by race and place," residents are considered beneficiaries, not leaders and deciders. Surveys, focus groups, charrettes, town halls, or even listening sessions are practices characterized by fixed notions of how residents are expected to show up in order to serve or confirm what is frequently a predetermined vision.

Staci Haines (2023), a leader in the field of somatics, says, "We become what it is we practice," prompting us to look anew at what constitutes practice. In an unpublished webinar, Haines asks, "What purposeful practices are connected to what's the difference we want to make in the world." If we are always practicing something reflective of our principles, then conventional community engagement practices repeat a racist, top-down, power-over model which "assumes that the repository of knowledge is in the planners" and lead organizers (Kennedy, 1996). In reasserting white dominant cultural practice of seeing Black and Brown residents not for the individuals they are, but as groups to be counted and controlled by limited and limiting interaction, such practices negate the breadth, depth, and humanity of who is in the room.

Take it from "T," a 54-year-old African American woman and veteran who grew up in Eastern North Philly. T was a member of the Community Action Team – aka the CAT – for Just Act's 2020–2022 project with Philadelphia's HACE Community Development Corporation called *Restore-Reimagine-Rebuild Rivera Rec and Mann Older Adult Center*. When asked about the role of community engagement in planning, she candidly declared:

> We are used to being told what to do, dictated to, told what we need and how we are going to get it. We are never truly listened to. People can't be rolled over all the time like we are rolled over.[2]

If transforming relationality is the keystone on which our swing to equitable democracy depends, community engagement practices must be rehumanized by creating conditions for new possibilities to emerge. In the rest of this chapter, I endeavor to make meaning of my decades-long experience collaborating with Black and Brown residents in neighborhoods harmed by ongoing systematic racial and economic discrimination and marginalization. To demonstrate how I have restructured neighborhood engagement practices in pursuit of the difference I seek to make in my city, I describe salient elements from the 2020–2022 project, *Restore-Reimagine-Rebuild Rivera Rec & Mann Older Adult Center* (*RRR*).

Structural Change Needs Structure

Restructure Language

bell hooks wrote, "Definitions are vital starting points for the imagination. What we cannot imagine cannot come into being" (hooks, 2018). Rehumanizing community engagement begins with consciously choosing the words "resident-driven" and "community-based" to reflect an embodied commitment to racial justice and dismantling structural inequality from the inside out. N, the Afro-Latina Story Engagement Team Coordinator for *RRR*, explained that "Just Act serves the needs right in the community, partnering with organizations and groups whose mission and heart are centered in community." While a language shift may seem slight, it is the opposite: as a declaration of values, renaming the process is an accountability practice.

Restructure Project Planning

RRR took place in the predominantly LatinX Fairhill neighborhood of Eastern North Philadelphia. Fairhill's poverty level is 40.6%, and, with adjacent neighborhoods, is known more for the drug markets and crime than the social capital – assets and untapped capacities – of those who live there. Here, "the reality of concerns surrounding local crime and the rippling effects of addiction coupled with limited recreation and educational opportunities served as the backdrop" (Semerod, 2017).

Step 1: Pre Show

RRR began as an invitation from the Hispanic Association Contractor Enterprises – aka HACE – who were managing over $15 million of physical renovations of a municipal building divided between youth recreation and older adults via Philadelphia's citywide Rebuild initiative, with support from the Philadelphia Association of CDC's (PACDC). From my 2017 project *Art-Powered Places*, also supported by PACDC, I knew that HACE was committed to ideological transformation at the individual, collective, and institutional levels as to why and how residents should be engaged. They had demonstrated intentionality and readiness to invest and commit quality staff time on an arts-based project led by residents wherein professional staff would function as listeners and guides bringing knowledge, strategies, and networks to support project actualization. Collaboration was "not just for project goals but to model the value of collective action" at a local level, supporting social cohesion and strengthening belonging that would be "effective in facilitating community change" (Semerod, 2017).

Imagine this:

It's February 2020, our first official Rebuild meeting after a year of pre-planning. We warmly greet each other as we gather around well-worn folding tables in the community room where, three years earlier, I had introduced them to arts-based tools and methods for collaborative planning. Harry, HACE's Director of Operations, bustles into the room, an oversized roll of paper under his arm. Harry grew up in Fairhill, and Rivera Rec was pivotal to guiding him as a young man towards the role he now plays as a neighborhood leader. Carefully, we each hold down edges of a technical blueprint, ink marking our fingertips. I had been invited to implement Just Act's cultural organizing and planning model to capture residents' visions for architectural renovations of the beloved Center. Naturally, I thought this blueprint would outline their dilapidated state. When Harry announced that these were the architect's final renovation designs, I was incredulous. I leaned in, trespassing forward as if a closer look would reveal otherwise. Alas, no. The project was over before it began.

***

Step 2: Establish Core Co-Creators

With architectural renovations complete, I was determined to block further "rolling over" residents and interrupt racialized capitalist practices where residents are seen only as the end user, not the designers and decision-makers. I suggested we build on the community visioning from Art-Powered Places, and invite residents to co-create their own "people's blueprint" for change to meaningfully address deep cracks and fissures in Fairhill's social architecture. Residents would collectively write a community and culturally responsive plan for remodeling Center programming rooted in their values and visions. The blueprint would also map out an alternative economic development plan, like a teaching artist model, wherein local residents and groups, identified by neighbors for their skills and talent, would be hired to teach programs expressly desired by their neighbors. With a shared commitment to developing a community-driven vision for change, the HACE staff embraced this shift. The project was able to begin.

Imagine this:

It is March 2020. Panic and fear of COVID-19 abound. Staring at your computer screen during the first meeting of the newly formed CAT, 12 Zoom squares hint at our social lives beyond the square: a white wall with a lone guitar propped in the corner; a cacophony of color on a bookshelf; a blur of indeterminacy as if caught by a slow shutter speed; a big fuzzy cat. How do we grow social solidarity amidst social distancing, disconnection, uncertainty, and fragmentation? Create online, embodied practices that prompt on-camera interaction so we can be in relationship to one another in the present moment while recognizing the constant, seemingly inexorable loss brought about by COVID-19. Bear witness to how others are experiencing the world while bringing forth our shared humanity.

***

The CAT was the wisdom centerpiece circle of doers and decision-makers: intergenerational, multiracial and cross-sector, comprised of local artists, community leaders, residents previously active in the shuttered Centers, with representatives of city stakeholder organizations and HACE staff. The CAT met weekly on Zoom for almost two years, collectively steering the project through 18 months of engagement activities: imagining, framing, designing, assembling, collaborating, executing, and evaluating. From initial wariness to genuine relationships, CAT members built bonds in artistic activism and care that exist to this day.

The CAT Practices

To develop trust and familiarity with creative strategies for engagement and action-planning, I facilitated arts-based activities during CAT meetings that would be featured in the project's future events, such as the Story Circle Process[3] and story data harvesting adapted from the Art of Hosting and Orton's Heart & Soul, alongside typical strategic planning tools like visioning exercises, neighborhood network mapping, and social power analyses. This unexpectedly participatory, creative approach resulted in new kinds of conversation, knowledge, and awareness while cultivating a shared sense of belonging and accountability. It cultivated collective experience with, and individual understanding of, the ways in which the structure of an applied arts process could productively counter isolation by growing social cohesion, enlivening meaningful participation, dialogue, and connection across differences. The CAT customized the entire project's voice and focus. For example, after the launch of each act, the CAT shared their felt-experiences and event observations then collectively made adjustments based on what had emerged. Declaring project ownership of the CAT, one member described it this way:

> The neighborhood is our business. The CAT makes sure the community is engaged, consulted and involved in decision-making in the neighborhood. We make sure that the people with the funds and power know they are not the only ones who are making decisions.

Widen the Project Planning Circle

Every step of my model expands who participates and what they practice when participating so as to alter habitual relationality, change the nature of the conversation, prompting new ideas and perspectives to emerge. To further expand the redistribution of power, project leadership, networking and relationship-building, I created a Story Engagement Team, aka the SET, consisting of eight residents who were intergenerational, multiracial, bilingual, and of varying physical abilities. After auditioning online, the SET trained with me to become an ensemble of keen listeners and improvisers, meticulously practicing Story Circle facilitation and story harvesting while learning how to perform story gift-backs.

During Act I, called "Fairhill Story Circles," each SET member sensitively supported participants to share stories about meaningful experiences at the Centers that yielded personal discovery or a sense of belonging. Animating competencies developed in rehearsal, the SET modeled empathy, curiosity, and respect for each teller's dignity, thus avoiding habits of "hegemony and domination of some members of the community" over others and promoting "equality in their interactions and relationships" (Seppala et al., 2021). Interrupting patterns of isolation, distrust, and ongoing trauma, coupled with cynicism and skepticism that resident voices would ever matter, the formation and animation of the CAT and the SET contributed to the co-creation of a localized, multiracial, democratic civic culture rooted in connection, mutual care, multi-vocality, and shared sense of possibility. Refounding democracy was in the making.

Step 3: The Acts, Restructuring How and Where Residents Gather

Act I: Story Circles and Gift-Backs

Brene Brown's comment that "Stories are data with a soul" has always spoken to my heart, and given credence to how I have designed practices for cultural organizing that purposefully build space for stories out of which emerges actionable data. "Each stage of the process [named] 'Act' created a more defined and formal path to organize the information gathered from participants so that it could be used to support resident-driven decisions for programming upon completion of the centers' renovations" (Semerod, 2022). Setting the stage for all project events, Act I upended assumptions about traditional civic and/or planning meetings, starting with the principle that all residents were civic artists who were invited to "Get in on the Act."

Decentralizing where community gatherings took place, the CAT identified and invited different organizations to host the Fairhill Story Circles so as to best reach and respect neighborhood stakeholders. The unlikely spaces selected to reach normally excluded participants ranged from an overgrown vacant lot animated by a teen girl soccer club to generic community rooms at older adult centers catering to the LatinX population where the bilingual SET members assured that all voices were heard.

Imagine this:

You walk up the steps of a sleek, modern building that houses Taller Puertorriqueno, a thriving Puerto Rican art gallery and education center, a cultural haven

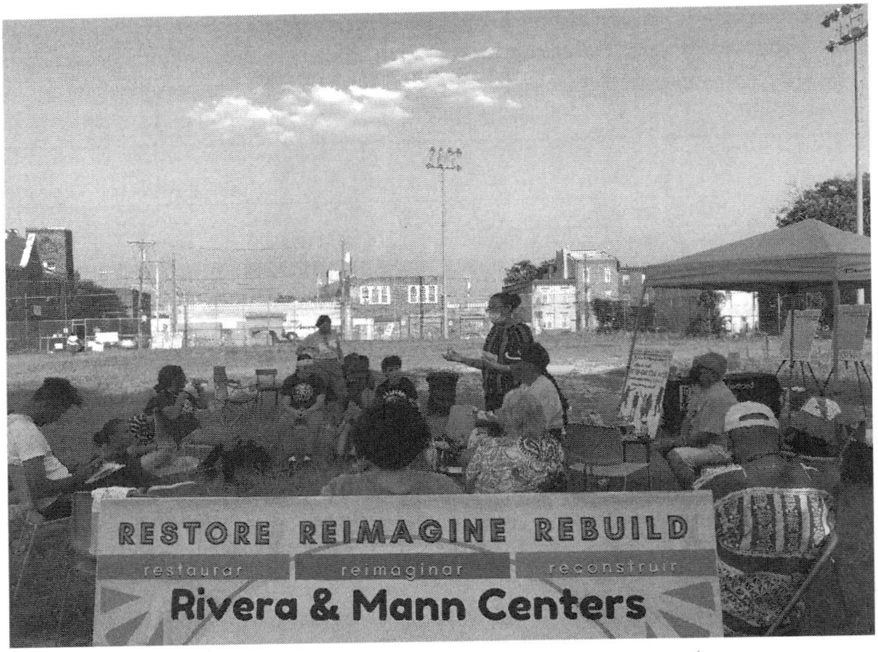

FIGURE 12.1 Amidst knee high weeds, in an abandoned lot, teen athletes from the neighborhood bounce from soccer balls to story circles. Photograph by Lisa Jo Epstein.

amidst aging row homes with gentrified housing poking up and the largest open-air, city drug market marking the adjacent neighborhood. The bright room undulates with an infectious beat from two African American master drummers, the sun rippling through floor-to-ceiling windows, while the enticing scent of locally made pastelillos entices you. A team of neighbors in matching bright yellow or turquoise T-shirts dot the space like fireflies, joyfully inviting you to sit in the constellation of small tables. Nourished by laughter, smiles, music and good food, you wonder how this could possibly be a community meeting.

***

In the Art-Powered Places model, participants and resident leaders consistently engage in small acts of healing and repair, demonstrating "social activism that is body-centered" (Menakem, 2017, p. 237). Act I opened courageous space for neighbors to meaningfully share the mic. Both online and in-person, emotional plurality bloomed, the rooms overflowing with a refreshing sense of ease and collective effervescence. People's bodies relaxed while remaining dynamically present, reminding us all that joy is a form of justice.[4] What emerged from the effusion of feelings and emotional responses was a waterfall of knowledge about important activities from the past, the impact of personal experiences at the Centers, and the values embedded therein. From re-seeing their past and present, neighbors were invited to organize around what neighbors were for, not fighting against, by articulating their visions for future programming to meet personal and collective needs in order to thrive.

Gift It Back

When piloting this model in 2015 to counter extractive engagement processes that depleted and defeated community members, I hatched the idea of "gift-backs" to literally give residents a gift at the conclusion of the Story Circles that acknowledged and validated individual and group contributions. To that end, pulling from my practices in Playback Theatre and Theatre of the Oppressed, I trained SET members to create short, performative gifts to reflect back the individual and collective consciousness of who was in the room, declaring that everyone's voices, vision, and emotions had a place in the planning process. One Act I participant expressed their felt-sense of how this process contributed to personal affirmation and communal connection when saying,

> I really appreciated this. It made me feel really safe and seen. Your tears during your story made me feel like I know you. Then how powerful it is when you get feedback through the giftbacks and to feel seen. I value this process.

Further demonstrating that the arts don't exist in isolation, but can support community resilience and unity, M, who is a 40-something LatinX man, drew a direct link between his experience in the Story Circle and gift-backs to everyday life:

> Imagine if a community had teamwork like that. And if a neighbor could collaborate, maybe there'd be less violence; if adults could express themselves with each other like in the Story Circles, maybe they'd better understand each other. If people could communicate and respond before you react, maybe you'd meet someone you didn't know that went through the same thing as you. I think more could happen in our community.

Act II: Data Jams

For Act II, I created a Data Jam board game, in collaboration with the CAT, to craft specific building blocks of the blueprint. To play the game, residents had to catalog, analyze, and make collective decisions about past and future Center programs, underpinned by the neighborhood's values as identified in Act I. Through acts of participatory play, the Data Jam served as another "wonder intervention" in community engagement default settings, offering fun and purposeful ways for participants to slow down and interact with each other in unexpected ways, yielding unexpected results (Davis, 2021).

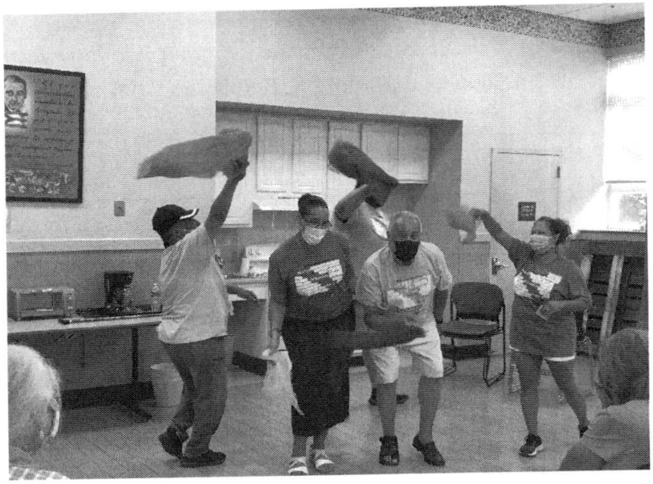

FIGURE 12.2 The Story Engagement Team dramatically gift back stories to participants through lively improvisation as part of the planning process. Photograph by Lisa Jo Epstein.

Whether a Data Jam session took place during a torrential downpour turning streets into rivers, or the thick heat of the second floor of an un-air-conditioned clubhouse packed with energetic kids and a sprinkling of caregivers, playing the Data Jam game delighted players and catalyzed a kind of focused aliveness and connectedness. “I felt electricity in the air,” said one Data Jam participant. “There was an enthusiasm there that I appreciated. I felt the positive activity, positiveness, that’s the vibe I got. And urgency.” Our Participatory Evaluator Mary Elizabeth Semerod called the Data Jam game an “interactive community-led needs assessment” that “reinforced the importance of arts-based participatory methods of community-based engagement to restore, reimagine and rebuild” (Semerod, 2022).

Lively conversation buoyed by faith in the power of shared humanity was coupled with a sense of co-responsibility for completing the game. One player explained the power of the participatory atmosphere where each simultaneously led and learned from each other in this way:

> I participated in the game, interacted with other players at my table . . . The woman sitting next to me was a really interesting person with some good ideas. It made me consider my position on things, whether or not they’re sound, whether you need to shift. You can glean a lot from other folks.

Equality of roles reigned within the clusters of players: each action step of the game served as a conduit for players to share their perspectives based on personal history, and to re-see their knowledge in relation to one another as key to building a new collective plan for the Center. As one CAT member summarized the Data Jam’s deliberateness in making neighbors feel that they had a role in program planning, she recounted that

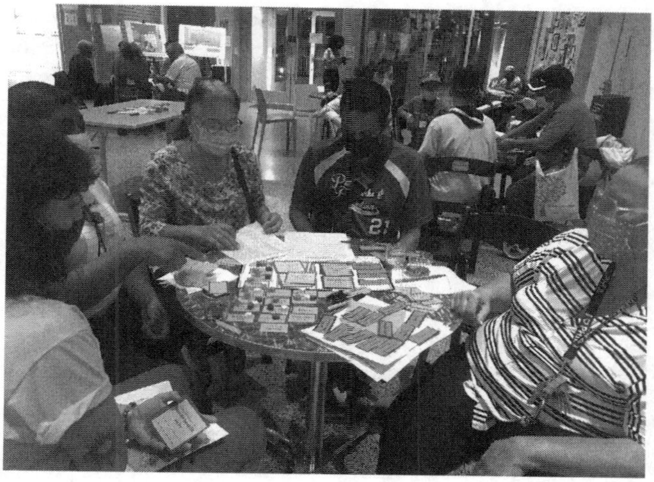

FIGURE 12.3 Playing the Data Jam Game moving meeples and tiles to identify what programs to preserve, prioritize and make possible. Photograph by Lisa Jo Epstein.

> the intimacy worked and made our guests not so one dimensional. Instead of picking just one activity, we got their perspective on three different activities per table, with some people engaging topics they may or may not have been familiar with.

Nobody was "there" to be counted, but there to collectively jam about what and who should count and why.

Act III: The Data Labs

For an artist, what is a lab? A place and opportunity for individual growth along with collective experimentation and exploration; for discovering new steps, then revisiting them to determine specific moves to be shared with the wider world. From my initial conversations with HACE, I had outlined a third act called a "Data Lab," that could be in person and online. While residents would shine as storytellers in Act I, and as action players in Act II, they'd serve as social architects in Act III. Once finished, they could use the blueprint to ask the city for robust reinvestment in people and programming to productively animate the architectural investments from the inside out, redressing the multi-layered harm caused by systemic racism and historic divestment and exclusion.

Imagine this:

An intersectional group of neighbors, local community organizers, youth-serving workers, and municipal staff, sharpies in hand, encircle oversized chart paper worksheets adorned with stacks of brightly colored Post-It packs: yellow for Action Steps, turquoise for Action Strategies, orange for Partners and Their Power, pink for People and Their Power, green for Resources. Similar people hubs hum throughout the room. Shifting focus from problem-solving to possibility-making, everyone concentrates on the task of deciding actions to be taken in order to create the desired programming and strategies to actualize them, dovetailing ideas and inspiration. They move from table to table, confirming or adding to each activity chart until the recurring rainbow of Post-Its proffers multiple pots of gold to be mined to actualize the people's blueprint.

***

The CAT and I wanted the Data Labs to make all of the 200+ voices from previous Acts visible and heard so that the city could no longer dismiss Fairhill residents' humanity, strength, resiliency, beauty, and social power. By acknowledging people's dignity and history, wisdom and creativity, as vital to growing the neighborhood's future health and well-being, the Data Lab process transformed participants' learned passivity to active engagement. "They didn't expect to impart what they themselves desired, or share their own knowledge," extolled one CAT member. "We [during the Data Labs] gave them that time, we gave them license to say what they needed and wanted, how they needed it and how they wanted it. They felt heard and saw what the Data Labs were all about, and that they had a role in rebuilding the Center."

The Power of Play

The engagement structures for creative, participatory play that characterized *Restore- Reimagine-Rebuild Rivera Rec & Mann Older Adult Center* demonstrated the healing potential of resident-led, arts- and community-based engagement for social justice where relationship is the project. It also underlined the urgency and challenges of bypassing habitual attitudes and practices for engagement that perpetuate dominant culture through systematic individual and civic silencing of Black, Brown, low-income residents and working families. If building an authentic, multiracial democracy that serves all to thrive and prosper is our guiding beacon, then we have to wake up to what has not been working and let it go. The palpable positive resident response to the activities of all of the Acts demonstrated that when we break up with a narrow definition of community engagement, and risk engaging with one another in unexpected practices, the felt-experience catalyzes shifts in the social architecture.

RRR began as, to paraphrase Monteiro from HACE, a seed idea of what equitable, community-driven, place-based, self-determination and development could be. After being handed "a done deal" on day one, we knew that growing people-power through programming needed to be part of the overall redevelopment equation. Otherwise, rebuilding the Center would be like "building a lighthouse with the light," as our CAT member T analogized a shiny rebuilt rec center without the community vision for change embedded therein. The three Acts succeeded in fostering awareness of relational practices – to ourselves, to each other, and to governing policies – through which participants gained knowledge and embodied understanding of the value of a felt-sense of mutuality, connection, and authentic solidarity.

Countering the extractive culture of conventional community engagement, Just Act's model offered a purposeful, creative framework for neighbors to get in better relationships with each other and with themselves through embodied critical reflection, connection, collaboration, and play. It invited a deepening of mutuality, while validating the whole person. Changes in the expected patterns of relationality offered everyone "the ability to be who we are in the face of others being who they are," which Rae Johnson advocates (2023). In this case, it showcased their capacity to co-design and lead their own neighborhood change. A Fairhill resident characterized the embodied social justice approach of *RRR* to imagine a different future as "an example of bringing the community together that's not just talking." And that

> it comes down to people. It involved another person touching their hearts. This process of engagement is more than inviting members to a meeting or an event but is gathering . . . gathering with. It drew us closer, and gave us a sense of empowerment. We are not alone. We all fit in but differently. We each have a small part to play in the community.

Prior to writing this chapter, I hadn't positioned my work as a social practice artist under the umbrella of "democracy." The word itself conjured thoughts of colonialism, oppression, genocide, and erasure, not liberation, freedom, and possibility-making. If, as I do, one agrees with numerous contemporary social thinkers that our imaginations have been colonized because of systemic power-over conditions and conditioning, impacting and inhibiting our everyday choices and actions, then this chapter has prompted me to decolonize my own thinking for how I describe what I do and why. I now see my commitment to creative cultivation of "horizontal relationships" that "foster pluralism and increase multivocality" through people and place-based structural change as refounding democracy in the making (Seppala et al., 2021, p. 11).

Notes

1 A principle promulgated by the Institute for Othering & Belonging.
2 I use the first initials of the speaker from personal conversations for privacy reasons.
3 In the late 1990s in New Orleans, I was introduced to the Story Circle Process by John O'Neal, one of the co-founders of this particular technique for bringing people together across differences and sharing equal space.
4 My assessment of what transpired is inspired by Tanmeet Sethi MD and her book *Joy Is My Justice: Reclaim What Is Yours* (2023).

References

Block, P. (2008). *Community: The structure of belonging*. Berrett-Koehler Publishers, Inc.

Brown, A. M. (2021). *Holding change: The way of emergent strategy facilitation and mediation*. AK Press.

Davis, J. (2021). *Tracking wonder: Reclaiming a life of meaning & possibility in a world obsessed with productivity*. Sounds True.

Duncombe, S., & Lambert, S. (2021). *The art of activism*. OR Books.

Emergent Strategy Ideation Institute. (n.d.). Retrieved December 26, 2023, from https://esii.org/.

Haines, S. (2023). *Embodied social justice certificate program*. Unpublished webinar.

hooks, b. (2018). *All about love: New visions*. William Morrow Paperbacks.

Hormazabal, M. S., Mollenhauer, K., Satu Miettinen, S., & Melanie Sarantou, M. (2021). *Arts-Based methods for decolonising participatory research*. Routledge.

Johnson, R. (2023). *Embodied activism: Engaging the body to cultivate liberation, justice, and authentic connection*. North Atlantic Books.

Kennedy, M. (1996). *Transformative community planning: Empowerment through community development*. http://www.plannersnetwork.org/case-studies-and-working-papers/transformative-community-planning-empowerment-through-community-development/

Kyodo williams, Rev. a. (2022). *Training the mind to transform*. Dharma Podcasts.

Menakem, R. (2017). *My grandmother's hands*. Central Recovery Press.

Othering and Belonging Institute. (n.d.). *Othering & belonging conference*. Home. Retrieved December 26, 2023, from https://belonging.berkeley.edu/.

Semerod, E. (2017). *Art powered places*. Evaluation Report.

Semerod, E. (2022). *Restore-reimagine-rebuild Rivera Rec & Mann older adult center*. Evaluation Report.

Seppala, T., Sarantou, M., & Miettinen, S. (2021). Introduction: Arts-based methods for decolonising participatory research. In T. Seppala, M. Sarantou, & S. Miettinen (Eds.), *Arts-based methods for decolonising participatory research*. Routledge.

Sethi, T. (2023). *Joy is my justice: Reclaim what is yours*. Hachette Go Books.

13

CREATING OUR NEXT LA

Art Animating Powerful Congregation-Based Campaigns for Justice

Karen Mack with Elizabeth Cho

I founded LA Commons in 2000, with the goal of using art and cultural approaches to build a stronger sense of community. After working for a decade in the nonprofit sector, including several years as a vice president at an incubator for start-up nonprofits, I was inspired to address the lack of connectedness that made it difficult to impact challenging issues in Los Angeles. At the time, processes that furthered engagement in democratic activity were few and far between because of limited bonds across organizations and, more importantly, individuals. I spent a seminal year at the John F. Kennedy School of Government at Harvard University, where of particular note I took a class with Dr. Robert Putnam studying approaches to building and strengthening these bonds – as he terms it, "social capital" – as a basis for writing the business plan for the organization.

My research and planning provided the foundation upon which to move forward. LA Commons was launched with a project called *Taking Flight: Migration Dreams*, which brought together youth and artists to gather stories from the largely immigrant community surrounding MacArthur Park. Bringing people together to illuminate these narratives through highly visible public art is a powerful strategy for strengthening the sense of connectedness. Our efforts within marginalized Los Angeles communities to make room for local residents – particularly youth – to assert their identities and ideas in a city where they are often rendered invisible have continued for more than 20 years. By engaging people in artistic and cultural expression that celebrates their unique stories, we create the basis for dialogue, interaction, belonging, and collective action.

Since that beginning, we have produced more than 80 collaborative, grassroots public art initiatives that advance the power of community members to play a role in bettering their neighborhoods. Over 40,000 of them have participated in LA Commons' programs, from that very first, major public art exhibition sharing

DOI: 10.4324/9781003475996-22

stories of immigration through art works in the trees of MacArthur Park, to the *Heart of Hyde Park* mural honoring residents at Crenshaw and Slauson, to Found LA walking tours from Lincoln Heights to Little Bangladesh. In the summer of 2022, we produced the 12th Annual Leimert Park Day of the Ancestors: Festival of Masks, bringing it back into the streets after two years of virtual presentations during the pandemic, as an opportunity for the community to come together to mourn, celebrate, and feel a deep sense of belonging.

This chapter describes our initiative, "Creating Our Next LA," a campaign designed during COVID to build on our artistic approach to community empowerment to engage people across Los Angeles in envisioning and working together in the political arena towards a more equitable city. Elizabeth Cho, LA Commons' Manager of Partnership Programs, led implementation of this initiative, moving it from a solid concept that involved leading organizations from across the city in a community storytelling project with youth and artists at the center, to an important element in an advocacy initiative to address key issues in Los Angeles and foster a culture of democracy in the process.

Elizabeth brought to this work a youth-organizing background from her time volunteering and observing organizations such as Gente Organizada in Pomona, California, and the Boston Youth Organizing Project. These organizations utilize Youth Participatory Action Research (YPAR) to involve youth in analyzing issues in their communities and creating action-oriented approaches in response to their findings. In 2019, for example, the youth of Gente Organizada collected over 500 survey responses from their peers about their mental health as the basis for a free, youth-centered mental health conference. Similarly, LA Commons facilitates opportunities for youth to survey their communities to identify important local issues. While not solely rooted in youth organizing and YPAR, LA Commons incorporates these approaches by involving youth directly in community development as they gather data from their neighbors to contribute to the design of artistic advocacy.

A seminal partner in this effort has been LA Voice, a network of Southern California congregations that functions as a political force to advocate for equity and abundance for all. Through Creating Our Next LA, we joined forces with LA Voice during 2022, an important election year, when we selected a new mayor and doubled down in the fight for housing and justice. Art has provided an effective vehicle for members of the congregations to express their visions and a touchstone for the creation of a platform that transforms these narratives into the basis for action.

This approach has potent value. With the massive global changes taking place – from COVID, to deadly fire seasons, to explosive inequality, to digital privacy concerns – the past is not an adequate template for where urban development needs to go. Rather than looking strictly to previous experience, taking dreams and desires more seriously as inspiration is key to manifesting alternatives of possibility as we negotiate our increasingly uncertain world.

After a brief overview of the challenges to democratic practices in Los Angeles, the sections that follow describe our approach and the evolution of Creating Our Next LA, which incorporated several practices aimed at giving participants, both individuals and organizations, venues for democratic action. Our process engaged community members from across Los Angeles in developing a joint visualization for the city's future. Then, the critically important partnership with LA Voice provided a bridge between cultural work and the powerful force resulting from community organizing across congregations of different religious faiths to enhance practices of democracy.

Democracy Is Challenging in Los Angeles

We are Los Angeles natives. I grew up in Compton, and Elizabeth was born and raised in Pomona, reflecting the far-flung nature of the 4,000-square-mile metropolis. Los Angeles County comprises a total of 88 jurisdictions including Los Angeles, which, with a population of 4 million, is the second largest city in America. This jurisdiction, spanning 500 square miles, sprawls from the shores of the Pacific Ocean, to the Santa Monica Mountains, to the flatlands of South LA. In addition to being the capital of the entertainment industry, the area is known for its exceptional ethnic and racial diversity. According to the 2020 census, the city's population is 47.5% Latino; 26.1% white; 9.6% Asian; and 8.9% African American. The size, landscape, and diversity of LA can make it difficult to feel a sense of place. And, unfortunately, elected leadership is rather limited for a city of this size, with just 15 city council members each representing around 270,000 people. At the county level, there are only five elected officials for 10 million people. With voter turnout chronically low, many residents are underrepresented by their political leaders.

Because of barriers to civic engagement, at LA Commons, we are passionate about fostering a deeper connection between Angelenos and their city through the arts and, in particular, lifting up the voices of those who are most marginalized. The initial plan for our organization was inspired by a class I took taught by Dr. Robert Putnam, whose research on the significance of social capital, or the bonds of trust that exist between people, in the functioning of democracy examined a range of strategies for strengthening this resource. In *Better Together – The Report of the Saguaro Seminar: Civic Engagement in America*, Putnam and the colleagues he convened from around the country note that the arts play a unique role in building social capital, particularly among groups of different races, religions, cultures, and socioeconomic status. He writes:

> The arts have a singular advantage in rebuilding social capital: Cultural activities are enjoyable and fun. Unlike attending meetings or voting – what we call "civic broccoli" because they're good for all but unpleasant to many – artistic performance is akin to civic fruit. . . . The enjoyable nature of the arts makes them perhaps the most promising, if neglected, means of building social capital. We recommend that America's cultural institutions and the people who work within them create opportunities for political expression, community dialogue, shared cultural experiences, and civic work – all with an eye toward making citizen participation fun.
>
> *(Putnam, 2001, p. 47)*

COVID as the Impetus for Angelenos to Envision Our Next LA

The mission of LA Commons is to engage communities in artistic and cultural expression that tells their unique stories and serves as a basis for dialogue, interaction, and a shared understanding of Los Angeles. Our Neighborhood Story Connection (NSC) program translates this mission into action through work by artists and local youth, ages 15–25, to engage community members in sharing their stories, which, in turn, are transformed into public artworks that illuminate local community culture, history, and a vision of the future.

Our work strengthens the sense of belonging felt by the broad range of stakeholders involved in the process. We train participating youth in effective ways to engage their neighbors; and we involve local organizational partners based on their vested interest in project outcomes aimed at enhancing connections between locals to improve their neighborhoods. They work with us to recruit artists and youth, access locations for the program workshops, find the sites for public art projects, and collaborate in hosting story summits and closing events. They also lend authenticity to the efforts, furthering acceptance and deep engagement by community members in the work to accomplish something meaningful and make their places better together.

In spring 2020, as the pandemic took hold, we devised the idea of Creating Our Next LA, which took key elements from our NSC programs as the basis for a multiplatform campaign to foster civic engagement, healing, and change through art and dialogue. Recognizing artistic participation as a valuable tool in this time of transformation, we leaned into our unique organizational strength, tapping the power of artists and the other super imaginers – youth – to help Angelenos envision a new, more just, and equitable future.

Our intention was to build on our process of bringing artists and young people together with fellow community members to uncover and uplift local narratives and increase the connections that are the basis of civic engagement. Creating Our Next LA extended this work to involve people from throughout Los Angeles by bringing collective, creative visioning to community events across the metropolis.

Gaining Momentum With Yo-Yo Ma

After a year of organizing people around the idea, the initiative gained momentum when we received a call from classical cellist Yo-Yo Ma's team in July 2021. They heard about Creating Our Next LA and wanted to explore a partnership as part of the Bach Project, a global effort in which the renowned performer links with local organizations in cities where he is playing Bach's *Suites for Unaccompanied Cello* to bring cross-sector groups together to explore the question: "How can culture help us imagine, create and build a better future than the one we are experiencing right now?" With this fortuitous alignment, in September 2021, we spearheaded a "Day of Action" with Ma, providing an incredible opportunity to engage local leaders in sharing their stories to fuel collaborative thinking about what it would take to advance a more people-centered LA. As Ma explained,

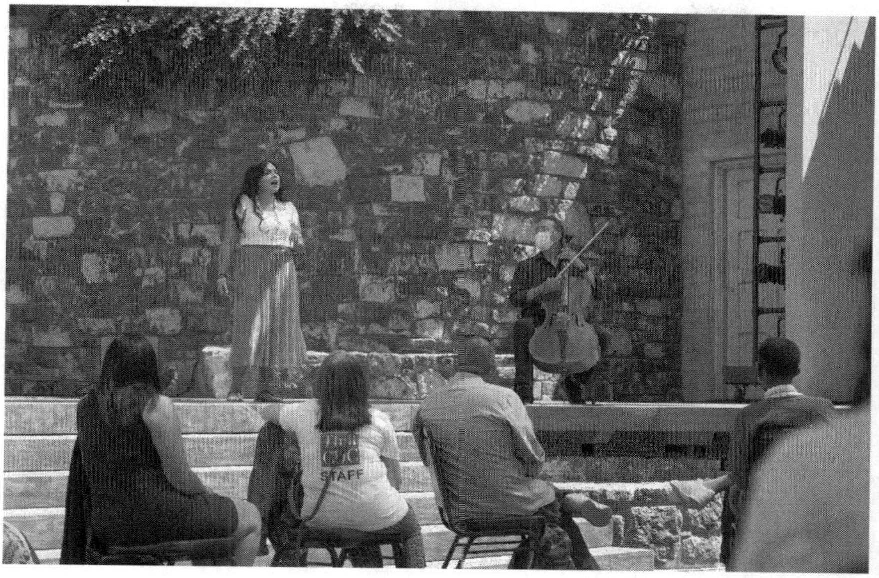

FIGURE 13.1 Yo-Yo Ma and Kelly Caballero perform at our Day of Action. Photograph by Halline Overby.

> The shared understanding that culture generates in these divisive times can bind us together as one world, and guide us to political and economic decisions that benefit the entire species. We are all cultural beings – let's explore how culture connects us and can help to shape a better future.
>
> *(Ma, n.d.)*

Our Day of Action brought together a strong cohort of community-based organizations actively working on key community development issues in Los Angeles, including housing, transportation, and arts and culture. These organizations included: Little Tokyo Service Center, Thai Community Development Center, the theater collective LA Poverty Department, Tia Chucha's Centro Cultural, Esperanza Community Housing, and CicLAvia. The shared visioning process involved key leaders from these partner organizations and resulted in inspirational songs, poetry, and art from artists hired to document the outcomes from the gathering. Former LA Poet Laureate Luis J. Rodriguez created an exceptional poem, "Grime and Gold: Imagine a New Los Angeles . . ." Here is an excerpt:

Let's draw the birds
of greater flight.

Let's sing what is often unsung,
let's dance as prayer and potion,

let's paint with cascades of colors,
let's perform till our hearts sing.

For a Los Angeles worthy
of its angels,
beyond the finite prisons of scarcity,
divisions, power
– all made up stuff –
yet cloaked over us
as if God-given and natural.

What's called natural is often unnatural.

The organic hand
of a man without a house
is a natural way
of dreaming and living,
of renewal
and abundance,
of intrinsic value,
what generates
over and over
the whirlwinds of change.

This phase of our campaign was instrumental in not only cultivating joy and healing among movement builders in Los Angeles, but also strengthening connections among this network of change workers, building power and a foundation for activating even more people towards civic action in the next phase of the process. We worked with this network to develop ways to use highly engaging art activities and installations to inspire continued civic engagement.

A Seminal Partnership to Advance Democratic Action

In Spring 2022, we joined with LA Voice to build on the Creating Our Next LA network in order to connect our creative vision and arts engagement with an organization specifically aimed at community organizing for transformative action. LA Voice is a multiracial, multi-faith community organization that awakens people to their own power, training them to speak, act, and work together to transform LA County into a place that reflects the dignity of all people. LA Voice is a part of PICO California, the largest faith-based community organizing network in California. PICO California was founded in 1994 as a project of the national Faith in Action Network.

Faith in Action, founded in 1972, developed based on the idea that people of faith have been at the center of some of America's most consequential fights for social justice, as faith institutions provide a venue where people can come together across differences to advance a shared vision for a more just society. They utilize a congregation-community model of community organizing, where values and relationship building are centered as congregation members are engaged to create a collective vision for their communities. Within this model, LA Voice provides leadership training for its congregation members that incorporates sharing individual and collective stories as a way to build the personal and public relationships that enable the development of actions, strategies, and campaigns around issue areas generated by the collective.

Similar to our approach with Creating Our Next LA, LA Voice had been engaging in deep listening and story-gathering across Los Angeles. In 2022, they developed the Power Campaign to understand the needs of their communities, research and develop policy solutions, and build campaigns to take action. In the first phase of their campaign, LA Voice leaders held over 2,000 conversations, including both one-on-one conversations and group sessions, asking congregation members two questions: "What is most negatively impacting you?" and "Where do you find hope?" Thirty-seven congregations from across LA County participated in this deep listening campaign, including All Saints Pasadena, Dolores Mission of Boyle Heights, Greater Zion Church Family in Compton, Homeboy Industries, Islah LA, Leo Baeck Temple, McCarty Memorial Christian Church (all four in LA), St. Luke Holy Baptist Church in Long Beach, and Temple Israel of Hollywood.

As a result of these conversations about the experiences of their members, LA Voice leaders ultimately identified two key issue areas that most concerned their communities: housing and economic stability. In the second phase of their campaign, they held research sessions with political and organizational leaders to inform coordinated actions around these issues.

Simultaneous to this work, LA Voice was developing a new youth organizing branch to engage and develop youth leaders as part of both their Power Campaign and general organizing efforts. As LA Voice youth came together, they expressed a desire to utilize art within their campaign to inspire and engage community members. LA Voice reached out to LA Commons to inquire about bringing art engagement to their work, and a natural connection was formed.

Youth at the Center of Power Building

Prior to our alliance with LA Voice, we were motivated by the opportunity to leverage the work done with our powerful organizational cohort to engage more citizens in Creating Our Next LA. From the first LA Commons project, young people have been at the center of our community engagement efforts. We have learned over the years that youth participation in our local arts programming not only strengthens their sense of belonging and self-agency, and their social and emotional skills, but, more importantly, empowers them as leaders to engage others in the efforts.

With this in mind, it was essential for us to involve youth as the heart of Creating Our Next LA as we sought to involve others, not to mention the opportunity

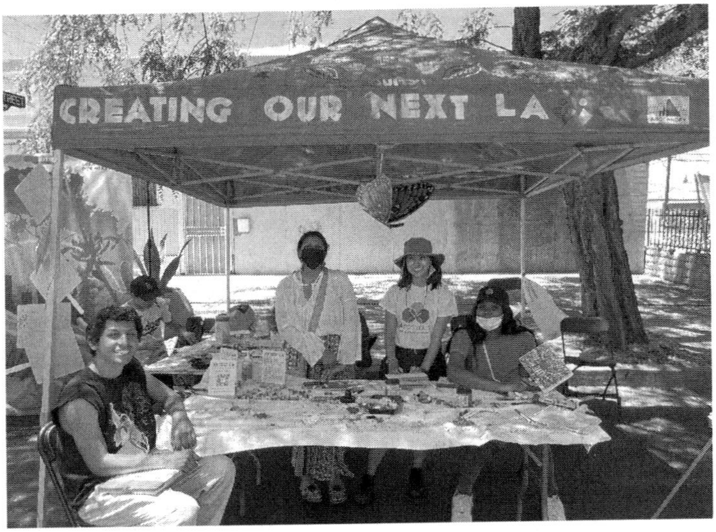

FIGURE 13.2 Youth Visionaries. Photograph by Karen Mack.

to introduce them to democratic ideas such as voting, local organizing campaigns, and civic discourse through conversations around a vision for a better future for Los Angeles. To uplift the role of youth in community engagement for Creating Our Next LA, we developed a component called Youth Visionaries, designating 15- to 24-year-olds as our core ambassadors. Many of the youth we engaged were previous participants in LA Commons' Neighborhood Story Connection programs. Within these neighborhood programs, youth gained experience in engaging with community members through story-gathering events. At these events, free food, art activities, and other resources are offered in exchange for community members' stories. Youth participants, with the support of a lead artist and LA Commons staff, developed questions about their neighborhood to use to interview elders, business owners, fellow students, and other stakeholders. Our youth participants have commented that these interviews give them more confidence in communicating with others and bring them closer to their community. From this program, we were able to recruit Youth Visionaries who could bring these communication skills to events throughout Los Angeles.

With the input of our partner organizations, we created a calendar of "pop-up activations" where Youth Visionaries, along with community artists, showed up at civic and cultural events to engage with community members, asking them, "What is your vision for a livable, healthy, and just Los Angeles?" Youth Visionaries and artists designed artmaking activities that would allow participants to artistically express their vision.

As an example, we were invited in spring 2022 to curate an installation and series of art activations as part of a countywide initiative to promote community well-being. We saw this opportunity as integral to Creating Our Next LA, as this time we had the chance to design a high-visibility installation for a major public space: Grand Park, in the heart of Los Angeles's civic center. Our concept was to create a "forest" of 84 live native oak trees, giving the public a way to envision Los Angeles as a site of creative healing and regeneration. The creation of this artwork provided a great opportunity for Youth Visionaries to staff art-making tables at Creating Our Next LA pop-ups throughout the County. By the end of the month, our urban forest represented a collective community vision for Creating Our Next LA, with voices ranging from Leimert Park poets to Skid Row artists and San Fernando Valley youth.

In June, Youth Visionaries analyzed community responses, categorized the input by issue area, and designed icons based on the most prevalent issue areas. These icons were then transferred as rubber stamps for continued artmaking with the community. Youth expressed that this artistic community engagement strengthened their ability to communicate and provided them with a personal connection to issues impacting Los Angeles. In reflective conversations, Youth Visionaries noted that community members at Creating Our Next LA pop-ups and cultural events generally enjoy artmaking, and thus artmaking booths were successful in bringing people in to then engage in civic conversations. The challenge was to integrate the input gathered as part of the artistic engagement activities into the policymaking process.

Integrating Art Into Policy Advocacy

In August 2022, our Youth Visionaries were invited to a youth organizing event with LA Voice. The collaborative event encouraged all participants to grow and learn in several capacities, inspiring organizers to think like artists and artists to think like organizers. The Youth Organizing Workshop introduced them to community-organizing concepts like power and relationship-building. Our Youth Visionaries received training in the "One-to-One" conversation that organizers use to connect with community members to encourage them to become civically engaged. While our Youth Visionaries had previous experience in community engagement through art, this experience with community organizers allowed them to deepen their communication skills by learning how to encourage action-oriented steps in conversations with community members.

Integrating this training right away, Youth Visionaries designed and led a creative visioning process with LA Voice youth organizers, wherein participants drew their vision for the world they wanted to create on cardboard tiles. Participants were led in this project by LA Commons youth leader Emily Rangel. After the youth drew their vision with paint markers and pastels, Emily led the youth in a brief meditation, wherein the youth closed their eyes, held their tile close to their chests, and meditated on their visions. Tiles were then pieced together into a collective quilt – our "Vision Quilt" – designed to travel to several additional LA Voice events within their Power campaign. Our youth participants expressed how this

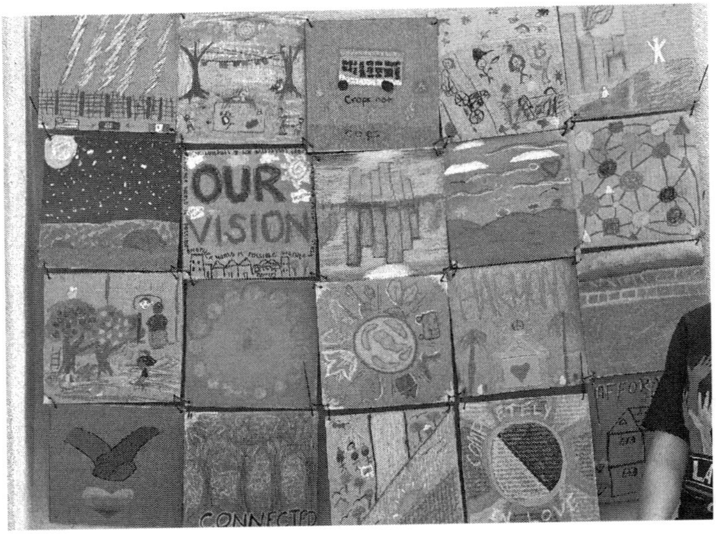

FIGURE 13.3 The Vision Quilt on display at an LA Voice event. Photograph by Karen Mack.

exercise made them feel hopeful, joyous, and empowered about building the future they wanted to see. When asked to reflect on seeing the collective quilt, the youth remarked that the quilt was a visual representation of "love in our communities" and the youth's "will for change."

Youth Visionaries brought the quilt to two additional LA Voice events – a collective voting meeting where community members voted on campaign strategy, and the Rally for the Dignity of All, where LA Voice leaders presented their agenda for housing and income stability, including policies and ballot measures on the 2022 ballot. At these events, youth from LA Commons and LA Voice grew their civic leadership skills as they engaged LA Voice members in a creative visioning exercise where participants were invited to add their tile/vision for LA onto the growing quilt.

This creative visioning process not only invoked civic discussion among participants, but enriched the democratic process by injecting a legislation-heavy, voter education event with a fun and inspirational activity. When asked, "What is the power of art in engaging with the community?" One Youth Visionary noted that artmaking activities are often immediately inviting and accessible, making them a successful entry point for civic engagement. Other youth participants noted the therapeutic qualities that artmaking has, calling art "nourishment and medicine for the soul." Families and youth may stay engaged with LA Voice because of the additional care and enjoyment brought by artmaking.

In October 2022, in partnership with the Music Center of Los Angeles County and artist Mandy Palasik of M/PAL Studio, LA Commons transformed the community responses for a healthy, just, and equitable Los Angeles into a large-scale art installation and community celebration at the major art complex owned by the County. Participants engaged in artmaking, poetry, and participatory dance to celebrate the collective vision of Los Angeles. On Jerry Moss Plaza, LA Voice displayed the Vision Quilt, shared information about the Power Campaign, and invited participants to pledge to vote, register to vote, or, if they were unable to vote, pledge to encourage others to vote.

LA Voice's Angel Mortel led the LA Commons partnership and had this to say about the importance of the partnership:

> As an organizer, I often encounter people who are tentative about civic engagement because they're not exactly sure how it connects to their daily lives. They see their community struggling with high rents, low wages, constant violence, environmental degradation, etc. and they feel powerless because it's not clear what they can do about it and where to begin.
>
> At LA Voice, we say the first revolution is internal. In other words, you need to first believe that a different world is possible. If you have a clear idea of the world that you want, then it's oftentimes easier to see what you need to do to fight for it.
>
> Using art, Creating our Next LA invited youth and adult leaders in the LA Voice network to imagine the world they want. Through the project of the "cardboard quilt," people were given a cardboard panel to draw and paint an image of the Los Angeles they want to build. We weaved those panels together into a piece that offered a powerful collective vision for LA Voice to put before us as we engaged people to get out the vote and advocate for affordable housing. The quilt has given us inspiration for the journey and the fight. We plan to display it at our public actions this year.
>
> The LA Voice-Creating our Next LA partnership offered a glimpse into the power that art has to invite and inspire civic engagement.
>
> *(LA Voice's Angel Mortel, personal communication)*

Advancing a Culture of Democracy

Creating Our Next LA is an example of the power of storytelling as a basis for civic participation. Storytellers get the opportunity to connect with their vision for our city and artistically render that vision. Power begins to mobilize as the narratives are connected and transform from the vision of one to that of many. Artwork becomes a potent symbol for this shared vision that brings together the varied hopes and dreams of people from across Los Angeles and furthers the sense of agency and belonging felt by those involved.

This artistic participation in movement-building organizations like LA Voice provides an accessible point of entry for people to join the dialogue; everyone is welcome to contribute their ideas and voice as the first step in building the political agency that is the basis for collective democratic action. They continue to leverage the storytelling and artistic engagement of their membership, building connectedness and fueling the advocacy efforts that are focused on achieving real wins in the fight for economic and housing justice.

On any project as complicated as Creating Our Next LA, in hindsight, there were aspects that could have been developed more to increase our impact. When we began the project, we did not have LA Voice on board, and as such could not anticipate and fully plan for how to integrate the goals of their listening campaign with our creative visioning project. With more time, not only might we have been able to integrate their civic goals more deeply into Creating Our Next LA, but we might also have been able to center our youth participants more and even integrate our two youth teams more. With a schedule full of community pop-ups, and the election date fast approaching, our team moved quickly to infuse the LA Voice campaign with artistic engagement, thus bringing direct civic engagement to the Creating Our Next LA project. With more planning time and more resources, our Youth Visionaries could have had even more agency in directing the project alongside the LA Voice youth organizers.

There is a common chant often heard at rallies and demonstrations across the world: "We are unstoppable; another world is possible!" For organizations like LA Voice, visualizing a better world is the first step towards action. Through the artmaking process, LA Commons' Youth Visionaries aided community members in envisioning a Los Angeles where all community members could thrive. By pairing this visioning with LA Voice's campaigns, LA Commons has been able to provide a clear pathway to engage newcomers to movement building, as well as continued inspiration for seasoned organizers.

References

Ma, Y.-Y. (n.d.). The Bach project about | Yo-Yo Ma. *The Bach Project*. Retrieved April 14, 2024, from https://bach.yo-yoma.com/about/

Putnam, R. (2001). *Better together – The report of the Saguaro Seminar: Civic engagement in America. John F Kennedy School of Government* (p. 47). Harvard University. http://robertdputnam.com/better-together/the-report/

14

WARM COOKIES OF THE REVOLUTION

A Case Study of Democratic Culture Through the Framework of Civic Health

Vincent Russell

Warm Cookies of the Revolution (WCR) is an arts-focused nonprofit organization operating predominantly in Denver, Colorado, that describes itself as a "civic health club" (Warm Cookies of the Revolution, 2013, para. 3). WCR produces creative, fun, and participatory community events (called "programs") meant to promote a participatory democratic culture in Denver and, more recently, rural areas of Colorado. The inspiration behind WCR is that residents have many spaces to develop their physical, mental, and spiritual health: gyms, therapist's offices, and places of worship, respectively. However, most cities lack spaces for citizens to exercise their *civic health* – the social capital, civic engagement, and political participation of a municipality, often measured by the extent to which citizens trust their neighbors, are active in their communities, and interact with their government (Fernandez et al., 2019).

The philosophy behind WCR's mission is that, too often, participating in the civic life of a community is difficult and boring. Rather than getting to shape and control government decisions, residents are simply "updated" on civic processes and decisions made by other people about issues as important as taxes, housing, schools, immigration, neighborhood development, and much more. As WCR (2013) explains:

> We all have the capacity to understand and take part in the decisions that affect our lives. . . . However, we all have such limited time and money as we work and raise families, and so, after spending it on what is necessary, we spend what is leftover on what we find fun. Civic life is currently boring and complicated, but it need not be. We need to meet people where they are and create beautiful and vibrant and fun new systems.
>
> *(para. 6)*

DOI: 10.4324/9781003475996-23

The eponymous "warm cookies" of the organization's name are served at each of its programs, and they are a symbol of its soul-nourishing and lighthearted approach to civic engagement. Evan Weissman, the founder and executive director of WCR, explained in a video produced by the organization why they serve cookies at their events:

> We're trying to make a revolution of values, a revolution of perspectives. What's going to be comforting? What's gonna keep us questioning, "Hey, what are the fun things? What are the cool things? What are the aspects we want to keep?" Like warm cookies. We want to keep those.
>
> *(as quoted in Russell, 2020, p. 224)*

WCR takes pressing cultural and political issues – such as immigration, racial justice, affordable housing, education, prisons, aging, media literacy, gender norms, and more – and combines them with sports, comedy, music, low-riders, magic, poetry, and food in a unique alchemy that fosters feelings of community connection among attendees and equips them with the capacities to imagine and build a more just, more loving, more democratic society. WCR's mission is to wed art with civic engagement, making programs fun while also connecting people with ways to take action in their communities long after any single program ends.

Since its founding in 2012, WCR has reached more than one million people through its in-person programming and media productions. The organization has partnered with hundreds of artists working in nearly every medium to make their programs engaging, creative, and – most importantly – fun. Along the way, it has established relatively stable funding streams, with an operating budget of $250,000 in fiscal year 2023. Funding sources include many individual, small-dollar donors; a modest amount of high-dollar grants from local and state foundations; some national grants and awards; occasional contract work for other organizations; and sales from WCR's merchandise. Because WCR does not rent any office space, it has little overhead costs, with nearly all their revenue going to artists and local residents to support WCR's programming. Many of WCR's programs have been hosted at the McNichols Civic Center in downtown Denver (a city-owned space for arts and cultural events), while other programs have occurred at venues across the city, including churches, community centers, libraries, parks, private residences, nightclubs, and even cemeteries.

In this chapter, I offer a case study of WCR and its efforts to promote civic health by developing participants' *civic imagination* – "the capacity to imagine alternatives to current social, political, or economic institutions or problems" (Jenkins, 2016, p. 29). I have served as a community-based researcher with WCR, as needed, since 2018, conducting evaluations of their programs – most notably as the evaluation partner for two participatory budgeting processes WCR implemented,[1] which I describe later. Years of collaborating with WCR have granted me insights into the organization, its programs, and its members.

Herein, I provide detailed descriptions of some of WCR's programs to illustrate ways the organization supports the flourishing of democratic cultures in Colorado. The chapter offers practical insights and inspiration for readers on ways that arts programming can contribute to cultures of democracy in local communities, as well as the challenges involved in such work, including WCR's recent efforts to address *civic deserts* – where residents have scarce opportunities for civic engagement (Shao et al., 2022) – in rural Colorado.

Civic Health

Much has been written in recent decades about the perilous state of democracy in the United States (for an overview, see the Editors' Introduction to this book). For instance, in 2018, nearly half of Americans (45%) reported that they were not at all engaged civically or politically (Jones et al., 2018). If civic participation is a measure of democratic culture and the health of a society, then a reasonable person might conclude that US democracy is, at best, deeply unwell, and at worst, terminally ill.

As civil society began to identify and address this public participation crisis, "civic health" emerged in the early 2000s as a term meant to describe the status of democratic culture by measuring the well-being of civic life and its salience for democracy (National Conference on Citizenship, 2006). The theory of citizenship informing civic health is that of participatory democracy, which emphasizes mass participation by the public in civic affairs (Fishkin, 2019). Theories of participatory democracy argue that as citizens interact with each other in the public sphere, they develop the capacities necessary to become competent political actors, engage others about social issues, and identify policies that promote the public good, thereby fostering a healthy democracy (Held, 2006).

Assessing the civic health of a community requires measuring three components: social capital, civic engagement, and political participation. WCR strives to promote civic health in communities by encouraging each of these components. Social capital is fostered as program attendees (referred to as "members") break bread with their neighbors and get to know each other; civic engagement is fostered as members learn about pressing issues in their community; and political participation is encouraged when members learn how to take action to address those community issues. However, WCR does not simply seek to engender political participation in a hegemonic governance system that is boring, difficult to access, and oppressive.

Instead, the organization encourages its members to ask critical questions about participation in what kind of political system, for whom, and to what end. WCR employs art and cultural practices to provide opportunities for members to develop their civic imagination around the kinds of communities and governance systems they want to see enacted, as they strive to practice and create just cultures of democracy. WCR's members are not only encouraged to practice such civic participation during WCR's programs. Oftentimes, WCR's programs feature other community-based organizations with which members can become involved so that they continue their civic participation even after the program concludes. Making civic engagement fun can increase the civic health of communities (Lerner, 2014), and WCR's programs – as I detail later – often are playful, creative, and fun (Russell, 2020).

A final significant component of WCR's programs is their embrace of diversity. People from marginalized communities often are overrepresented at WCR's programs (compared to local community demographics), in part because WCR strives to ensure its programming is culturally responsive to people from those communities. All are welcome at WCR's programs, and this is communicated through the provision of food at its programs, providing free childcare to foster a family-friendly atmosphere, offering pay-what-you-can pricing for members, and the presence of language interpreters for people with low levels of English fluency (Russell, 2020). WCR's events have featured Mexican dance performances, Southeast Asian choirs, multilingual poetry readings, and much more. Cultural diversity is incorporated through WCR's collaborations with other community-based organizations that serve marginalized populations, such as when a local organization that serves immigrants and refugees in Denver asked WCR to help organize programming to promote participation in the US Census. WCR then worked with the organization to create promotional videos of local immigrants and refugees sharing testimonies about why the census was important to them.

WCR's heartfelt celebration of diversity is significant because of its role in fostering multiple cultures of democracy (rather than a single democratic culture). That is, WCR does not endorse a one-size-fits-all vision of civic health and democratic culture; instead, each member and community group is encouraged to find what speaks to them at WCR's programs, thereby charting their own path toward increasing civic health. For the refugee group I mentioned earlier, the program was about increasing participation in the census; for LGBTQ groups, it may be about promoting safety at house balls and drag shows; and for historically Black neighborhoods, it may be about addressing the causes and effects of gentrification and displacement. As long as people want to have fun and imagine a better world, WCR is there to help them weave a tapestry of approaches to and behaviors for improving civic health and promoting social justice.

Giving a Damn in Denver, Colorado

WCR's promotional materials and merchandise are emblazoned with the tagline "Warm Cookies of the Revolution: Giving a Damn in Denver, Colorado." The organization has been "giving a damn" since 2012, beginning with the programming that established its reputation: in-person arts-based events.

In-Person Arts-Based Events

WCR has hosted more than 250 in-person programs, some of which have been standalone events, while others have been a series of programs. For instance, one of the standalone events was the Tax Day Carnival, where WCR organized a carnival to celebrate putting collective values into practice through paying taxes. Members were treated to acrobats, stilt-walkers, jugglers, an illusionist, face-painting, and games of chance. Members also could stop at stations to learn about what their tax dollars fund, who makes those decisions, and even philosophies of tax resistance. Members could participate in a poll to vote for what they would like their tax dollars to fund: education, environment, the arts, healthcare, housing, or the military. The informative stations included posters and infographics designed by local artists, and they were staffed by volunteers who could answer questions from passersby.

Other in-person programs have been part of ongoing series, such as Stupid Questions, Stupid Talents; Civic Stitch n Bitch; Bring Your Government; and the Show and Tell Mixtape. At the Stupid Questions, Stupid Talents events, members were invited to attend discussions with local government employees about the basics of city infrastructure, with each event focusing on an essential service, such as water, housing, transportation, parks, libraries, and more.

At Civic Stitch n Bitch, members can participate in hand-occupying crafts while hearing from community members, activists, and experts. As WCR explains in one of its promotional slideshows, the events are for "woodcarvers and whittlers, crocheters and quilters, finger painters and sketchpad drawers, magic card trick people and pencil and quarter knuckle flippers (you know, like Ice Man in *Top Gun*)." The programs provide craft materials for anyone who wants to learn a new hobby, and professional craftspeople attend to guide members in their learning. Activists and community members have given talks at these events on a range of social issues, including immigration, fracking, racism, feminism, and aging, among others. The conversations that occur during the program are meant to provide opportunities for members to meet others in the community and take civic action after the program ends.

At the Bring Your Government series, members are invited to dream big about the communities in which they want to live while using LEGO blocks to build their ideal community. Members are asked to imagine what a community based on justice, health, science, or some other value might look like. In addition to everyday people who attend, WCR invites stand-up comics to keep spirits high, as well as a range of professionals (e.g., archaeologists, computer programmers, musicians, and activists) who pitch their visions of how to organize communities for the common good. The programs sometimes include elected representatives, candidates for local office, and local government officials who offer their visions of the city. Bring Your Government provides opportunities to explore innovations in democratic practice (e.g., rank-choice voting) and interact with lawmakers in a convivial, creative atmosphere.

Another ongoing program series is the Show and Tell Mixtape. At these events, members create an intergenerational mixtape of music, or show-and-tell about an object that represents their generation. Prior to the program, members are asked to identify a song that was meaningful to them, either because of an important time in one's life, or because it defines the person and their generation. They then attend the program, play the song, and explain why they chose it. The Show and Tell

Mixtape is intended to promote intergenerational communication, usually in the context of a particular social issue or community. For instance, a 14-year-old girl attended a Mixtape program about LGBTQ life, and, hearing stories from others in the LGBTQ community, made the decision to come out about her sexuality for the first time that night. The student later shared:

> I was always afraid of who I am and always looked down on myself. After that moment [coming out at the Mixtape program], with such amazing people, I've learned that it's okay. No labels have to be put on who I love, and that's okay. I've wanted to do this – to express myself – for years. From now on, I'm free . . . . That night was so cool, and I've gotten a lot of hugs, and that's all a girl like me needs.

Another event, which has grown into an annual tradition in Denver, is La Raza Park Day. For many years, WCR has worked with low rider designers and car clubs because of the highly technical and beautiful artwork required for creating such unique vehicles, and because many of these artists are located in areas threatened by gentrification. In 2019, WCR and Chicane/Latine organizations and activists successfully pushed Denver's city council to proclaim every August 25 "La Raza and Barnum Park: A Cruise Down Fedz Day" (Sylte & Cole, 2019). The proclamation honors the many generations of Chicane residents who have and continue to cruise up and down Federal Boulevard (colloquially known as "Fedz," a main transportation artery in Denver that connects multiple immigrant communities) to show off their cars and spend time with family and friends.

At La Raza Park Day, members can watch low riders cruise down Fedz, see the cars up close, and talk with the artists who designed them. Attendees are treated to mariachi bands, Indigenous dancers, luchadores, and much more. One might stop at a table to sample Latin American cuisine, or purchase goods from local vendors, craftspeople, and artisans. Importantly, La Raza Park Day is not just another cultural street festival. To promote civic health, WCR ensures that residents can connect with local activists and/or city officials to discuss the city planning/zoning process. These connections foster conversations and political actions that address the vulnerability of Latine artistic and cultural enclaves in Denver. In recent years, the politics of La Raza Park Day have evolved into conversations about regional reparations: What does the City of Denver owe neighboring areas to which displaced people have relocated? Thus, La Raza Park Day celebrates and preserves Latine culture in Denver (and surrounding areas), while at the same time promoting civic health by fostering community engagement in urban planning.

This Machine Has a Soul

A final significant program that WCR organized is This Machine Has a Soul (TMHS) – a multiyear arts-focused experiment in community-based participatory budgeting. TMHS is unique from the other programs because of its scale, duration, and focus on organizing for policy change. Participatory budgeting is a public deliberation process that involves residents controlling the allocation of a portion of a public budget in their geographic locale (e.g., neighborhood, school, or city; Marquetti et al., 2012), and the process has been found to promote social justice, increased government transparency, and increased public participation in civil society (Baiocchi, 2003; Bhatnagar et al., 2003; Wampler, 2010).

In 2018–2019, WCR formed a coalition of nonprofit organizations to allocate $60,000 in grant funds through participatory budgeting in two areas of Denver. TMHS required a year of planning, and, once launched, then involved thousands of residents in weekly work for another year as they implemented participatory budgeting. Participants deliberated to identify community needs; propose potential projects that could address those needs; develop these project ideas into full-fledged project proposals that included justifications, designs, and price estimates; vote on which projects they wanted to fund; and then implement the chosen projects. TMHS participants conducted community outreach, door-to-door canvassing, and tabled at public events to solicit their neighbors' input and encourage their participation in the process.

Simultaneously, WCR worked with multimedia artists to develop an installation about the themes of collective decision-making, community control of public budgets, and social justice. Artistic creations provoked consideration about who controls how tax dollars are spent, and the often opaque and disempowering ways budgeting decisions are made (Beaty, 2018). Organizers wanted to demonstrate to city officials the feasibility and benefits of making participatory budgeting permanent.

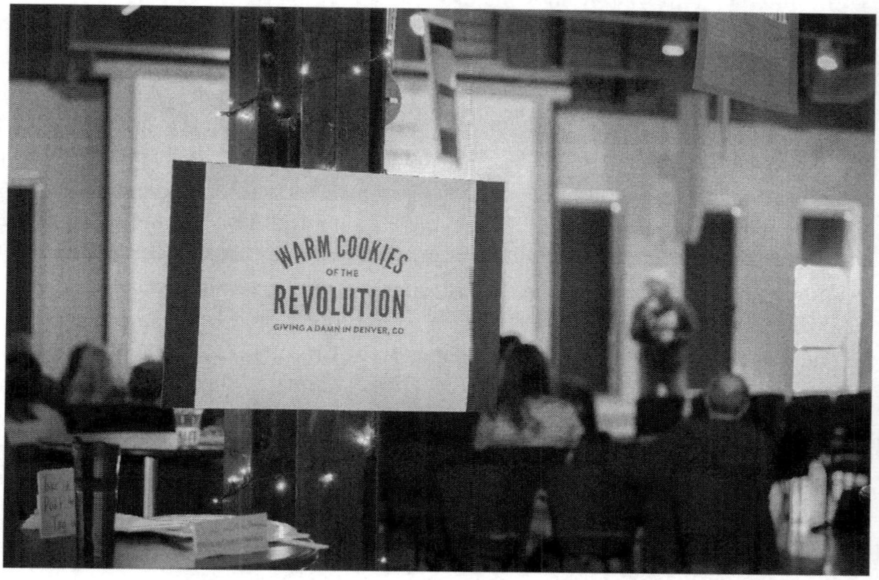

FIGURE 14.1 A sign for Warm Cookies of the Revolution at one of its programs. Photograph by From the Hip Photography.

After successfully completing the two PB processes in 2019 by allocating $60,000 to community improvement projects, WCR worked with community organizers to press Denver officials to adopt PB permanently. They used media coverage, citizen pressure, and meetings with city officials in their advocacy campaign to approve PB. In 2020, despite the COVID-19 pandemic, WCR and its allies secured a historic people's victory when Denver's City Council announced that it would allocate $1.7 million of city funds through a pilot PB process. Thus, WCR's efforts fostered meaningful policy change, creating the first PB processes in the state of Colorado.

WCR has remained engaged with Denver's PB process, securing city contracts to recruit and train resident leaders who are committed to distributing the funds equitably. As of 2023, Denver's city budget had a total of $3.4 million committed to participatory budgeting this year and next year, suggesting that WCR's playful approach to promoting civic health is creating lasting change as it reforms institutions.

Media Productions and the COVID-19 Pandemic

The mainstay of WCR is its fun, creative, in-person programming. However, beginning in 2020, the COVID-19 pandemic made it unsafe to organize large gatherings of people. WCR, therefore, pivoted to creating multimedia productions, including videos that could be shared online, and self-publishing two board books. Prior to the pandemic, WCR had worked with creators to produce brief (typically 1 to 3 minutes long), promotional videos that captured exciting moments during its in-person events. The pandemic caused WCR to shift its attention to producing longer videos and collaborating with numerous artists to share their civically minded work.

One example of WCR's video programming is the Community Almanac series (The Community Almanac, 2021). The four-episode series was inspired by farmers' almanacs of old – tomes of knowledge gained from hard-fought, grassroots experience that offered practical recommendations for applying that knowledge, thereby transferring cultural traditions and knowledge to future generations. Each 30-minute video addressed a different social issue (housing, climate, food, or health) and employed the metaphor of a tree (roots, trunk, branches, and leaves) to understand community as a holistic element, with each issue contributing to the overall health of the community. Every video includes artists' ruminations, performances, and media about the chosen topic/theme. The videos were so popular that Rocky Mountain PBS (a network of PBS member stations serving Colorado) licensed them and began broadcasting the videos over their airwaves to hundreds of thousands of viewers.

Finally, WCR has expanded not only into digital media production but also book publishing. In 2021, the organization self-published two board books. Although board books are typically associated with children's literature, WCR's publications are intended for all ages and explore themes of democracy, poetry, art, and community health. The first book, *We Trust Our Wings*, is available in English or Spanish and includes local photographer Juan Fuentes's uplifting black-and-white portraits of urban settings, cultural celebrations, and everyday people. The book also features a poem about the beauty and power of community written by Colorado's poet laureate Bobby LeFebre.

The second book, *Vote Every Day*, which is available in eight languages, reads as WCR's manifesto, written in the fun, playful style that permeates all of its work, including lighthearted illustrations of community life and civic engagement. *Vote Every Day* explores what it means to be "civic" and how regular people can use their power to create the communities they want. The books are sold on a pay-what-you-can basis, and WCR has donated many copies to community organizations, public libraries, schools, and other cultural institutions.

As the risks of the COVID-19 pandemic recede, WCR's pivot into multimedia production appears to be permanent. In the early days of the organization, WCR hosted, on average, three in-person programs a month – nearly one in-person event each week. However, now that the organization has grown and established itself over more than a decade, it has shifted its focus onto higher quality, more impactful in-person programming (e.g., approximately one in-person event every two months) while continuing to produce videos that share WCR's unique take on civic health to audiences across and beyond Colorado.

Conclusion

Since launching in 2012, Warm Cookies of the Revolution has been working diligently to improve Denver's civic health through fun, civically focused cultural events, and it has no plans on slowing down. Having established itself as a cultural institution in the Denver metropolitan area, WCR has begun to expand its engagement to other marginalized communities around Colorado. Its latest initiative – Future Town – promotes civic arts in Colorado's rural civic deserts, including the towns of Greeley, Leadville, and Loveland. As the organization begins to operate in these communities, WCR's members can look forward to more programs, more videos, and, of course, many, many more cookies.

Note

1 To learn more about those participatory budgeting processes and my research partnership with WCR, see Gardner and Russell (2020), Russell (2021, 2023), and Russell and Gardner (2019, 2021).

References

Baiocchi, G. (2003). Participation, activism, and politics: The Porto Alegre experiment. In A. Fung & E. O. Wright (Eds.), *Deepening democracy: Institutional innovations in empowered participatory governance* (pp. 45–76). Verso Books.

Beaty, K. (2018, August 15). Need help understanding the city budget? Grab a toy car and get to work. *Denverite*. https://denverite.com/2018/08/15/need-help-understanding-the-city-budget-grab-a-toy-car-and-get-to-work/

Bhatnagar, D., Rathore, A., Torres, M. M., & Kanungo, P. (2003). *Participatory budgeting in Brazil*. World Bank. https://siteresources.worldbank.org/INTEMPOWERMENT/Resources/14657_Partic-Budg-Brazil-web.pdf

Community Almanac 4: Health & leaves. (2021). *On Vimeo*. https://vimeo.com/channels/1732318.

Fernandez, K., Robichau, R., & Alexander, J. (2019). Fostering civic health: An analysis of the generative and mediating activities of community-based organizations. *The American Review of Public Administration, 49*(7), 762–776. https://doi.org/10.1177/0275074019854177

Fishkin, J. (2019). Democracy when the people are thinking: Deliberation and democratic renewal. *Proceedings of the American Philosophical Society, 163*(2), 108–121.

Gardner, T., & Russell, V. (2020). *Cole has a soul 2018: Participatory budgeting research and evaluation report*. https://scalar.usc.edu/works/participatory-budgeting-2019/index

Held, D. (2006). *Models of democracy* (3rd ed.). Stanford University Press.

Jenkins, H. (2016). Youth voice, media, and political engagement: Introducing the core concepts. In H. Jenkins, S. Shresthova, L. Gamber-Thompson, N. Kligler-Vilenchik, & A. M. Zimmerman (Eds.), *By any media necessary: The new youth activism* (pp. 1–60). New York University Press.

Jones, R. P., Cox, D., Griffin, R., Najle, M., Fisch-Friedman, M., & Vandermaas-Peeler, A. (2018). *American democracy in crisis: Civic engagement, young adult activism, and the 2018 midterm elections*. Public Religion Research Institute. https://www.prri.org/wp-content/uploads/2018/10/Civic-Engagement-NovB.pdf

Lerner, J. (2014). *Making democracy fun: How game design can empower citizens and transform politics*. MIT Press.

Marquetti, A., Schonerwald da Silva, C. E., & Campbell, A. (2012). Participatory economic democracy in action: Participatory budgeting in Porto Alegre, 1989–2004. *Review of Radical Political Economics, 44*(1), 62–81. https://doi.org/10.1177/0486613411418055

National Conference on Citizenship. (2006). *America's civic health index: Broken engagement*. http://www.ncoc.net/index.php?download=2gpcfl256

Russell, V. (2020). Keeping warm cookies: Cultural discourses of fun talk in public participation. *Journal of Civil Society, 16*(3), 216–233. https://doi.org/10.1080/17448689.2020.1788247

Russell, V. (2021). *Making space for marginalized voices: Deliberative activism in participatory budgeting* (Publication No. 28543024) [Doctoral dissertation, University of Colorado Boulder]. ProQuest Dissertations and Theses. https://www.proquest.com/dissertations-theses/making-space-marginalized-voices-deliberative/docview/2572572933/se-2

Russell, V. (2023). Communicating about social justice in participatory budgeting in the United States: 'Coming together' to benefit communities. *Journal of Applied Communication Research,* 1–20. https://doi.org/10.1080/00909882.2023.2178856

Russell, V., & Gardner, T. (2019). *Auraria participatory budgeting 2018 research and evaluation report*. https://doi.org/10.13140/RG.2.2.18940.90249

Russell, V., & Gardner, T. (2021). Money, speech, and power: Participatory budgeting as free expression. In S. Jovanovic (Ed.), *Expression in contested spaces: Free speech and civic engagement* (pp. 109–124). Lexington Books.

Shao, C., Kwon, K. H., & Nah, S. (2022). Civic life in rural America revisited: The role of social and mobile news on civic participation. *Journal of Broadcasting & Electronic Media, 66*(2), 278–299. https://doi.org/10.1080/08838151.2022.2086255

Sylte, A., & Cole, T. (2019, August 5). Denver City Council issues proclamation to make August 25 'A Cruise Down Fedz' Day. *9News*. https://www.9news.com/article/news/

local/next/denver-city-council-issues-proclamation-to-make-august-25-a-cruise-down-fedz-day/73-da65abb4-91cf-4ad8-8a69-85056fda82fa

Wampler, B. (2010). *Participatory budgeting in Brazil: Contestation, cooperation, and accountability*. Pennsylvania State University Press.

Warm Cookies of the Revolution. (2013, March 22). *About*. http://www.warmcookiesoftherevolution.org/about-us/

15

CIVIC ARTISTS REIMAGINING DEMOCRACY

Johanna K. Taylor, Amanda Lovelee, and Mallory Rukhsana Nezam

Our dream is for government staff to fall in love with their work again and for communities to believe in their civic systems again. We envision that artists with a permanent role in connecting government and community can achieve their civic goals to foster a culture of democracy. As CAIR (Cross-sector Artists In Residence) Lab, we work collectively to support artists embedded across sectors from biotechnology to transportation as they collaborate with professionals and communities to shift how public administrators and other government officials collaborate with community members and civic groups.

The field of cross-sectoral artists in residence encompasses the work of deep collective reimagining, initiated by artists, that buttresses democratic processes and creates pathways to collectively redefine how people live, work, and interact. The impact of this work is recognized in the *process* of creation, often through the collaboration itself, rather than any final *product* that is produced. This arts-led collaborative process is where change can happen, where relationships are built, and how a culture of democracy is fostered in every industry that shapes some aspect of daily life. This arts-engaged approach creates a more equitable and just society.

Why Government?

We are inspired by the work that artists do every day to ask deep questions of their collaborators and take risks that can spark big ideas to answer wicked problems or shift minute ways of working within an organization. This work is long standing yet diffuse and hard to track, as artists often also hold full-time jobs in scientific or technical fields where they bring their artist lens to the work but do not hold the title of "artist" while on the job.

DOI: 10.4324/9781003475996-24

From our perspective as artists, researchers, and field builders dispersed across the United States, we identified government spaces as productive opportunities for promoting an emphasis on the impacts of artists in cross-sector collaboration. During the COVID-19 pandemic, public trust in government eroded as public health systems crumbled and calls for racial justice mounted. At the same time, unprecedented levels of federal financial support moved into state agencies and local municipalities that gave civic leaders the leeway to decide what their communities most needed to revitalize their daily lives in a time of crisis. These quickly distributed funds led to the need to bring more collaborators into conversation to establish new program models, new engagement tactics, new internal systems. Because Artist in Residence in Government (AIRG) programs had already gained some traction over the previous decade in cities such as New York and Boston, with support from the National Endowment for the Arts as well as city budgets, desire to experiment with this model to address local needs increased. At the same time, ArtPlace, a national organization supporting arts in equitable community development initiatives, was sunsetting, thereby leaving gaps between artists, community organizers, city staff, and others who needed a place to ideate in collaboration. In the post-pandemic era, the need to experiment with bringing artists and art processes into civic systems more formally is even more imperative as pandemic supports are removed and broad swaths of groups feel disenfranchised from their leaders.

Artists in Residence in Government

Artists repair eroded civic systems through residencies in government that prioritize cross-sector collaboration, equity, and trust building. They catalyze new practices that help to address core and chronic civic challenges from public health to environmental justice. Over the past decade, formal AIRG programs increased in number, a model tested mostly within city governments but also at statewide levels. Federal residences currently are under consideration. Each AIRG program is unique, designed to respond to specific social, cultural, political, and environmental contexts. Artists are embedded in government agencies from transportation to public health to immigrant affairs, collaborating with staff to address a particular issue (Taylor, 2021). Incorporation of an artist resident can shift how systems operate internally and make government work more impactful externally. Typically, artists are in residence part time, over a set period averaging one to two years, though their roles are frequently extended to allow for continued impact.

This work reimagines democracy in action by making poetry out of policy, collaborative paintings out of parks, and sculpture out of sanitation maintenance. Artists currently are in residence across the United States, from big cities (Boston, Los Angeles), to small towns (Granite Falls), to state agencies (Washington, Minnesota). Programs are beginning to be recognized in cultural policy scholarship as a part of the policy toolkit (Lithgow & Wall, 2017; Taylor, 2021), with cities producing detailed program evaluations for the field (Sherman et al., 2021).

Mostly, however, it is being advanced by practitioners across sectors around the country who are tracking it in reports and through informal networks.

Reimagining Democracy in Action: Art Methods and Civic Impacts

We are inspired by the stories that we hear in talking to artists and government staff across the United States. The work does not look the same from one government context to another, but the ways in which artists approach their work share many similarities. Artists ask complex questions and bring creative thinking that can identify root problems facing democratic processes. Once surfacing the underlying challenges that have been overlooked, artists build capacity to bring diverse stakeholders together for a meaningful process of collective problem-solving using their arts practices.

In analyzing residencies, we identified nine different creative methods being used by artists that can lead to impacts in governments (summarized in Table 15.1). Often multiple methods are implemented simultaneously, but each individual

TABLE 15.1 Cross-sector collaboration: Art methods and impacts

Art Method	*Impact*	*Example*
Experimentation	Improve problem-solving	Benny Starr & US Water Alliance National
Collaborative performance	Validate the labor of civic workers	Mierle Laderman Ukeles & NYC Department of Sanitation New York, NY
Storytelling	Humanize government	Alan Nakagawa & Los Angeles Department of Transportation Los Angeles, CA
Deep listening	Long term cross-departmental collaboration	MAPC Boston, MA
Slowing down	Uncover the beauty of civic systems	Marcus Young & City of St. Paul (Sidewalk Poetry) St. Paul, MN
Prioritizing process	Systems change	Amanda Lovelee & City of St. Paul (Pop Up Meeting) St. Paul, MN
Curiosity and reuse	Make government systems relevant and exciting to people	Sto Len & NYC Department of Sanitation New York, NY
Community building, internal and external	Unite diverse networks	Amanda Lovelee & City of St. Paul (Urban Flower Field) St. Paul, MN
Asking questions	Expand what is possible in order to shift collaborators to focus on core issues	Anu Yadav & Department of Mental Health Los Angeles, CA

impact is instrumental, so we address them individually in this chapter and provide a specific example to demonstrate the impact in action.

Experimentation

In the artistic process, the freedom to experiment allows artists to experiment through trial and error, freeing themselves from a fixation on what they think the product should look like. In an applied artistic context, this might look like a printmaker testing the viscosity of a print ink on ugly prints before determining how to make them beautiful. Trial and error is essential to the ultimate success, i.e., finding the right thickness of the ink. Additionally, the artist might find unexpected information along the way, like the need for a new color of ink.

Government can also benefit from a mindset that is open to informed experimentation, unafraid of taking risks to find solutions for core problems. As One Water Artist in Residence at the US Water Alliance, hip-hop artist Benny Starr reflects, "the artistic process . . . gives way to a blueprint of sorts . . . how we can all step up to be courageous and daring." Hosting public meetings in new locations to engage new populations may take a few months to get right, yet taking the risk may ultimately result in higher engagement. Conversely, not trying sells the process and the outcome short. Starr observes, "as an artist, one of our essential roles comes from our tedious observation, which allows us to process and alchemize many experiences, failure chief among them, into creative expressions that communicate all the possibilities of our existence" (Benny Star, personal communication, April 26, 2023).

Collaborative Performance

Mierle Laderman Ukeles has been working as artist in residence in the New York City Department of Sanitation since 1977 and is a pathbreaker in building spaces of collaboration for artists and government. Her work celebrates unseen labor that is crucial in sustaining all city residents.

At the Department of Sanitation, Ukeles began to work at a massive city scale by engaging workers across the agency. Over years of art performance, she shifted mindsets within the department by inviting all of the employees into collaborative spaces to become co-creators with her. In *Touch Sanitation* (1979–1980), she shook the hands of over 8,500 workers, saying "thank you for keeping New York alive" to acknowledge their daily labor as essential. She documented the meetings in maps, photos, and detailed notes about the workers' stories. Sharing the documentation of these collective performances became opportunities for participating employees to see their own labor as part of an essential collective, as well as public celebrations of all sanitation workers as vital to sustaining the daily lives of everyone in the city. The impact of this work continues and was reinvigorated during the COVID-19 pandemic, when the "thank you for keeping New York alive" message was placed on billboards and in subway signage as a constant reminder to government staff and residents alike.

Deep Listening

The Community Engagement and Arts and Culture Departments at the Metropolitan Area Planning Council (MAPC, 2023) in Boston have long been exploring the ways to work together. Through deep listening, they have been able to form a powerful long-term, cross-departmental collaboration. MAPC's Arts and Culture Department plans projects and runs an AIRG inside their department. The resident artist's experience starts with an onboarding phase that often involves meetings with different departments, deep listening and learning about what MAPC does. Through deep listening, the artist often ends up working across departments, uncovering shared challenges and complementary approaches. Artists have fostered interdepartmental collaboration by bringing partners together from different teams to work together.

A similar method prevails in the collaboration between Community Engagement and Arts and Culture, which uses deep listening to invite the departments to recognize that engagement is a necessity central to their practice, rather than a budgetary bonus. The teams codified creative engagement as an arts and planning method (MAPC, 2023). The regional plan MetroCommon 2050 includes a strategy to engage art throughout including documentary film and a request for proposals for artists to communicate systems and areas for action.

Curiosity

The New York Department of Sanitation sees one challenge they face as getting New Yorkers to "reconsider their own role" in the relationship between themselves, their trash, and those who make it disappear. The curiosity of Sto Len, the department's 2022 AIRG, has helped to make government sanitation systems relevant and exciting to people. His curiosity about a system that most people overlook uncovered unique elements of the department's work and displayed its importance to New Yorkers and sparked their curiosity in it.

Len considers the department's material and personnel as his artistic materials. He established the Office of In Visibility to highlight the department's workforce through public events, resurfacing old videos that are entertaining and informative, and prints that are remixed from old posters. In Privy Pit, a public engagement series, a community member could decorate a trash can to make it fun to use or attempt to not throw anything away for a day. Len's palpable interest to uncover and learn from department materials finds its way into the art he creates and the engagement opportunities he hosts, which ultimately improves residents' understanding of the Department of Sanitation's role in their lives and their own relationship to waste systems.

Storytelling

Oral history is foundational to Alan Nakagawa's practice. He was trained in oral history and artmaking and sees the value of listening and storytelling as connecting both practices, he explains that "listening is the key . . . I seek for some sense of honesty or truth" (Nakagawa, 2022, p. 136). He has built deep collaborative relationships, working with government staff to discover truths about themselves and their agency that led some to honest tears. He progresses from listening to building narratives and telling stories that respond to what he heard to form alliances and advance government goals.

Nakagawa worked on staff for Los Angeles Metro before transitioning into a series of nine artist residency positions over six years. Appointed Los Angeles County Creative Strategist in the Department of Transportation in 2015, he assumed it was because of his prior government experience, but he was told that it was because of his listening abilities. He was able to bridge gaps, bringing the LA Ghost Bike community into DOT decision-making to continue to memorialize bicyclists while also improving roadway safety. He created new cultures of relationship building through story, making welcoming spaces uniting artists, community, and transportation staff the first step in every policy initiative (Nakagawa, 2022).

Community Building

Urban Flower Field was a gathering space built in a fenced-off gravel lot that the City of St. Paul struggled to activate and that the community was angry about. The temporary public art project was ultimately cared for by the community who also fought to integrate it as a city park. City Artist in Residence Amanda Lovelee knew that she needed partners when she started thinking about design of the quarter block lot. Like most artists would do, she drew on her connections in the community to pull together many different partners across different sectors including permaculture, landscape design, biology, education, local businesses, artists, and residents. Working with Professor Adam Kay at the University of St. Thomas, the public art project became a scientific research site, leading to two research projects conducted over four years with findings published in a scientific journal. Countless community art events were hosted in the space.

AIRGs allow cities to benefit from artists' vast connections within their own communities and across many fields. Artists not only have a seat at the civic table in these programs but tend to bring in other new and diverse voices. Artists are natural community builders, both shaping internal collaborations and breaking down silos within government and also shaping unique outside partnerships. Urban Flower Field won multiple awards and raised operating funding from multiple fields and partnerships. Artist creativity lies not solely in art making but also in uniting diverse networks and building community across unexpected divides.

Prioritizing Process

We are used to thinking of art as a product, an object that holds value and meaning. Yet art can be both product and process, where the real value is in the process of community connection. Amanda Lovelee's Pop Up Meeting was a popsicle truck designed to bring underrepresented voices into the City of St. Paul's work. It was a tool that dramatically expanded the city's systems for community participation. Pop Up Meeting changed how St. Paul approaches community engagement by bringing community meetings to where people already are – the neighborhood park, the schoolyard – rather than requiring them to attend a formal public meeting. The truck made participating in the civic process fun, accessible, and easy while rewarding residents for sharing their community expertise with a locally made popsicle.

Lovelee was in residence in St. Paul for seven years and created many projects, but she thinks that the biggest impact she had was on internal systems change. AIRGs have the unique opportunity to explore within a system, ask questions, and test ideas. With time, the unique internal position that artists in residence operate from in collaboration with government staff provide the collective ability to change civic systems from within. Pop Up Meeting has also become a model used in other cities across the country.

Slowing Down

Viewed from the outside, cities seem slow to change and slow to operate; yet internally, systems are always functioning. Replication of the structure of these systems is considered to be efficient. St. Paul Artist in Residence Marcus Young slowed down this repetition by looking at systems and asking why things were done in particular ways.

Young began his work getting to know the city and the people who make it run by following staff on their daily tasks. He followed a public works employee working on the sidewalk replacement program and noticed that after a contractor finished a sidewalk section, it was stamped with their name and date. Marcus asked if other messages could be stamped on the sidewalk, and Sidewalk Poetry was launched.

Since 2008 more than 1,200 poems have been stamped into sidewalks, including 73 poems written by St. Paul residents. The project has continued past Marcus's time in the city, and now everyone in St. Paul lives within a ten-minute walk of a Sidewalk Poem. Slowing down the simple process of replacing sidewalks has turned the streets of St. Paul into a book of poetry, uncovering the beauty of civic systems.

Asking Questions

The Los Angeles County Department of Arts and Culture has been operating the Creative Strategist program since 2018 and is a part of the countywide Cultural Equity and Inclusion Initiative, which aims to "improve inclusion in the wider arts ecology for all residents in every community." That vision inspires every artist appointed to ask who is being included in the work of the agency they are partnering with and how to expand access to services for all residents.

Theatre artist Anu Yadav centered this mandate to ask questions about equity and inclusion in her work with the Department of Mental Health. Through her questioning, she learned that medical industry practitioners were included as prospective partners and had established department relationships, but many of the non-Western clinics that are the primary providers for many Angelenos were overlooked. Yadav's questioning led her to build relationships with many wellness practitioners in this expanded field, mapping these prospective contractors and collaborators to meet the department's new strategic plan goals in the *Healing Through Story* toolkit (Yadav, 2020).

A Personal Experience With Culture Change

In the following paragraphs, CAIR Lab member and co-author Amanda Lovelee describes her personal perspective on experiencing culture change in civic institutions and clarifies the difference between an artist in residence and more traditional, product-focused art. Artists have the power to change internal cultures within civic settings to create a new culture, reshaping government slowly from within.

> Everyone including artists, partners, and funders are looking for the money shot of a project with a simple tagline. Like pairing "Pop Up Meeting – bringing underrepresented voices into urban planning one popsicle at a time" with a picture of the cute red truck next to me handing a survey and a popsicle to a community member. I never thought I would be known as the "popsicle person," nor did I realize my real change work would be internal culture change. But how do you photograph culture change? It is easier to talk about the product than the process. Traditionally, artists have been paid for products like a painting or sculpture.
>
> As an artist who has spent more than a decade embedded in government, I see that some of the real magic happens on the inside, where systems change work happens. The largest gift I was given as an artist in residence was time. I was not given much direction and was able to follow what made me curious and pursue the sweet spot where my curiosity aligned with the city's unrecognized needs. While participating in an under-attended city meeting, I realized that the city needed to make community engagement more equitable, fun, and easy. I transformed a city-owned truck into a nationally known project that highlights the need to make civic participation accessible and impactful. Handing out popsicles in exchange for participating in a mobile city meeting was fun, but my real pride came in seeing how the deeper community input was able to change the mind of one planner or one public works engineer about the value of community engagement in their daily work. Pop Up Meeting changed the city's internal system, changed staff mindsets, changed how the city does community engagement.
>
> Internal culture change also happened in Urban Flower Field, a fenced-off gravel pit turned into a temporary gathering space, park, and science experiment.

Yes, the published scientific research and the awards we won for design were amazing, but I will never forget the email I received from a landscape architecture firm. They wrote:

> Thanks for pushing our maintenance team to use movable furniture at Urban Flower Field and saying it was part of the art when you were told no. When the furniture was not stolen or vandalized after a summer you showed our maintenance team what is possible. I was allowed to add movable furniture to a permanent design of a downtown park. Thanks for changing the city.

The public documentation of the park includes images of plants in bloom and the Fibonacci-inspired mural behind it, but this email shows the true impact. While the park is temporary, the process of creating it changed a system, a bureaucratic rule, to create new, more accessible approaches in the city.

Futurecasting Democracy and the Field of Cross-Sector Artists in Residence

Public trust is at an all-time low across the United States. People feel abandoned as pandemic sources of financial support are canceled, even as food and housing costs increase, childcare opportunities are extremely limited, and available jobs pay low wages insufficient to support a family. Simultaneously, corporations report huge profits and their leaders are awarded enormous bonuses. Public protests at government offices are ignored as legislatures promulgate more restrictions on voting and the rights of women and marginalized groups. The country is increasingly polarized. The future of democracy is in crisis.

The cluster of art methods we describe reflect the powerful impacts of AIRG programs and similar opportunities that embed artists across sectors. Traditional public art projects are valuable and can impact the built environment and community engagement of a place, but AIRGs can change culture to affect how civic systems function and how government agencies connect with the communities they serve. This is why CAIR Lab pursues our goal of artists in residence at all levels of government to promote democracy through action.

Uniting artists, public administrators, and communities together in cross-sector collaboration is an opportunity to disrupt expected modes of government operations to create invitations to rebuild trust. Bertelli (2022) discusses the power of the work of public administrators in promoting democracy and aligns well with our goals for artists in government. He delineates measures to enhance accountability and internal processes which will make public administrators more responsive to the people they affect in their work. Inclusion of an AIRG in these agencies would provide a new avenue for them to reimagine internal systems based on care, equity, and other values prioritizing the impacts of their work on the public. Through cross-sector collaboration models such as AIRGs, civic systems can interrogate how public values are prioritized, by whom, and for whom, by looking at civic processes and reimagining ways of working to be more accountable.

We envision residencies beyond the government sphere transcending all sectors of civic life. While artists have been working across industries for decades, recognizing their impact and their potential for the future can lead to more democratic outcomes. The process-based work of cross-sector artists in residence emphasizes artist-led collaborations with practitioners in diverse sectors that advance change, both internally and externally to the place of work. Now is the time to dream big, to draw on a legacy of artists advancing cross-sectoral change to collaboratively shape a future where artists lead at all levels of government and across all parts of society to shape our civic life for a more equitable and just society.

References

Bertelli, A. M. (2022). *Democracy administered: How public administration shapes representative government*. Cambridge University Press.

Lithgow, M., & Wall, K. (2017). Embedded aesthetics: Artist-in-residencies as sites of discursive struggle and social innovation. *Seismopolite: Journal of Art and Politics*. https://www.seismopolite.com/embedded-aesthetics-artist-in-residencies-as-sites-of-discursive-struggle-and-social-innovation

MAPC. (2023). *What is creative engagement*? Arts and Planning Toolkit. Metropolitan Area Planning council. https://artsandplanning.mapc.org/creative-engagement/

Nakagawa, A. (2022). *A.I.R. head: Anatomy of an artist in residence*. Writ Large Press.

Sherman, D., Montgomery, D., & Bruck, C. (2021). *How artists change the city: Three year program evaluation*. The City of Boston Mayor's Office of Arts and Culture. https://www.boston.gov/departments/arts-and-culture/boston-artists-residence-air

Taylor, J. K. (2021). Art practice as policy practice: Framing the work of artists embedded in government. *The Journal of Arts Management, Law, and Society*, (4), 224–237. http://dx.doi.org/10.1080/10632921.2021.1925193

Yadav, A. (2020). *Healing through story: A toolkit on grassroots approaches*. Los Angeles County Department of Mental Health. https://www.healingthroughstory.org

16

"THE MOST OPTIMISTIC WAY I HAVE OF ENVISIONING OUR COLLECTIVE FUTURE"

Bronwyn Mauldin and Artists 4 Democracy

On a sunny Southern California Sunday two days before the 2018 midterm elections, two chartered buses filled with artists and art students drove down the freeway from Los Angeles into Orange County, where first-time candidate Katie Porter was running for Congress. A small group of artists-turned-activists had recruited the canvassers and raised money to charter the buses from art galleries Wilding Cran, Blum and Poe, Night Gallery, Ochi Projects, and Ghebaly Gallery. They had partnered with Swing Left, a progressive political group founded after the 2016 presidential election, who had the infrastructure and connected us with the campaign. Before heading out to canvas door to door, Porter boarded the bus to thank everyone.

Wearing wide-brimmed hats and slathered with SPF 50, some on the bus were visibly nervous. Few if any had ever canvassed for a candidate for public office. The next day, some 30 of them returned on their own to canvas again.

This was the moment when Artists 4 Democracy (A4D) found our groove. Porter won her election, flipping the long-red district to blue as part of a wave that began to stem the tide of rising authoritarianism in American politics, and artists had played a role.

In this chapter we share the story of A4D. It's a story of how artists as a distinct group of people with a specialized set of skills and talents can manifest their ideas in tangible ways to build a more inclusive and just democracy. It is equally a story of how artists are ordinary people living the same busy, complicated lives as everyone else. Some of our most important contributions have been to join with others to engage in rather mundane tasks that, when we do them in a spirit of empathy, mutual respect, and radical practicality, can help strengthen democracy.

***

DOI: 10.4324/9781003475996-25

Ask ten artists to define democracy and you'll get at least a dozen answers:

"Democracy is where the communal and the individual intersect."

"Everybody has a voice. Everybody has a vote."

"It's about consensus and compromise. Everyone has a say but not everybody gets exactly what they want."

"The consent of the people being ruled."

"It's the most optimistic way I have of envisioning our collective future."

One thing all of us who are members of A4D agree on is that "voting" is not a synonym for "democracy." It's only one critical component of how we make democracy work in the United States. Nevertheless, we are all artists and members of an activist group that has been organizing get-out-the-vote activities with art schools and art students since those historic 2018 midterm elections.

Each of us traveled our own personal and artistic journey that converged in the wake of the 2016 election. Some had years of experience as activists on issues from healthcare to housing to immigrant rights to cancellation of debt in the Global South. Some had volunteered before for political campaigns. Some had worked in government. For others, the election of a would-be autocrat as president spurred them to take organized political action for the first time. This election had revealed the fragile infrastructure underpinning democracy.

The election "started this whole kind of hysteria," says A4D member Lynne Berman. "We went into complete fear and anxiety. What the fuck just happened to our world? And what can we do about it?"

We also agree that the democracy most of us took for granted until November 2016 was not the best democracy possible. A4D's work to get out the vote is not an effort to recreate the status quo, but to truly engage artists and art students in the long-term struggle to make democracies more just.

***

A4D emerged from a group founded in November 2016 by seven artists and an architect in a meeting at the Hammer Museum in Los Angeles. They christened their new organization the Artists' Political Action Network (APAN) and put out a wider call to artists to gather on February 12, 2017, to discuss what they could do collectively in response to the rising threat to democracy.[1]

To do its work, APAN organized itself into committees focused on women's issues, immigration, the environment, racism, and electoral politics. There was a "maker" committee and another focused on mass communications. A4D member Sarana Mehra describes the tone of those early APAN meetings. "There was a shared feeling of panic. There was this feeling of wanting to do something but not knowing quite what to do."

As weeks turned to months and APAN subcommittees continued to meet, individual artists began to drift away. Some launched individual art or "artivist"[2] projects focused on the issues they cared about. Many simply did not have the time or energy for ongoing planning and organizing meetings. Within a year, APAN had dwindled to a handful of people.

A few original APAN members continued to experiment in a series of actions that functioned as a fact-finding period to arrive at our core mission. A4D member Ry Rocklen led a project to make T-shirts and banners to support a local resident who had been snatched off the streets by Immigration and Customs Enforcement (ICE). A4D member Kysa Johnson helped organize an artist panel about the culture wars of the 1980s at the Museum of Contemporary Art (MOCA) in downtown Los Angeles. We co-hosted an event on immigration law at the Los Angeles Contemporary Exhibitions (LACE) gallery. A4D members Berman and Deborah Aschheim began taking materials to demonstrations so people could make their own signs, adding an element of joy and pleasure to events built on protests that had emerged from anger and fear.

This emerging new organization needed a new name. Sitting in the nearly empty Ivanhoe restaurant over guacamole and chips one afternoon, Johnson, Mehra, and Rocklen brainstormed ideas, scribbling on napkins and searching URLs. They wanted a name that reflected the new direction they were moving in, that centered on the thing they cared about most: democracy.

"How crazy it was that as artists you're meant to be the radical side of society, and in that moment the most radical thing for us was protecting democracy itself," says Mehra.

In some ways, these early months reflect what was happening across the United States. The Indivisible Guide – a highly influential call to progressive activism published as a Google doc on December 11, 2016 – was burning its way across the internet, inspiring creation of new grassroots groups in cities, towns, and rural communities. Workers at federal agencies (and their imitators) were launching alt-style social media accounts. Every weekend there was another protest on the next emerging crisis, people pinging from one demonstration to the next in hand-knit pink pussy hats.

As the 2018 midterm campaign was heating up, Swing Left reached out to us. They saw artists as one community among countless others across the United States to be mobilized for political action. When artist Patrick Jackson organized an art sale fundraiser at Ghebaly Gallery for first-time congressional candidate Katie Hill, A4D was on hand to register voters. Artist William Kaminsky was heavily involved with the Hill campaign at the time and helped facilitate the connection. This would turn out to be the largest single fundraiser of Hill's campaign. A4D partnered with other groups including Walk the Walk, who raise money for grassroots organizations doing voter education in historically disenfranchised communities of color that are led by people from those communities. A4D cross-promoted Walk the Walk's fundraising events to our artist community, and several members of A4D did volunteer work with them.

We set up tables to register voters on the campus of California Institute for the Arts (CalArts), located in the historically red district where Hill was running. A4D participant and CalArts faculty member Scott Benzel went door-to-door in the dorms to register voters. Turnout by CalArts students increased by nearly 44% compared to the 2014 midterms, and both Porter and Hill were elected to Congress. Our experiments led us to a simple but profound discovery: we could create meaningful on-ramps to the democratic process for artists and art students.

"It's less about telling people what to do than it is about convincing the people who already know what to do how to do it," says A4D member Lisa Anne Auerbach. She introduced us to the concept of "radical practicality" and we have embraced it, taking pragmatic action that can ultimately lead to profound change, working with whatever material is available.

"As artists, we're used to making something out of nothing," Johnson says. "We understand that when you have these big ideas and concepts, you have to do a lot of really mundane, practical things to get them out into the world. To make this thing that when other people see it seems like magic, the artist knows it took me a month of going to the hardware store to buy materials, building a stretcher, priming the canvas, all that messy work."

"It takes a certain stamina," Berman says. "It's not sexy or glamorous, and you're not going to get a career boost out of it."

Flush with success after the 2018 midterms, A4D members reached out to Frieze, which was launching its first Los Angeles art fair. We were given space for a "Democracy Shop." Members and supporters of A4D made original works, including limited-edition poster prints, T-shirts and hats, zines, and postcards. Proceeds from each sale were split 50/50 between A4D and the artist.

We started planning for the next presidential election, designing a tour of art schools located in swing districts across the United States. We would partner with local artists to give talks on campuses about their work and their views on democracy and voting. We would bring in local issue-based activist groups to do voter registration. We were given space for a Democracy Shop at the second Frieze Los Angeles, where we raised even more money to fund our upcoming tour.

It was February 2020.

***

Like everyone else who could, A4D pivoted online. Our virtual meetings became a mix of election-year planning and mutual support for each other as human beings struggling to cope with the upheaval of the pandemic. We even gained a few new

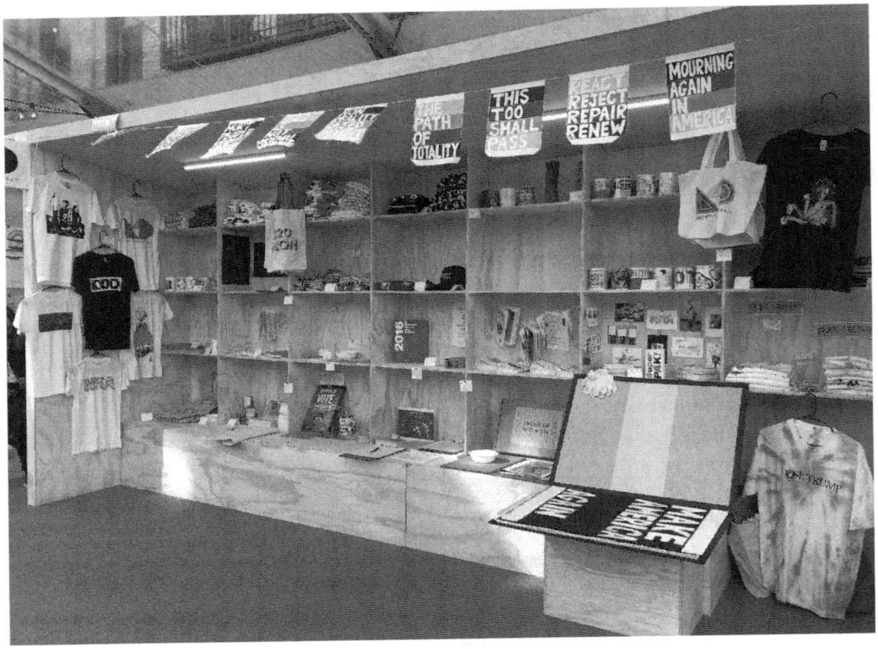

FIGURE 16.1 A4D's "Democracy Shop" at Frieze Los Angeles in 2020. Photograph by A4D member Kysa Johnson.

members. Filled with a mix of hope and dread for the upcoming election, we dug deep into our networks to create a series of seven virtual talks by artists who wanted to contribute to our work to defend democracy: Ruben Ochoa, Amir H. Fallah, Kandis Williams, Scott Benzel, Christina Quarles, Lauren Halsey, and Laura Owens. Each talked about their work and their values, and the sometimes circuitous, sometimes very direct relationship between the two. Halsey's *Summaeverythang* community center was providing organic produce to residents of Watts and South Central Los Angeles, while Ochoa's newest works highlighted the invisible labor of immigrant street vendors. The series of talks showed how artists can model their values of inclusivity and social justice as individuals while also taking action on those values through their work. Each talk was introduced by an A4D member and concluded with information about how and why to register to vote. Art professors from the University of Nevada, Las Vegas; Rhode Island School of Design; University of California, San Diego; and others incorporated our talks into their course syllabi.

"As an art student, you are looking at these people in the art world who are living the life that you hope to have, and you admire them," says Johnson. "They represent something to you that is good. To have that voting message come through them can have a greater impact."

For the artists who gave the talks, it was an opportunity to speak openly about the political content of their work that the art press doesn't always want to explore, says A4D member Melissa Passman. "We gave them an opportunity to have a more direct conversation and get that on the record."

Auerbach takes it a step further. "I would argue that much art, even non-politically themed art, is political. Even the decision to be an artist in the period of twentieth century capitalist ideology is political."

At the same time, Mehra, who manages A4D's social media, launched our "POV" (Protest, Organize, Vote) initiative. In the pandemic pivot to online, she had doubled down on building our Instagram network, identifying organizations who shared our values and cross-promoting events with Advice, Black Lives Matter, RiseUp, Walk the Walk, and others. She invited artists from anywhere to send recorded short videos explaining why they protest, organize, and vote. Artists from across the country – from Georgia to Texas to Oregon to Connecticut – participated, from art students to blue-chip names.

In early 2021 we launched a newsletter modeled on the artist talks. Each issue shares actions that artists can take to help strengthen democracy, including information about legislation in the works. We also profile an artist whose work reflects democratic values. Performance artist and Pulitzer Prize finalist Kristina Wong, an elected member of the Koreatown Neighborhood Council in Los Angeles, encouraged artists to run for public office. Ukrainian-born artist Julia Tcharfas called on the global arts community to help keep Ukrainian culture alive by sharing and highlighting the work of its artists, filmmakers, and writers at a time when Russia is trying to destroy not only the country but its language, history, and culture.

When the GOP tried to do an end-run around the democratic electoral process and recall California Governor Gavin Newsom in 2021, A4D was there with our "TOTAL NO RECALL" online campaign.

We were finally able to be back on campus in the fall of 2022, in time for the midterm elections. We taught a series of hands-on workshops for making signs, zines, costumes, and videos with students at the CSUN (California State University, Northridge) Art Gallery. Berman organized a Festival of Voting with students at Cal State LA (California State University, Los Angeles). We traveled to CSUB (California State University, Bakersfield), where three deep-red congressional districts converge, and spent a day encouraging art students to vote. (The Art Department at CSUB cancels classes on Election Day to ensure students can vote.)

Nearly one-third of undergraduate students attending California State colleges are the first in their family to attend college. This was a group we particularly wanted to reach. Our workshops provoked conversations with them about the issues they cared about most deeply. We discovered that art galleries can be a critical locus of democratic action, a center for free speech on campus, but only if faculty, staff, and students activate them. Several A4D members also did independent get-out-the-vote workshops, lectures, and exhibits with students at community colleges, universities, and high schools in Georgia, North Carolina, and across Los Angeles County.

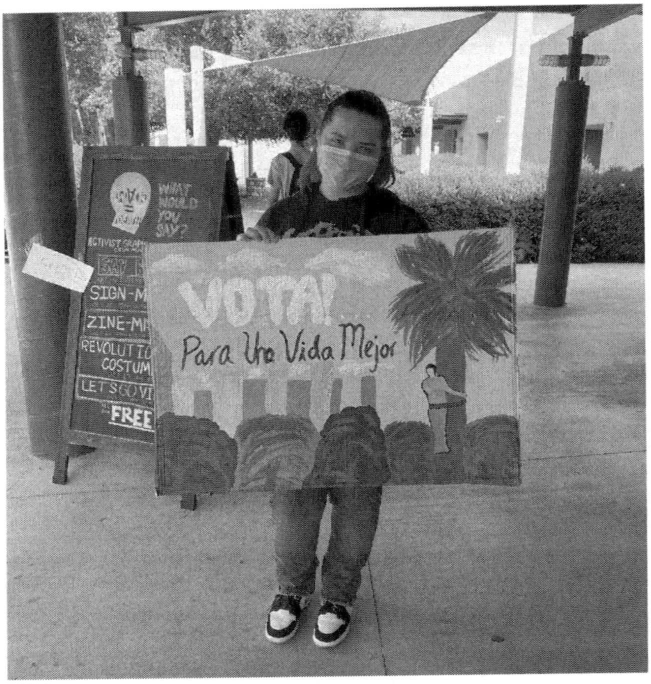

FIGURE 16.2 A student at California State University, Northridge, poses with the sign she made in an A4D Sign-Making Workshop in 2022. Photograph by A4D member Deborah Aschheim.

By stepping up and doing the work of organizing events and activities, by sharing timely information about everything from protests to voting and recommending places to give time and resources, we created opportunities for other artists to step in occasionally and contribute to defending democracy. For the members of A4D, this came at a cost. Time spent organizing was not spent on our individual artistic practices or our loved ones. At the end of 2020, many of us were exhausted and burned out. We rallied in 2021 for the California gubernatorial recall election, and again for the 2022 midterms, as we will for the 2024 presidential election, and for the election after that. But we have learned to pace ourselves, even as we continue to work to build the better democracy we envision, one where all people with the right to vote have equitable access to the ballot box as well as the knowledge, skills, and confidence to exercise that right.

***

Over time A4D's work has moved up and down the continuum between partisan and nonpartisan. We have made these decisions situationally, based on what is most urgent in the moment and what is the most pragmatic way to achieve our goal of working toward a more just democracy. Even our legal structure was debated at length and ultimately driven by radical practicality. At first we pursued registering as a Super PAC, but federal election laws would limit who we could accept money from and require significant, intrusive data collection about donors. Advised by Passman, an attorney, we decided to register as a 501(c)4 nonprofit, rather than the better-known (c)3 model. The tradeoff is that while (c)4 organizations can engage in far more partisan political activities, our donors cannot take a tax deduction, and we are ineligible for most foundation or government grants.

Our on-campus events required us to be nonpartisan, but this also turns out to be radically practical. Working with young art students, we have discovered how deeply wary they are of political parties. Nonpartisan outreach can be more effective for getting students civically engaged in ways that are meaningful to them, rather than telling them who to vote for in the next election or promoting a specific political party. Art students want to speak their truth, so we show them how voting is a tool for doing that. In our hands-on workshops, we invite them to choose an issue that matters to them, then make a sign, zine, costume, or video to express their views.

Then we always return to voting. Not just voting for the candidates they support, but protecting the right to vote by exercising that right and encouraging their friends and family to vote too. As A4D member Futernick says, "None of the rest of what makes up a democracy happens without voting. That's the thing that feels especially fragile. It's hard to think about anything else right now."

Johnson adds, "We want to reach this pool of people who are about to start voting but might think they can't make a difference, who are disillusioned with the system."

"Art students can be apathetic, but they can be convinced to participate," says Auerbach. "It doesn't take that much effort to show up. So you may as well because the alternative can be that you and people you love are going to be harmed."

Berman sees our fundamental task as "getting art students engaged in some kind of activity that involves them in a creative process that makes them feel energized to participate and, hopefully, to become curious and ask questions."

"A4D specializes in democracy education and voting literacy," says A4D member Lee Webster. "There's something about it that's so simple and so direct, but so needed."

Focusing on elections, as Aschheim says, is about flexing our power where we can. "We don't get to do it with other powerful people like Elon Musk or Jeff Bezos. Elected officials are the one group of people who have power over us, but where we have power over them."

***

"Artists are deeply affected by a lot of civic issues but don't necessarily feel empowered to do anything about it," observes Futernick. This drives the deep cynicism about politicians and the political system we sometimes see among fellow artists.

Taken as a group, artists are generally perceived as having views well to the left of so-called "average" Americans, and many artists embrace this outsider status.

Nevertheless, while many artists may not see their personal views reflected in state and federal laws, major national polls show that:

- 71% of Americans support equal marriage for LGBTQ+ and straight people[3]
- 71% of Americans want stricter gun laws[4]
- 61% of Americans believe abortion should be legal in most cases[5]
- 61% of Americans have changed their behavior because of their concerns about the environment[6]
- 57% of Americans believe voting is a fundamental right for every US citizen and should not be restricted[7]
- 43% of Americans would prefer that our current healthcare system based on private insurance be replaced by a government-run system[8]

When artists opt out of voting because they believe elected officials and the government do not reflect their views, they create a self-fulfilling prophecy. "When I hear artists say that whoever is President doesn't matter," says Rocklen, "it gets me fired up for people to be that pessimistic and dismissive of the power of politics."

A4D is working to reverse this vicious cycle and transform it into a virtuous one where artists vote, then help other artists and art students vote as well. Philadelphia-based artist Jessica Gath founded the initiative 5 Million Strong[9] on the fact that there are more arts and culture workers in America (4.9 million in 2021)[10] than there are physicians (761,700)[11] or oil and gas workers (106,440).[12] Why shouldn't we organize ourselves to fight for better wages and working conditions, to fight for our values, just like they do?

A4D believes in the radically practical act of showing up to vote and helping others do the same. We believe in the radical practicality of providing artists with on-ramps to all the different ways they can engage in democracy, from protests, to meetings with elected officials, to running for public office. When more people who share our views show up and stay engaged, we can change laws so they reflect our beliefs. We can change the names and faces of the people making those decisions so they look more like the rest of America.

***

A4D had to go through a period of uncertainty and experimentation to discover our mission. We tested new ideas, discarded what did not work, then honed the ones that do. Thinking about engaging in democracy as an ongoing practice rather than a one-time task or goal helps us to persist. It keeps us motivated when our candidates lose an election or when morally corrupt politicians stoke fear against people we love as a cruel strategy for getting elected.

We have learned that giving people something to paint, sing, play, or make inspires a spirit of generation and builds enthusiasm, which can translate into action. Art can counteract the feelings of being shut down and oppressed that lead to inaction and, at worst, cynicism. A4D works to help people build a sense of agency through arts activities merged with civic engagement.

We have learned to plan for fallow periods where we step away from our organizing activities. We give ourselves permission to be human beings with complex lives. We create opportunities and infrastructure that allow other artists to step in and out of democratic activism when and where they can. In order to do the best work we can around elections, we also have to make time for art, our vocation.

We have discovered that artists have a role on both sides of the electoral system: the money side and the people side. Blue-chip artists and collectors can and should donate cash, artwork, and their clout for political fundraisers. If they do not put their resources behind the candidates and activist organizations who share our values, then our opponents will use their wealth to harm us all. We say this despite our deep frustration that money still plays such a pivotal role in electoral politics.

We will continue to criticize our imperfect elected officials and the flawed policies they enact, even as we encourage artists and art students to engage actively and continuously with our democratic processes toward a better future. As political communications strategist Anat Shenker-Osorio has said, "Our opposition is not the opposition. It is cynicism."[13] A4D's collective hope for the future is not a blind wish that everything will somehow all work out. It is firmly rooted in our critique of the injustice, violence, and environmental degradation around us, combined with our belief in our ability to make real, meaningful change by working with our arts community.

Notes

1 K. Andrews et al. The artists' political action network issues a call to action. *365 Mission* [blog]. Retrieved April 21, 2023, from https://356mission.tumblr.com/post/156723801920/the-artists-political-action-network-issues-a.

2 A. Funderburk (2021, May 17). Using art as a means for social change, artivists can change the world. *Art & Object*. https://www.artandobject.com/articles/artivism-making-difference-through-art.

3 J. McCarthy (2022, June 1). Same-sex marriage support inches up to new high of 71%. *Gallup*. https://news.gallup.com/poll/393197/same-sex-marriage-support-inches-new-high.aspx.

4 S. Burnett (2022, August 23). AP-NORC poll: Most in US say they want stricter gun laws. *AP News*. https://apnews.com/article/gun-violence-covid-health-chicago-c912ecc5619e925c5ea7447d36808715.

5 H. Hartig. *About six-in-ten Americans say abortion should be legal in all or most cases*. Pew Research Center. https://www.pewresearch.org/fact-tank/2022/06/13/about-six-in-ten-americans-say-abortion-should-be-legal-in-all-or-most-cases-2.

6 National tracking poll #2207099, crosstabulation results. *Morning Consult*. Retrieved April 21, 2023, from https://assets.morningconsult.com/wp-uploads/2022/08/11140636/2207099_crosstabs_MC_ENERGY_SINGLE_USE_PLASTIC_Adults_v1_CC.pdf.

7 V. Gomez & C. Doherty (2021, July 22). *Wide partisan divide on whether voting is a fundamental right or a privilege with responsibilities*. Pew Research Center. https://www.pewresearch.org/fact-tank/2021/07/22/wide-partisan-divide-on-whether-voting-is-a-fundamental-right-or-a-privilege-with-responsibilities.

8 M. Brenan (2023, January 23). Majority in U.S. still say gov't should ensure healthcare. *Gallup*. https://news.gallup.com/poll/468401/majority-say-gov-ensure-healthcare.aspx.
9 *5 million strong*. Retrieved April 21, 2023, from https://5millionstrong.art.
10 The U.S. arts economy in 2021: A national summary brief. *National Endowment for the Arts*. Retrieved April 21, 2023, from https://www.arts.gov/sites/default/files/National-Brief-final-3-16-23.pdf.
11 Physicians and surgeons. *Occupational Outlook Handbook*, U.S. Bureau of Labor Statistics. Last modified September 9, 2022, from https://www.bls.gov/ooh/healthcare/physicians-and-surgeons.htm#tab-6.
12 NAICS 211000 – Oil and gas extraction. *Occupational Employment and Wage Statistics*, U.S. Bureau of Labor Statistics. Last modified March 31, 2022, from https://www.bls.gov/oes/current/naics3_211000.htm.
13 A. Giridharadas (2022). *The Persuaders: At the front lines of the fight for hearts, minds, and democracy* (p. 230). Knopf.

EDITORS' SUMMARY AND CONCLUSION

As editors, it was a joy to work with the visionary authors in this volume – artists, scholars, and activists who have articulated work that has not received the attention and support it deserves. We hope this book has provided readers evidence of the skillful ways artists' practices have and can contribute to cultures of democracy. Beginning with Maryo Gard Ewell's Foreword, we've read how artists from the early part of the 20th century produced cultural programs in the United States that conspicuously promoted democracies and democratic ways of living on multiple levels of community and civic life. These were surely not unique but point to a long tradition of such work that has been relegated to the margins of creative cultural practices and of history.

Continuing and growing threats to the very fabric of democracies around the world call for every sector and professional practice to contribute to weaving a culture of democracy in every community. There is reason to fear major world powers may again fall to fascism and authoritarian rule to the benefit of corporate global capital, oligarchs, and strongmen political rulers; to the denigration of labor and hard-earned social supports, civil, and political rights. A mere two centuries or so of liberal democracies in the face of thousands of years of human civilization that were dominated by oppressive authoritarian regimes can easily succumb. Artists, and their creative work, have served these regimes and institutions of power and privilege. Clearly, there are exceptions, and we hope these exceptions grow to more than a footnote in history, to a powerful force in communities around the globe.

We hope this book makes a contribution to a long-standing and global discussion around the realities and possibilities of artists aligning with the broader interests of their communities, challenging self-serving interests of power.

The six practices we delineated in the Introduction that we found are shared across democracy and ways artists and cultural organizations engage in

DOI: 10.4324/9781003475996-26

community-building work, are well integrated in the work described: storytelling and the construction of narratives that promote empathy; a built environment that fosters equitable interactions; distribution of power that builds bridges; discourse and deliberation that fosters learning; advocacy and organizing to mobilize action; and active engagement in governing and electoral processes. We have read here about how artists' practices can contribute to all of these threads to weave more equitable cultures of democracy.

The book led with Part One on Place-based Actions, seeing the ground – the physical spaces people share on which communities exist – as a fundamental building block for democracies. Democracies, in the formal political sense, are place-based, formed around spatial delineations, and generally include place-based representation. In the introduction to this section, Jeremy Liu and his father John K. C. Liu illustrate how locally based community work by artists help weave social and civic fabric. They add to the metaphor of weaving from the book's title, describing culture as the warp to democracy's weft. From their decades of experiences in community development, they call for the need to recognize the "cultural" in every community's development, and they highlight what they call the "energizing effect of process over end result." Through the thoughtful practice of weaving, cultures and democracies gain strength.

Contestation of power and place is common in place-based democracies as explored by D'Arcy Molan, Katya Johanson, and Emily Potter in Chapter 1. In settler-colonial rural Australia, Indigenous families, farmers, and recreation-seeking newcomers engage in what these authors call "democratic spectacle." Through the co-creation of multimedia events, grain silos become both object and symbol in the weaving of a richly layered civic life. Meena Natarajan, in Chapter 2, writes about the work of Pangea World Theater in Minneapolis in a neighborhood left in ashes after the police murder of George Floyd in 2020. With Indigenous artists, and employing theater and public art practices, Pangea prepares the ground for equitable rebuilding through cross-cultural relationship building and democratic practices applied to planning, development projects, and collective action. Creative recovery following natural disasters in the Australian state of Victoria, as described by Anna Kennedy-Borissow in Chapter 3, illustrates how combining a spirit of resilience with transformative recovery builds on democratic practices and creates a healthier civic community. The authors of Chapter 4 describe how Writers Room in Philadelphia widens circles of urban spatial justice while building models for sharing living spaces and sharing stories. Engaging in practices of democracy, including shaping narratives, design of the built environment, deliberation, and organizing, these authors describe ways of braiding stronger civic fabric in a contested urban neighborhood.

Introducing Part Two on Aesthetic Strategies, Diane Ragsdale and Shannon Litzenberger provide theoretical underpinning for how creative processes and collective practices model ways of worldmaking and provide rehearsal for the world they would like to make. Ragsdale and Litzenberger describe the aesthetic practices in the chapters that follow as "pre-figuring functioning democracies." In a contemporary world of increasingly "pernicious polarization," they reflect on how these aesthetic practices counter this disturbing trend, shift relationships, and provide ways to manifest pluralism. Western ways of knowing that separate knowledge from responsibility (among many other things) are reconnected through the process that weaves meaning-making with practices of embodied co-creation.

Andrea Assaf, in Chapter 5, traces her personal creative journey in protest movements and the performing arts describing the practice of decentering dominant cultural narratives and systems of power to shape equitable democratic ways of working and living. She uses Story Circles, collective dramaturgy, ensemble process, co-creation, and other techniques to create a microcosm of a more desirable world and to rehearse one's places in that world. Heather McLean, working in the settler-colonially named Kamloops, British Columbia, co-creates comedic performances via webinars with Indigenous collaborators to advance suppressed Indigenous perspectives. In Chapter 6, she describes these webinars that address climate and housing crises while confronting a neoliberal university setting that neutralizes democratic principles and practices. In the third and final chapter in this section, Rui Gonçalves Cepeda, working in Portugal, illustrates how, by building on centuries-old traditions of bullfighting, audiences co-create and perform artwork while they erase the image of the bullfighter. Co-curation of this public spectacle engages participants to challenge public policies while reshaping cultural practices.

In Part Three on Learning Environments, introduced by Susan Badger Booth, civic education goes beyond the classroom and learning about the machinery of governments. Booth expresses optimism seeing increased participation in democracies by young people. She advocates the value of active participation in democratic practices both in classroom pedagogies and through experiential field work in their communities. In the four case studies in this section, Booth observes how storytelling, culturally responsive teaching, questioning power, giving voice, seeing multiple viewpoints, and collective decision-making are shared pedagogical approaches as well as learning outcomes. Students in each of the environments are not just observers but creators and co-creators who experience democracy in action.

In the photography-based project, Doing Visual Politics, in Chapter 8, artists-teachers-authors Alan Hill, Kelly Hussey-Smith, Marnie Badham, Shehab Uddin, and Sagar Chhetri reframe photography as a relational practice in which students and their audiences come together around shared concerns. Teachers and students in three South Asian-Pacific countries co-create work and exhibitions as forms of civic action. Maria Asp and Sonja Kuftinec, in Chapter 9, animate cultures of democracy through transforming space and place, questioning power, and sharing newly devised stories. Their focus on Indigenous stories take on additional meaning in their Minneapolis setting, where students become familiar with these places and their meaning. Through the Ray of Hope Project and Women Composers Festival, based in Connecticut, Alika Hope and Penny Brandt use music and storytelling to teach, practice, and model democracy. Stories of Black leadership in abolitionist movements in the United States in the early 19th century provide a beginning place for students who take charge of how these narratives take on new relevance in their own experiences in the contemporary world.

In the introduction to Part Four on Civic Processes, civic leader and poet Roberto Bedoya summarizes how the five chapters stitch civic imaginations and cultural practices into a variety of civic processes – the systems of democracy. Artists working in and around the formal practices of policymaking, public administration, and electoral processes, he says, bring to life the idea of "We the People." He describes this as "helping to sculpt our democratic best selves."

In Chapter 12, Lisa Jo Epstein, a Philadelphia theater artist, brings creative practices into community engagement in urban and community planning. She views relationships as both the process and product of democratic action. Karen Mack with Elizabeth Cho, in Chapter 13, employs Story Circles and other creative activities to organize for direct action and advocacy while building agency in Los Angeles neighborhoods, especially among youth. In Chapter 14, Vincent Russell describes the work of Colorado-based Warm Cookies of the Revolution, an organization using arts activities and fun – and, of course, freshly baked cookies – to bring people together through deliberative practices and processes related to local issues of the day. Getting inside the administrative machinery of local government, the artists' work described in Chapter 15 by Johanna K. Taylor, Amanda Lovelee, and Mallory Rukhsana Nezam, explores ways in which artists build transparency and trust – and ultimately, greater participation – in municipal governments. Finally, Bronwyn Mauldin, with Artists 4 Democracy, takes us on a journey of local elections in Southern California where artists bring their unique talents to make a difference in multiple dimensions of electoral processes.

Reflecting on the three major threads of democracy, described in the Introduction – ideals, norms, and systems – these authors have shown how their work builds on all of them. The culture of democracy we have advocated may be most squarely found in the norms, as they speak to how people practice and maintain democracy on a daily basis. However, these artists, and their work, grow from the ideals while building and improving the systems in multiple ways towards more just and equitable democracies. The ideals, norms, and systems are interwoven with creative cultural practices as civic fabric.

The remarkable work of these artists and organizations, however, remains on the margins of the formal arts and cultural sectors in the seven countries from which they hail. We argue that the strength of democracies is dependent on the kinds of creativity that can invigorate cultures of democracy in daily life. These interlocking threads of culture and democracy – the warp and the weft – form the fabric of communities that can move them towards just and equitable futures. Advocates of democracy should look to find allies and valuable resources among the culture bearers and artists in their communities. Philanthropic, educational, and social justice entities working for progressive change and espousing principles of democracy, we argue, should similarly turn their attention to the work of building a culture of democracy.

INDEX

Note: Page numbers in *italic* indicate a figure on the corresponding page.

Printed in the United States
by Baker & Taylor Publisher Services